British television drama

For Toni who has been very patient

British television drama

Edited by
George W. Brandt

*Senior Lecturer and Director of
Film Studies, Drama Department
University of Bristol*

Cambridge University Press

*Cambridge
London   New York   New Rochelle
Melbourne   Sydney*

Published by the Press Syndicate of the University of Cambridge
The Pitt Building, Trumpington Street, Cambridge CB2 1RP
32 East 57th Street, New York, NY 10022, USA
296 Beaconsfield Parade, Middle Park, Melbourne 3206, Australia

First published 1981

Phototypeset in Linotron 202 Palatino by
Western Printing Services Ltd, Bristol

Printed and bound in Great Britain
at The Pitman Press, Bath

British Library cataloguing in publication data
British television drama.
   1. Television plays – History and criticism
   2. English drama – 20th century – History
   and criticism
   I. Brandt, George W
   822'.02   PN1992.65   80–41031
ISBN 0 521 22186 2 hard covers
ISBN 0 521 29384 7 paperback

Contents

Acknowledgements

Like most books and like all anthologies, this volume is the product of the collaboration of a good many people. Its shape has resulted from an exchange of ideas between the editor and the eight contributors of essays on individual television dramatists. Indeed, many of the playwrights discussed have been generous in giving their time as well as supplying otherwise unavailable material to the writers of these essays.

I should like to acknowledge the help given at different times by the following: my colleague David Ponting in the Drama Department of the University of Bristol, who allowed me to draw freely on his ideas as well as his library; Graham Murdock, Research Associate at the Centre for Mass Communication Studies, University of Leicester, who brought to my attention research material I might otherwise have missed; and Richard MacDonnell, Regional Executive of the Independent Broadcasting Authority, who gave me a good deal of useful archival information. I wish to thank them for their valuable advice.

I also owe a debt of gratitude to the following for supplying information for the various critical appendices: Enid M. Foster of the British Theatre Association; Barrie MacDonald, Librarian of the IBA; Mary Welsh and Michel Petheram of the BBC Reference Library; Sandra Archer, Librarian of the British Film Institute; and Ian MacDonald, the BFI's Television Information Officer.

Jeremy Bolton, of the National Film Archive, enabled contributors to the volume to view a number of classical TV programmes not available elsewhere, and Bridget Carter of the BBC Photographic Library helped me to find illustrations for this book. Thanks are due to the BBC for use of BBC copyright photographs. Permission to reproduce BBC copyright photographs has also been granted by Ray Brooks, Carol White, James Ellis, Brian Blessed, Helen Mirren, John Stratton, Colin Farrell, Francis Matthews, Paul Copley and Janine Duvitski. Every effort has been made to seek permission from the other subjects of the photographs to reproduce those in which they appear.

Permission to quote from published sources has been granted by the following: Faber and Faber Ltd (*Through the Night* and *All Good Men* by Trevor Griffiths and *The Art of Television*), The British Film Institute (interview with Dennis Potter), William Heinemann Ltd (*A Survey of Television*), the Independent Broadcasting Authority (1979 handbook, *Television and Radio*), Stuart Hall (*Television as a Medium and Its Relation to Culture*), The Hutchinson Publishing Group Ltd (*The Popular Arts*), Focal Press Ltd (*Television in the Making*), Allen Lane/The Penguin Press (*The New Priesthood*), Pelican Books Ltd (*Discrimination and Popular Culture*), The British Academy of Film and Television Arts (*Journal of the Society of Film and Television Arts*), Marion Boyars Publishers Ltd (*Cathy Come Home* and *Edna the Inebriate Woman*), Michael Joseph Ltd (*The Television Playwright*), Tavistock Publications Ltd (*Sanity, Madness and the Family*), Calder and Boyars Ltd (*Smiling David*), John Calder (Publishers) Ltd (*The Two Generations* and *In Two Minds* by David Mercer), Temple Smith Ltd (*Sex, Violence and the Media*) and the editors of *Theatre Quarterly* (extracts from various journal numbers).

Permission to quote from unpublished manuscripts has been given by Jim Allen and his agent Judy Daish, by Peter Nichols and his agent Margaret Ramsay, by Alan Plater and his agent Margaret Ramsay and by Yorkshire Television, and by Jeremy Sandford and his agent Norman Thompson.

I also wish to acknowledge information received from Penry Jones, IBA; Elaine Steele, Writers' Guild of Great Britain; and Rod Allen, the publisher of *Broadcast* at the time in question. It is hardly necessary to point out that while the book owes much of the quality it may have to the above informants, its shortcomings must be laid entirely at the door of the editor.

Notes on the contributors

S. M. J. ARROWSMITH was born in Birmingham, took a first degree at Cambridge in English Literature in 1974 and then obtained his Ph.D. at the University of Exeter with a dissertation on Hollywood narrative. He has been an archivist and a film scriptwriter among other things.

MARTIN J. BANHAM is Senior Lecturer in Drama and Director of the Workshop Theatre in the University of Leeds. Publications include books on Osborne and on African theatre. He has worked extensively on television, in the area of schools broadcasting, as presenter of Yorkshire Television's *My World*.

GEORGE W. BRANDT worked for the National Film Board of Canada after the war as researcher/editor/director; he has been teaching in the Drama Department of the University of Bristol since 1951, where he has initiated theoretical as well as practical media studies which have supplied many graduates to the communications industry. He finds time occasionally to do stage and TV film directing in a professional, rather than a university, context.

EDWARD BRAUN lectures in modern theatre, film and television in the Drama Department of the University of Bristol. His published works include two books on the Soviet theatre director Meyerhold – the standard English edition of his writings on theatre and a critical biography. He has also written a study of directing in European theatre.

ALBERT HUNT read Modern Languages at Balliol and has taught in adult education in Shropshire, at Bradford College of Art and the Victorian College of the Arts, Melbourne, his interests ranging over literature, theatre and the mass media. His production of original plays with the Bradford Art College Theatre Group, especially *John Ford's Cuban Missile Crisis*, has been widely noted.

PAUL MADDEN was educated at Liverpool Collegiate School, the University of Keele and the School of Management Studies at the Polytechnic of Central London. The National Film Archive's Television Officer 1970–80, he organised the first retrospective of British television drama at the National Film Theatre in 1976. He writes regularly on television in various publications.

BRIAN MILLER was born in Calgary, Alberta, in 1941. His first play was produced by Granada in 1961, and since then he has had a number of plays and adaptations produced on radio and television in Canada and Britain. Joining the BBC in 1963, he has lived in Bristol since 1965.

KHALID EL MUBARAK MUSTAFA is a well-known Sudanese playwright and the Director of the Institute of Music and Drama in Khartoum. He wrote both his Master's and his Ph.D. dissertations at the University of Bristol, the latter dealing with British television playwrights.

PHILIP PURSER has contributed television criticism to *The Sunday Telegraph* since its inception in 1961. Before that he was on the staff of the *News Chronicle*; before that, with the *Daily Mail*. He is the author of a number of television scripts, six novels, two biographies and a vast amount of miscellaneous fact and fiction. He lives in Northamptonshire.

1   Introduction

GEORGE W. BRANDT

Television drama is the liveliest of the arts. People who go to the theatre only once or twice a year, or to the cinema two or three times a month, make a habit of viewing several television plays every week.[1]

Television drama does not exist. It never has existed. And as an act of primary creation, rather than as a means of communication, it cannot exist. The profession has been pursuing a mirage.[2]

IT WOULD BE ABSURD to claim that television drama is being ignored in Great Britain. Viewing figures are staggering: *The Forsyte Saga* reached an average weekly audience of no fewer than 15,630,000 persons.[3] According to Manuel Alvarado and Edward Buscombe, well over half of the top twenty most popular TV programmes consist of plays; they say that 'in one average week we counted over 80 separate drama productions on television, including in that figure programmes such as situation comedies'.[4] The ready availability of television drama has implications that go far beyond how people choose to fill their leisure time. 'What we now have is drama as habitual experience: more in one week, in many cases, than most human beings would previously have seen in a lifetime.'[5]

As early as 1960, Harold Pinter estimated that in order to match the audience of 6,380,000 viewers who saw his *A Night Out* on *Armchair Theatre*, his stage play *The Caretaker* then running at the Duchess Theatre would have to stay on for thirty years![6] David Jones, who became a *Play of the Month* producer after having been a director with the Royal Shakespeare Company, made this telling comparison between traditional and electronic forms of drama: 'One Sunday night transmission of "Play of the Month" reaches four million people; it would take the Royal Shakespeare Company four years, playing in all its theatres, to equal that figure.'[7]

However, though this fact of cultural life at the popular level is universally acknowledged, sections of the intellectual Establishment are still averting their eyes from it. The modest role that television drama plays in university syllabuses is clear evidence of this. How many English Departments consider making a TV play a prescribed text? In the hierarchy of British cultural values, the verbal arts still tend to come first – more than in France, for instance, where the cinema has enjoyed the support of artists and intellectuals almost from the start. Apollinaire was a film buff at a time when no educated Englishman would have admitted to a liking for the flicks; he doted on Feuillade's *Fantômas* serial. A play text, even one written for television, is clearly an ordering of words on paper – but these words demand to be read visually. That seems sufficient to make television drama academically suspect.

What is perhaps more surprising is that journalists, too, should for a long time have vied with one another in denigrating television as the goggle box, the idiot's lantern, chewing gum for the eyes or moving wallpaper. There have been television critics ready to foul their own nests – like Maurice Wiggin, who commented,

The television playwright must . . . remember that he is writing for the least co-operative audience in the whole history of entertainment . . .
  Writing for television is a self-denying exercise, quite possibly intolerable for a young man, or woman, brought up with an overdue regard for the beauty of words. You must forget everything about 'fine writing', forget that there was ever such a word as style. This is a department of literature, I suppose, but the word 'literary' is an insult to a television playwright.[8]

This flippant attack, penned at an early stage in the development of TV drama, need not be taken too literally. But there were bigger guns blasting away. Philip Abrams, Fellow of Peterhouse, Cambridge and Assistant Lecturer in Sociology who was happy to be described as 'almost a television addict', contributed a chapter on radio and television to *Discrimination and Popular Culture*, a book published in 1964. It was a serious piece, concerned with the values that broadcasting spreads throughout the community. In it the writer claimed that the broadcaster in radio or television (no distinction was made between the two media for the purpose of the argument) would stand a good chance of being successful in the fields of information and education; but that 'wherever he tries to fill the third role, that of entertainment, the chances are that he will fail and that radio and television will prove less adequate media than many others'.[9].

What led the writer to this astonishing conclusion? According to his definition (he is not talking exclusively about drama), radio and television 'have four qualities which distinguish them from all other mass media. They are universal, continuous, public services for domestic consumption.'[10] No one would wish to quarrel with so comprehensive a description. Difficulties begin with the conclusions drawn from this premise.

First, *universality*. Since the audience comprises, at least potentially, a large part of the country as a whole, we may as well admit that working to the 'highest common factor' may in practice mean staying within the confines of a not very golden mediocrity. The argument is like that advanced against the cinema in its heyday when it was said that it appealed to a public with a mental age of fourteen – frequently not without cause.

But as the history of the cinema shows, there is another, more positive, side to this working for a mass audience. The very fact that from the 1920s to the 1950s an ever eager market made a high level of film production not merely possible but commercially imperative provided the necessary base for the masterpieces of such film-makers as Chaplin, Ford, Lang, Hitchcock, Renoir and von Stroheim (to mention only a few of the culturally OK names). Universality of appeal didn't exclude quality. When Abrams argues that 'so far as these media are concerned the acceptable and the authentic ought to be thought of as mutually exclusive goals' (p. 55) he is begging at least two questions. What is acceptable in audience terms – ratings or prestige? And what precisely does authenticity mean? Clearly we are in a realm where aesthetics, morals and a cluster of socio-political values overlap. Are we talking about an authentic reflection of life? Authentic in terms of typicality? Or with some deep poetic or imaginative validity? Or do we mean the advocacy of authentic values? The more the formula is held up to inspection, the more it falls apart. Although Abrams is not defending an elitist cultural position – indeed, he is explicitly taking the *opposite* stand – he nevertheless seems to end up by championing Establishment values: 'Purporting to reflect the world the entertainment offered by these media offers a definition of the world which is not the world known to most people and which rests on values alien to most people and certainly alien to the professed ideals of most educators and public men' (p. 12).

Next, the *continuousness* of television. Of course, if drama is put cheek by jowl with current affairs programmes, quiz shows, gardening talks and weather reports, there cannot be quite the same sense of occasion you get from a visit to the theatre or the cinema. True, the British cinema also used to have continuous programmes before the war: two feature films with full supporting programme (newsreel, cartoon, 'interest' film and trailers for forthcoming attractions). But the ceaseless flow of images on the domestic screen is a different matter altogether. Sets left on early in the evening pump out material so heterogeneous that the impact of any single item is liable to be blunted. The concentrated attention that good (which does not necessarily mean serious) drama demands is that much harder to achieve.

If we grant this drawback we are still a long way from conceding that 'continuity . . . serves to compound the trivialising tendencies of universality' (p. 58). What the complaint against the trivialisation comes to is an unacknowledged quarrel with popular affluence (such as it is). It is implied that viewers should have less choice; they should savour more fully what little they get; enough is, or should be, as good as a feast. The puritanical undertone is audible to the sensitive ear.

Then there is the question of the *domestic* setting. In a general sense one must agree with Abrams that broadcasting, 'through its special character, acquires strictly non-aesthetic, social and psychological functions which other media do not have (or do not have to nearly the same extent)' (p. 61). But is it true that home viewing is *necessarily* unselective, that the cosy or distracting atmosphere of the family living-room is bound to weaken the impact of drama? We are back to the 'trivialising' argument – a half-truth that paradoxically almost justifies poor programme quality because 'it really doesn't matter anyway'. The valid non-aesthetic functions of TV do not displace the strictly aesthetic ones.

Another way of denigrating programme content, in a compound of the 'continuous and domestic' argument, is to say, as Abrams does, 'A good deal of what is communicated . . . not only is ephemeral (as a result of the "one transmission only") norm of broadcasting performance which is itself a by-product of universal coverage), but ought not to pretend to be more than ephemeral.' (p. 61).

Apart from the fact that nowadays successful plays are frequently repeated unless there are impediments of the kind that will be noted later on, it is quite wrong to confuse the ephemeral with the trivial. Ben Jonson had the answer to that one when he wrote in defence of his masque *Hymenaei* in 1606, 'howsoever some may squeamishly cry out that all endeavor of learning and sharpness in these transitory devices . . . is superfluous, I am contented these fastidious stomachs should leave my full tables and enjoy at home their clean empty trenchers'.[11]

I don't wish to press the analogy between the Jacobean court masque and today's television drama too far. But an ephemeral art form need not be aesthetically inferior to more long-lasting forms: short-lived is neither beautiful nor ugly, it's simply short-lived. Anyway, does a stage play with a long run but with an audience far smaller than that commanded by the domestic screen really sink into the public consciousness any more deeply than its ephemeral rival? There is no answer to that; we are dealing with imponderables. But I suspect that the unspoken assumption underlying such a comparison is the expectation that if you missed the play early in its run, or if you had liked it so much that you wanted to see it again, it would still be there for subsequent visits.

Finally, the *public service* nature of television. Of course there are limits to what can be put on to the domestic screen if its controllers are themselves ultimately accountable to the public. To admit this is far from agreeing with Abrams that what 'impairs television drama . . . is the very mythology of impartiality that contributes so much to the high standards broadcasting achieves in its documentary activities'.[12] There is a confusion of ideas here. The same forces that impart a bias under the guise of objectivity to overall drama programming (rather than to individual dramas) also colour the documentary presentation of the world on television. Total objectivity is a will-o'-the-wisp. Nor is there all that much to choose between the public stances of the BBC and ITV, although the latter is not a public service organisation: the myth of impartiality informs the programming of both. But would a ruthlessly commercial television service be more likely to produce good drama? Not so, if American TV experience of the sixties and seventies is anything to go by.

The whole argument against television drama boils down to the theoretical assertion that it *cannot* be first-rate: *ergo* it isn't.

I have dwelt on Abrams's essay not in order to single it out as an example of anti-TV drama bias but because it articulates a point of view that used to be general not so long ago among educators and spokesmen for high culture.

A factor in the relative disesteem that television drama has been suffering from in comparison with the theatre is the different, and generally less satisfactory, kind of criticism it receives. TV reviewers are given grossly insufficient column space for a start. (Not that anything like adequate space is given to straight drama criticism either in the daily or Sunday press. Which of today's drama critics doesn't look back longingly to the elbow-room the *Saturday Review* allowed George Bernard Shaw and Max Beerbohm, enabling them to devote a thousand words or more to one single play?)

But regardless of whether TV and radio critics are treated badly or well by editors, the function of television reviewing is intrinsically different from the reviewing of stage plays. It is here, and not in the plays themselves, that the ephemeral nature of the medium is a handicap. By the time the review appears the broadcast has already receded into history. Since the review cannot serve as a shopping guide in the way a theatre criticism does for the wavering playgoer, one may wonder what purpose the television critic serves. Some justify their existence by the creation of a personal style, by being amusing – like *The Guardian*'s Nancy Banks-Smith. Some do in fact aim at creating a climate of opinion favourable to the reception of mature works. The drama-minded among these are, of course, stymied by the TV critic's task of having to write knowledgeably about all subjects that pass across the small screen. This is as unreasonable as expecting theatre critics to include some paragraphs on adult education, public affairs and sporting events in their columns.

The one major attempt in this country to give TV criticism a powerful voice ended in failure. The television quarterly *Contrast*, published by the British Film Institute as an 'independent critical magazine', began its career in autumn 1961 with a generous subsidy from the BBC and Granada Television; eighteen issues later, in spring 1966, it had to suspend publication, defeated not only by the economics of magazine publishing but also by the inherent paradox of writing at length, with a considerable time lag, about irretrievable events. *Contrast* couldn't hope to duplicate the success of its elder cousin in the media field, the

BFI's magazine *Sight and Sound* which had been appearing since 1932.

In a piece entitled 'The Critical Problem', the editors of *Contrast* came to grips with the unsatisfactory state of TV criticism at the time.[13] Of course the ephemeral nature of small-screen offerings was mentioned; so was the artistic immaturity of the medium (that part of the argument at least is ancient history); so was the shying away by reviewers from hard technical analyses, sheltering behind an essentially literary approach to an audiovisual medium. The TV critic's jack-of-all-trades role was castigated.

In the light of the working conditions prevailing then (and nothing much has changed since), it's not surprising that no very mature critical tradition had developed in relation to TV drama. A pioneer of consistent TV criticism with a strong drama bias like Philip Purser, associated with *Contrast* from its very first issue and a contributor to the present volume, is one of the exceptions that prove the rule.[14]

Is the criticism of television drama really such a specialised discipline? Indeed, is there such a thing as television drama as a wholly separate dramatic genre at all? Not all practitioners or theorists would agree that there is, as the Tony Garnett quotation at the head of this chapter shows.

Much ink has been spilt comparing this form of drama with its two elder relatives: the vastly senior one of live drama enacted on a stage, and the one projected on to a cinema screen which began around the turn of the present century. Little comparison has been made with radio drama, for excellent reasons. The latter, a 'theatre for the blind' (blindness has in fact often served as a motif in radio drama),[15] evidently differs from dramatic genres in which the visual element is an important means of signification.

However, the various attempts to define television drama – showing just how it differed from the others and was *sui generis* – have usually failed to take into account its rapid evolution. As a result, theories put forward with great conviction proved shortly afterwards to be largely out of date. Such speculations have not been unlike the theorising that was fashionable in the early days of the cinema. In the days of the silent film, largely under the influence of the theory and practice of the great Russian directors Pudovkin and Eisenstein, *editing* was seen as the quintessential element of film-making. But with the coming of sound, which brought back the old elements of dramatic significance of dialogue and music as well as the new element of sound effects; with the greater camera flexibility resulting from the development of more sophisticated camera vehicles, including the crane; with the introduction of the zoom lens and wider aspect ratios which have profoundly affected the whole concept of *mise-en-scène*, the old certainties about what was and what was not cinematic have ended up in the dustbin of outdated theories. Editing remains, of course, an important aspect of film art – but not, as Pudovkin had claimed, its very foundation. Similarly, yesterday's confident assertions about what is and what is not televisual have turned out to be merely interim statements.

The fact that television drama started out as a live medium gave it an obvious initial link with the theatre. It is significant that the first drama ever transmitted by the BBC in 1930, i.e. long before the beginning of regular transmissions, was an 'experimental' broadcast of Pirandello's one-act stage play, *The Man with a Flower in His Mouth*. It was probably the first play to have been televised anywhere. The rudimentary state of the art ruled out anything like a theatrical impact. *The Man with a Flower in His Mouth* had been

chosen for its suitability in view of the limited resources at the producer's disposal. Lance Sieveking's services were recruited as producer . . . and the cast of three were Gladys Young, Earle Gray and Lionel Millard . . . The distinguished artist, C. R. W. Nevinson, was persuaded to paint four canvases to be used as 'settings', and an improved 'theatre' was built . . .

The size and range of the fields in which the producer worked were not extensive, being represented by the head-and-shoulders picture of the actor . . . and, alternately taking his or her place, items of scenery or captions or inanimate objects of about the same size and seen at the same distance.

In this brave effort, a member of the cast began the dialogue as he was seen on the screen. He continued as he was faded out of vision and in his place came a small setting to create the scenic illusion. Occasionally the screen showed an expressive view of a pair of hands resting on a table or holding a tumbler as the dialogue continued. The gestures and changing expression of face were frequently visible, which was unfortunately more than one could say for some of Nevinson's 'scenery' . . .[16]

The BBC started its regular TV transmissions – the first such service in the world – on 2 November 1936. Between that time and the cessation of television broadcasting on 1 September 1939 – an unavoidable war casualty – drama was an important feature

1 *The first television broadcast ever of a play – Pirandello's* The Man with a Flower in His Mouth – *produced as an experiment in 1930 by Lance Sieveking, shown here with a 'caption' during rehearsal.*

of programming. Cecil Madden, Programme Organiser and Senior Producer during that period, has explained, 'I created the slogan "a play a day", and it was a very good one. Some plays were short, some plays were very long, but the drama was there right through.'[17] In 1937 there were no fewer than 123 drama transmissions, including repeats. Many of these, it should be noted, were very short indeed – between ten and thirty minutes in length.

The first original TV plays went out that year. J. Bissell Thomas's *The Underground Murder Mystery* was transmitted on 21 January; it had a running time of a mere ten minutes. Agatha Christie's *The Wasp's Nest* ran for twenty-five minutes, and S. E. Reynolds's *Turn Around* lasted half an hour. But the vast bulk of drama televised by the BBC before the war consisted of stage plays more or less adapted for the new medium. Indeed, the regular programme *Theatre Parade* presented weekly studio excerpts from current West End plays. Prewar TV drama productions included such sterling theatrical material as *Once in a Lifetime* by Kaufman and Hart, Flecker's *Hassan* and *The Insect Play* by the Čapek brothers. Some attempts were made to exploit the new medium creatively. Thus, in a production of *Murder in the Cathedral* the Tempters were presented as ghosts whispering in Becket's ear; and in *Journey's End* film shots of trench warfare and devastated areas were inserted in order to open up the action which on stage was wholly confined to a dug-out. These were tentative nods in the direction of a slightly more cinematic approach to TV drama. Two original plays appeared on the screen in 1939: *Rehearsal for Drama*, a thirty-five-minute play by Roy Carter and E. Wax, and *Condemned to be Shot*, a twenty-minute piece by R. E. J. Brooke. But it must be admitted that the amount of original playwriting on prewar television was miniscule.

When the BBC resumed television broadcasting one year after the war – on 7 June 1946 to be precise – adaptations once again loomed large: plays such as *The Man Who Came to Dinner*, *Rosmersholm*, *Mourning Becomes Electra*, *The Merchant of Venice*, *Everyman*, *Love for Love* – all good solid stage material. John Dighton's *The Happiest Days of Your Life* did in fact start out as a TV play in 1947 – only to transfer presently to the Apollo Theatre where it lived on for 604 performances. The link between the small screen and the theatre was still close. Some very few plays were in fact written for the medium, but Robert MacDermot, Head of Drama in 1948, put his policy in these terms:

I knew that it wouldn't be possible – nor, indeed, desirable – to concentrate exclusively on new material. I realised that the television audience would always need a staple ration of 'Shaftesbury Avenue Successes', but I was anxious that, in time, these would constitute not more than fifty per cent of our total output . . .

Of the remaining fifty per cent of plays, it was my aim to make half of them specially written for the medium and the rest admittedly written originally for the stage or screen but *not yet seen on either*.[18]

It was premature to claim at this embryonic stage, as one writer did, that these plays conceived only at one remove from the stage had 'blended the technique of the theatrical art with the ingenuity of the cinematic craft to create an interpretation foreign to both. That is drama as it should be in television, a medium with an infinitely greater canvas than that of the theatre or cinema.'[19]

How was television seen at the time by such practitioners as were given to generalising their experience? The technical constraints that guided notions about the 'inherent characteristics' of the medium were the following. First, TV was still monochrome (although the inventor J. L. Baird had been experimenting with colour years earlier). Second, the 405-line standard (adopted before the war and returned to when service was resumed) gave a low-definition image. Third – and from a playwriting point of view this was the most significant consideration – television drama went out *live*. There wasn't any of the post-production manipulation of recorded images and sound that was, and is, the essence of film-making.

These constraints were reflected in the advice given to aspiring TV playwrights. Some of the dramaturgic implications of poor image quality were spelt out as follows:

Obviously limitation of space is paramount. Even in the larger studios where, at any rate, one really big set can be built, one gains little, for you cannot pack it all on the screen at once. The further back you take your camera the less detail becomes recognizable. In the same way there should not be too many characters on the screen at once. Scenes between twos and threes are what television wants: quiet, intimate stuff which the camera can get right into. Five people on the set for any length of time is [sic] a producer's headache, meaning constant re-grouping and cutting from shot to shot in order to show viewers what the characters look like in close-up.[20]

Indeed, the close-up was considered *the* characteristic TV shot.

For the script writer the most exciting feature of television is its power to get right into a thing and focus attention on visual detail. It is fascinating to make use of this close-up view of the world, using vision, just as much as sound and dialogue, in revealing character and plot. The isolated close-up of some object, or subtlety of facial expression which would look overdone if magnified on a cinema screen, or would be lost in a welter of other detail if shown there in a more reasonable size, becomes perfectly natural on television.[21]

The fact that broadcasts were live affected the playwright in a number of ways. There was, for instance,

the problem of change of costume or make-up. In a stage play an actor has a ten- or fifteen-minute interval in which to grow old. In film he can take several hours. One five-minute interval is the average allowed in a television play. Often inexperienced authors will jump to 'the next day' quite forgetting their heroines have not only to get out of their evening clothes, but quite possibly rush to the other end of the studio where the next set is built.[22]

Live transmission meant constraints not only on the actors but on the technical crew as well – points with which the TV playwright of that era was supposed to acquaint himself. 'A longish sequence of rapidly changing shots so familiar in film "montage" is not practical. After three or four different shots in quick succession the cameramen, vision mixer and controlling engineers must be given time to take a breath. A change of shot every thirty seconds is a possibility but a little breath-taking.'[23]

In retrospect the disadvantages of live transmission would seem greatly to outweigh its advantages. Yet at the time this hazardous, only partly controllable method had its advocates: 'There is always something of a gamble about a television play, a gamble out of which the vast majority of productions come with flying colours. Naturally the artists – and the producer – are nervous. But I believe the best acting only springs from artists who are nervous – which after all merely means that their sensitivity is in a heightened state.'[24]

From the strictly dramaturgic (as against the production) point of view, the following considerations had to be borne in mind.

First, live electronic transmission committed the writer to a studio concept. This meant preferring the trained actor to the 'real' character who might perform well enough in his own environment but who would be lost inside a studio. (The cinema had gone through these problems more than once. What would have become of de Sica's neo-realist masterpiece *Bicycle Thieves* if he hadn't cast the non-professional actor Lamberto Maggiorani – a real industrial worker – in the principal role?) As well as limiting the casting possibilities, studio production would naturally tend to favour interior rather than exterior settings; it implied a whole series of spatial constraints.

At its best, television has only relative mobility and its action moves from set to set, or from set via film sequence to set. Within each set the action is usually pegged to a room, an office, a shop, or some other unit until it moves on to the next scene and is pegged there. It cannot (as in the film) move down corridors, along roads, and up hills or down precipices.[25]

Live studio transmission meant certain temporal constraints as well. There was bound to be some bias towards 'real time', the actual time of performance more or less coinciding with signified time, although there might be such elisions as we find in the stage drama of all periods (e.g. in Strindberg's *Miss Julie*, an actual performance time of some eighty minutes represents the events of a whole midsummer night – without the spectator being all that conscious of time-compression while watching the play).

'Real time' need of course operate in a television play only *within each scene*. Time-lapses might well be implied by the juxta-position of one scene with another – although in the early days of TV drama production, as we have just seen, there were severe limitations on these suggestions of time passing if actors had to change in a frantic hurry. The point is that the notion of time in TV dramaturgy at that point was more like that of the theatre, which conventionally observes 'real time' within each act (though usually not for the play as a whole), rather than that of the cinema, which, by assembling individual shots into se-quences, is able to make a totally free construct of time that obeys the laws of drama rather than the clock.

The novice playwright would also be informed that, apart from spatial and temporal limitations supposedly inherent in his field, there were thematic restrictions characteristic of the BBC in its role of Auntie.

The BBC often has to turn down good writing on grounds of unsuit-ability of subject matter. Television is very much a family entertainment . . . No one wants bad language or strip-tease by their firesides. It is not only our children, it is not only our mothers and aunts who may happen to be staying with us, nor the lonely spinster we happen to have invited in from the flat opposite, who must be protected – it is we ourselves who do not wish to be embarrassed by our friends' embarrassment.[26]

Television drama began to lift off into a more original sphere from 1951 onwards when, with Michael Barry as Head of Drama and Donald Wilson as Head of the Script Department, writers were put on staff who it was hoped would turn into television playwrights by story-editing other people's scripts and by staying close to actual production. The payoff of this policy was the rise to prominence of Nigel Kneale, whose science fiction serial *The Quatermass Experiment*, directed by Rudolph Cartier (July–August 1953), has been described as 'undoubtedly the most revolutionary original television drama event to that date'.[27]

Although ploughing much the same furrow as the cinema, which was producing a rich crop of mutants and space visitors in the fifties, *Quatermass* captured the popular imagination with its fast-moving action that articulated hidden fears and vibrated with symbolic overtones. The Thing from Outer Space that clung to the wall of Westminster Abbey, threatening mankind with instant destruction, was talked out of its nefarious designs by the hero. An optimistic, essentially liberal reading of the predicament of our times prevailed. *Quatermass II* was the inevitable sequel (November 1955), to be followed in turn by the demon-infested *Quatermass and the Pit* (December 1958–January 1959), both serials again directed by Rudolph Cartier. Other writers establishing themselves in television in the early fifties were the teller of thrilling tales Francis Durbridge, the versatile John Elliott, who was also to do a stint of top-level administration for the Corporation, and Iain MacCormick, whose *Good Partners* (June 1954) was the first full-length play – with a running time of eighty-nine minutes – to have been specially written for the BBC.

In 1954 Ted Willis launched *Dixon of Dock Green* upon a public that was glad to welcome such a reassuring image of the police into its home. Dixon, embodied by Jack Warner to the point of total identification, proved to be a long-staying visitor; indeed, police (and hospital, veterinary and other medical) series were to be a staple of TV drama. In the same year Nigel Kneale provided a spine-chilling corrective to cosiness with his dramatisation of Orwell's *1984* (12 December 1954), which was a less upbeat fable for our times than *Quatermass*.

A major influence on the tone as well as the quality of TV playwriting was the arrival of Independent Television, which began broadcasting on 22 September 1955. A great many fears had been voiced publicly and privately before commercialism was allowed to trespass into a field where the BBC had hitherto enjoyed a monopoly, in which non-competitive situation it had endeavoured to maintain somewhat high-toned 'standards' along the lines first laid down by Lord Reith. The coming of commercial TV didn't change everything, of course. Even those companies particularly devoted to drama – ATV, Granada, ABC, Associated Rediffusion – didn't emancipate themselves totally from dependence on the theatre: in fact, ATV had a contract with H. M. Tennent's for a regular supply of stage vehicles to be adapted for TV. Nor did the newcomers provide an instant explosion of masterpieces. However, the aggressive seeking out of the mass audience needed for a high income from advertising gave playwrights an incentive to write in a distinctly more popular vein.

One result of the competition for new playscripts was a massive injection of transatlantic material. At that time Canadian and American broadcasting companies were producing far more scripts dealing with facets of contemporary life than were being turned out in this country. The American writer Paddy Chayefsky had called on TV playwrights to look for material in the 'marvellous world of the ordinary'. His *Marty* had proved that the hopes and dreams of a very ordinary guy could be as moving as high-flown fantasy. One British writer to take this lesson to heart was Ted Willis, who was, of course, predisposed to be sympathetic to the Chayefsky message. Willis's *Woman in a Dressing Gown* – who was as ordinary as Marty but perhaps a shade less marvellous – made quite a stir when it was presented by Associated Rediffusion in July 1956; one critic hailed it as 'a television masterpiece'.[28]

But North American influence went beyond merely inspiring British television playwrights at a distance. In 1957 the BBC purchased for transmission thirty-five drama productions from the Canadian Broadcasting Corporation, thirty of which had been produced by one Sydney Newman. ABC acquired a large number of American and Canadian scripts for restaging on its *Armchair Theatre*. A more significant import was that of Newman himself, who was tempted across the ocean to take over *Armchair Theatre* in person. He used this key position to make profound changes in British television while with ABC from 1958 to 1963. Then the BBC, recognising his dynamic impact, lured him away from ABC in turn and made him Head of Drama.

Newman had a background in film-making with the National Film Board of Canada (where its founder John Grierson once said to him early in his career, 'Newman, you've got a B-picture mentality!').[29] He was whole-heartedly committed to capturing the largest number of viewers possible. His principle was that 'truth and audience identification are the first necessities for winning and holding an audience'.[30] Addressing a writing seminar in 1961 he said,

In an odd way, I am not fundamentally interested in the art of television. I am not fundamentally interested in camera work: nor indeed in the spoken word . . . I do like art that has something to say and art that is of use . . . I think great art has to stem from, and its essence must come out of, the period in which it is created.[31]

During the Newman era not all *Armchair Theatre* productions were either contemporary or British; nevertheless, there were a great many original plays by up-and-coming or established writers that exemplified his policy. Names like Alun Owen, Giles Cooper, Clive Exton, Bill Naughton, Peter Luke, Angus Wilson and Robert Muller come to mind.[32]

Nor was the upsurge of fresh television playwriting confined to the commercial sector (where Granada, too, was a great promoter of new plays by such authors as Peter Nichols, Rhys Adrian and Patrick Hughes): the BBC hadn't been idle under the vigorous Barry regime. Thus, Donald Wilson could write in 1960, 'In the year ending March 1960, BBC Television produced 265 *new* dramatic works, ranging in length from half an hour to ninety minutes and covering an immense variety of style and theme. In total screen time, this was the equivalent of 85 full-length stage plays or 110 feature films.'[33]

Yet another innovation was to change the ground rules of the game drastically: this was the arrival in 1958 of videotape. The recording of the TV image (as well as sound) on magnetic tape meant that repeats of a higher technical quality than had previously been available as telerecording on film ('kinescope' in American usage) were now available. But far more important was the opportunity it brought of bypassing the need for transmitting programmes – notably drama – live. Henceforth a play could be recorded in sections and then edited – with some difficulty initially when videotape had to be cut physically but with virtually the freedom of film editing once electronic editing had come in. At a stroke this exploded the mystique of the live broadcast which had supposedly given viewers the exciting sense of an event taking place here and now. (Actually, the impact of a show recorded earlier is identically that of one going out live, since the viewer is only concerned with the virtual and not the literal present.) From now on, writers were offered a degree of flexibility in play structures inconceivable in the days of hurried costume changes and actors rushing from set to set.

Following the recommendation of the Report of the Pilkington Committee on Broadcasting published in 1962, another major change was to leave its imprint on television. This was the opening of the BBC's second channel on 20 April 1964 (in fact transmission broke down on the opening night). The new channel provided fresh programme openings; it was also a technical change for the better in that it adopted a 625-line standard which gave considerably better definition. The market for drama (as well as other material) expanded, and some of the received wisdom about the limitations of the TV image became obsolete.

BBC-2 was the outlet for a new single drama spot called *Story Parade*, which was followed by *Theatre 625*. A more important step in the long run was the setting up under the Newman regime of the *Wednesday Play* on BBC-1, the title of which was altered to *Play for Today* in 1970 when transmission was shifted to Thursdays. Much of the history of British TV drama is tied up with this programme spot. Shortly after it began on 28 October 1964 the *Wednesday Play* made a name for itself, not least for its determinedly here-and-now approach and the commendably high number of scripts specially written for the medium. Among the authors it featured were Simon Raven, Julia Jones, Dennis Potter, John Hopkins, Michael Hastings, Nell Dunn, Paul Ableman, David Halliwell, John Mortimer, Simon Gray, Ray Lawler, Charles Wood, Jeremy Sandford, Michael Frayn, Jim Allen, John Osborne and others – for once literally – too numerous to mention. It's a roll-call of television writers of distinction, many of them playwrights in other media as well. Their work was presented by talented directors of the order of Ken Loach, Waris Hussein and Jack Gold. No less significant for the high quality of the *Wednesday Play* were its (relatively small number of) producers, such as Irene Shubik,[34] Peter Luke, James MacTaggart and Tony Garnett. Particularly the latter two gave this single play spot a lively reputation for concern with current issues.

When Sydney Newman was the BBC's Head of Drama, he made an administrative change in what had become a cumbersome machinery by subdividing the Drama Department into three sections, i.e. Plays, for the production of single, self-contained dramas; Series, for productions with recurrent characters but self-contained episodes; and Serials, plays the action of which would be continuous from episode to episode. He also brought over from ABC a breakdown of the amorphous post of producer from which were hived off: (*a*) the producer *proprement dit* who co-ordinated all the functions of the team – clearly a job of paramount importance, particularly in series and serials; (*b*) the director who actually directed cast and crew in the studio and on location – the man at the sharp end; and (*c*) the story editor who advised and guided the writer and who had a decisive influence when there was more than one writer working on a series.

The story (or script) editor was to become a key figure in the writing of TV drama. As Robert Buckler puts it,

the script editor is in the classic middle man's position. He's neither the unstinting champion of the writer nor the obsequious front man of the management. He has no immediately classifiable skill and is therefore frequently suspected of having none . . .

Some argue that the editor should have had writing experience, others that the preconceptions arising from that experience only get in the way. There are those who claim that the editor should be middle-aged, a not too successful writer perhaps, and those who say that he or she should be young, a graduate, full of enthusiasm. In the end, the only real qualification is the capacity to come up with the scripts . . .

At various times the editor thus finds himself required to be ideas man, skim reader, bureaucrat, talent scout, critic, rewriter, diplomat, censor, and, ultimately, defender of the completed script.[35]

A vital fact in dramatising the contemporary scene was the changeover, for substantial sections or indeed the whole of a programme, from recording directly on to videotape to recording on to film; in the early days this was done on to 35 mm film, then on to the cheaper 16 mm gauge associated with lightweight filming equipment.

In other words, television drama was no longer synonymous with studio drama. Film inserts as such weren't new in television; as we have seen, their use goes back to the pioneering days. But whereas in the past short film clips had served as continuity bridges between two studio shots or to establish an unavoidable exterior, there was now an increasing tendency – strongly championed by Tony Garnett among others – to exploit the cine camera's ability to poke its eye into any situation anywhere, in preference to the electronic camera's slow-moving studio-bound domesticity.

Whether or not this brought TV drama any closer to 'reality' in any substantial sense, it was certainly a shove in the direction of surface realism. It allied drama more closely to the documentary. Indeed, it made redundant the older conceptions of the TV documentary, described as follows in the mid-fifties: 'The production of story documentaries is complicated by ordinary television standards and it makes heavy demands – a big studio, elaborate film sequences, large casts, multiple sets, the maximum number of camera, film and sound channels, complicated equipment moves.'[36]

The new flexibility made it possible, in the manner of Italian neo-realism, to bring in non-professionals, to tap greater spontaneity in the actors, and to give a greater feeling of verisimilitude to a production all around. Plays would still be transmitted electronically; but the creative problems of writing, directing and production generally would be those of film, thereby making the domestic screen into a mini-cinema. In practice the studio wasn't to vanish as a drama venue by any means; but the whole world was potentially becoming a stage for television drama.

The producer most closely associated with the use of film on the *Wednesday Play*, Tony Garnett, worked with authors like David Mercer, Nemone Lethbridge, Charles Wood, Jim Allen and Jeremy Sandford. The play that epitomised this veristic trend was Sandford's *Cathy Come Home*. Produced by Tony Garnett and directed by Ken Loach, when it was transmitted on 16 November 1966 it entered into television mythology instantly. There is no need to enlarge on it here, since it is discussed elsewhere in this book.[37] In any case, the degree of 'realism' achieved by it and the earlier *Up the Junction*, written by Nell Dunn and also directed by Loach (3 November 1965), outstripped such earlier front-runners of naturalistic drama as Alun Owen's prestigious contributions to *Armchair Theatre – No Tram to Lime Street* (18 October 1959), *After the Funeral* (3 April 1960) and *Lena, Oh My Lena* (25 September 1960). The advantage of the later productions lay neither in greater authenticity of dialogue nor in subtler depiction of character, in both of which Owen had excelled, but rather in the observational freedom and the appearance of unmediated reality that lightweight film equipment was making possible.

While the single play was going through a Golden Age in the late fifties and the sixties, series and serials were nudging their way forward into immense popularity, to the point of posing a threat to the single play in the seventies.

This development was common to both the BBC and ITV. The BBC started *Z-cars* in 1962, a series originated by Troy Kennedy Martin that was to give work to a number of writers; in this distinctly post-Dixon view of the work of the police in a northern New Town – a view not initially popular with the force – great stress was laid on recognisability. Recognisability was also the keynote of the longest-running of all serials, Granada's *Coronation Street*, which had begun its screen life even earlier – on 9 December 1960. This evergreen saga of a working-class street has seen generations of writers come and go since Tony Warren first created it, abetted by John Kershaw, John Finch, Jack Rosenthal and others. At any one time the scriptwriting team would be plotting out the next six episodes, three months ahead, the team consisting of about a dozen writers.[38] It's interesting to recall that this serial, which has long since become a national institution, met with a mixed reception at its launch. The *Spectator* applauded it, the *New Statesman* was dismissive. Opinions have been divided ever since, but the fascination exerted by what's been called Television's Most Famous Street over whole strata of viewers is not in question. There have been addicts so bemused by the naturalism of *Coronation Street* that they believe its denizens to be not fictitious creatures but flesh-and-blood characters whose lives just happen somehow to be chronicled on the TV screen. A regular flood of letters offers them advice, help and sympathy in their trials. But the admirers of this, the greatest of all British soap operas, aren't confined to any one segment of the educational or social spectrum: none other than Poet Laureate, Sir John Betjeman, has said, 'Manchester produces what to me is the Pickwick Papers. That is to say, *Coronation Street*.'[39]

It is no accident that the tone of this serial reflects the ethos of an independent company determined to win large audiences. The populist drama of ITV has helped Auntie to rid herself of some of her Reithian reflexes. Mid-sixties serials like *Mogul, Dr Finlay's Casebook, The Power Game, The Troubleshooters* and others were aimed at the mass viewing public in a ratings game which made it possible at other times to take a chance on the not-so-popular single play.

Yet another technical innovation was to affect drama – the coming of colour. BBC-2 had started transmitting in colour in July 1967; a full colour service began on 2 December of that year, using the West German PAL (Phase Alternation Line) system. By the end of 1969, BBC-1 and ITV had joined the party and were all fully colourised.

This change may not at first glance seem to signify much for the television playwright. But soon enough broadcasting companies felt the urge to exploit to the full an innovation for the sake of which viewers were being asked to buy new sets and pay higher licence fees. Years before, the introduction of Technicolor and other colour systems in the cinema had been an invitation to lavish spectacle; history was to repeat itself in television. Colour is a designer's dream. True, the first of the high-class costume dramas, the BBC's *Forsyte Saga*, was a black-and-white affair. (Immensely successful, with splendid performances and high production values, this serial proved a blockbuster for the export market; it was shown in the United States, Portugal, Hungary – even in the Soviet Union, where it was transmitted in a dubbed Russian version; by 1970 the BBC reported that some 160,000,000 viewers in forty-five countries had seen this instant classic.) But colour was a major feature, appealing to domestic viewer and overseas buyer alike, in such costume serials as the BBC's *The Six Wives of Henry VIII*, ATV's *Edward VII*, Thames Television's *Edward and Mrs Simpson* and *Jenny* (the story of Churchill's mother), and – last but not least – London Weekend's fictitious evocation of an Edwardian upper-middle-class household, *Upstairs Downstairs*, originated by the actresses, Jean Marsh and Eileen Atkins.[40]

Important though colour has been in churning the nostalgia wave, it would be an error to attribute the latter entirely to technology. There are too many other indicators, in the arts, in fashion and politics, suggesting that the backward glances cast at a mythological past spring from deeper insecurities. Nostalgia drama satisfies the need to imagine a dreamland of stable class and other relationships as a consolation for the turbulent present. According to Anthony Sampson,

there can hardly be a decent-sized mansion that has not by now been besieged by the cameras for yet another re-creation of Victorian, or eighteenth-century life . . .

And no doubt all this nostalgia captures folk-memories of ancient hierarchies and loyalties, even among people whose parents and grand-parents never stayed in a great house, whether as a governess or as a chatelaine. [41]

The great predominance of series and serials during the seven-ties, particularly on ITV but also on the BBC, has often been commented on. Observers rarely fail to point to the situation in the States, where the single play has virtually been killed off to make way for machine-made series and serials with high gloss, canned laughter and routine violence. The threat to the single play is primarily economic: an easily marketable product is an attractive proposition if ratings or overseas sales appeal are the programme executives' prime motivations. But there may be other factors at work as well. Drama content is more controllable in the series format with its narrow guidelines laid down for the writer or writers. At times when the 'message' play can stir up hornets' nests of letter-writing pressure groups, retreating to the safety of story-edited, prepackaged drama may seem an easier option.

A decline in the quantity and quality of the single play has been frankly recognised as a danger to television drama. In reply to the question whether he thought single plays might go, under econ-omic pressure, Shaun Sutton, BBC Television's Head of Drama, had this to say,

Well, it would be a tragedy if they disappeared, for they are the life-blood of drama . . . If you have a total output of series only, crime series, social series and all the rest of it, however good they are, you would be seeing one sort of drama all the same length, all very careful not to offend or overstep any social barriers. [42]

Much the same view has been expressed by Renée Goddard, then Head of ATV's Script Department: 'The single play is the one that in the end will influence the standard of writing. I think there should always be enough slots for single plays to keep up the standard of production in everything: producers, designers and cameramen, the lot.' [43]

The danger of a surfeit of series and serials has been pointed out by John Kershaw, too, one of the original *Coronation Street* writers: 'The popular arts (and high among them are serials) tend to make a virtue out of seeing. They celebrate the infertile, stag-nant *status quo*. There are, of course, worthwhile popular intel-ligences but popularity itself ought not to be the only or principal aim of the arts.' [44]

But we must not overstate the case against series. One particular branch, the situation comedy ('sitcom' for short) has usually been regarded as inherently conservative: after all, laughter is the punishment society metes out to social deviants, according to Henri Bergson. That was not, however, the effect of *Till Death Us Do Part* (which began on 22 July 1965); in it the authoritarian lower-middle-class anti-hero Alf Garnett, magisterially impersonated by Warren Mitchell, was held up to sharp ridicule. The series, which from the start drew audiences of over 18,000,000 viewers, was written by Johnny Speight, whose own working-class background enabled him to give great accuracy and bite to this picture of reaction in low places.[45] If the reception of the series was said to be ambiguous, some viewers actually identifying with the odious though comical Alf, the intention of the message was plain enough. 'At his best, its author, Johnny Speight, had the courage to use as the basis for ferocious humour our suppressed hates and guilts, our prejudices spoken and unspoken; racial prejudices, social prejudices, and all the rich stew of unreason which simmers away in the minds of most of us.'[46]

Not only have series often been very good in themselves (*Steptoe and Son* by Ray Galton and Alan Simpson; John Cleese's *Fawlty Towers* are outstanding examples), they have also provided useful employment and worthwhile writing experience for authors of single plays. Writers of the calibre of John Hopkins and Alan Plater worked on *Z-Cars*, and Jack Rosenthal, an early member of the *Coronation Street* team, was later to distinguish himself with *Bar Mitzvah Boy* and other award-winning TV plays.

The serial is a somewhat different matter. It can look back on a long ancestry not only in radio and the cinema but in literature too. The three parts of *Henry VI* are a history serial. The TV serial shares with the nineteenth-century novel published in instalments the cliffhanger ending for each episode. More significant than a bias towards suspense is the chance it gives the writer to paint a broader canvas, to develop stories of greater complexity than the single play permits. The time dimension built into the viewing experience can itself be used creatively in that the passing of a week between episodes makes the viewer actually share a sense of time passing with the characters on the screen.

The pressure of series and serials on TV playwriting may – I put it no higher than that – have tended to weight the scales in favour of naturalism. Exceptions to this generalisation can be found of course. Dennis Potter's *Pennies from Heaven* (7 March–11 April 1978) featured thirties songs dubbed over the miming of actors so deliberately unconvincing as to serve as a complex alienation device.[47] But the appeal of the most popular series rests on the mirroring of everyday reality: *Coronation Street* is a glaringly obvious example. 'Newspaper writers have criticised its authenticity at their peril . . . The week Britain went decimal, one of the country's first 50p pieces was passed over the Rovers Bar and into Annie Walker's till . . . and into the conversation in the Snug. "If it happens in life, it can happen in *Coronation Street*" is the yardstick.'[48]

The search for authenticity is not confined to stories of contemporary life. The same concern for correct detail has gone into the making of more upmarket serials such as Simon Raven's *Edward and Mrs Simpson* (Thames, 1978). This has its implications for the writer no less than for the rest of the production team. Andrew Brown, the producer of the serial, had this to say about the period research underpinning it: 'It was vital that we presented the story as accurately as possible. We could not stray from the truth, or distort it. Every aspect of the scripts had to be scrupulously researched, and that standard had to be maintained on all aspects of production.'[49]

Now this has its admirable side. The impact not only of escapist or nostalgic pieces but also of socially relevant plays like *Cathy Come Home* derives precisely from their realistic surface texture. Nor is naturalism peculiar to television: novel, theatre and cinema have long been travelling along the same road. There is, however, the significant difference that whilst other art forms have been trying for decades to break away from a naturalism increasingly felt to be a constraint, television on the whole has remained faithful to it.

As a matter of fact, in the fifties it was believed that naturalism was *the* style for television drama. In the opinion of Howard Thomas, then Managing Director of ABC, 'Television drama is not so far removed from television journalism, and the plays that will grip the audience are those that face up to the new issues of the day as well as to the problems as old as civilisation.'[50]

Sooner or later a quasi-journalistic approach was bound to run into a blind alley. Oddly enough, it was on the normally naturalistic *Armchair Theatre* slot that the hitherto naturalistic playwright Alun Owen tried to break out with *The Rose Affair* (8 October 1961). This retelling of the old tale of Beauty and the Beast featured blatantly stylised devices – such as Betumain, the 'Beast', wearing different masks. In the theatre not a single eyebrow would have been raised; on television it was a revolution. Press reaction to the play was mixed; but the *Times*, *Daily Telegraph*, *Daily Sketch*, *Daily Herald*, *Daily Worker*, London *Evening News*, *Spectator* and *Yorkshire Post* ranged from the warmly approving to the ecstatic. Sydney Newman, champion of aggressively realistic drama, backed the play whole-heartedly:

> *The Rose Affair*, I think, is the always-hoped-for, sometimes-achieved best we can do; Alun Owen has written a really demanding play which holds so many possibilities that it defies definitive interpretation. It is the sort of play which should be put on every year for four or five years, interpreted by different directors with different casts; by the end of that time I believe it would have become a television classic.[51]

A more theoretical impetus to the debate about style was given by another refugee from the naturalistic camp, Troy Kennedy Martin, the originator of *Z-Cars*. His polemical article 'nats go home', published in the theatre magazine *Encore*,[52] remains one of the few declarations of literary principle in the history of British TV drama. Kennedy Martin demanded two things of the TV play of the future: that it should break away from the theatre and that it should abandon naturalism. Greater camera freedom and release from the constraints of real time would ally the 'new drama' more with the cinema; but he rejected the Hollywood emphasis on the close-up as a 'subjective' device. He advocated using the camera 'objectively' instead. Television drama was challenged to join the mainstream of the English creative life of the last 250 years in which naturalism had merely been a backwater; and in this effort all the resources of lighting, sound, editing were to be deployed. He conceded that this might ultimately make TV drama a director's medium like the cinema; meanwhile writers would have to be the spearheads of innovation.

This polemic was vigorous rather than rigorous. What exactly did its author mean by the objective use of the camera (other than preferring medium long shots and long shots to coming in closer?) But it was widely noted and helped to shake up seemingly fixed dogmas. Following this still essentially aesthetic polemic, naturalism has been attacked from a more political stance by Raymond Williams, Stuart Hall, Colin McArthur and others.[53]

Stuart Hall has challenged naturalism as the dominant language of TV (not merely TV drama) on the grounds that 'television is technically and socially a *thoroughly manipulated medium*. The utopia of straight transmission, or the "naturalistic fallacy" in television, is not only an illusion – it is a dangerous deception.'[54]

Why dangerous? Precisely because it is a style that pretends we are being shown unmediated reality – which of course we are not. Regardless of style, any portrayal of reality is constructed; it has a built-in point of view. This applies even to such non-fiction items as the news; how much more to drama, which is inevitably an artefact. The seamless portrayal of reality in which the painter becomes invisible *may* be a subtle endorsement of the *status quo*. It may crush the viewer with a sense of the way things (inevitably) are, instead of showing how they might be.

Hall had earlier criticised *Coronation Street* along comparable lines:

for the working-class audience the depiction of a life similar to their own yet lacking the intensity and the complications of experience can itself be a form of relaxation – a playing-through of experience at precisely that speed which is calculated not to disturb. And for the middle-class audience . . . the images of neighbourliness and co-operation may be exactly the wrong sort of compensation and consolation.[55]

So far the argument is plain: the surface texture of naturalism prevents the viewer from grasping the inner contradictions, the social tensions that haven't as yet risen to the level of consciousness. But what becomes of it when it's turned against precisely those plays that do show social conflict and question the *status quo*? Is naturalism absolutely incapable of adopting a resolutely critical stance? According to some, it is. Jim Allen's *Days of Hope*,[56] which had its fair share of flak from the right, also drew fire from some leftwing critics:

the film falls within a bourgeois conception of history in which the past is understood as having a fixed and immutable existence rather than being the site of a constant struggle in the present. And it is this conception of history which places *Days of Hope* firmly within the most typical of the BBC's varieties of artistic production: the costume drama.[57]

Such a blanket condemnation can easily become formalist. Can style be divorced from content? When this question was discussed at the First Edinburgh International Television Festival in 1977, Dennis Potter (not only a playwright but also an experienced professional critic) contributed a paper in which he struck a balance between form and content in TV drama.

Most television ends up offering its viewers a means of orientating themselves towards the generally received notions of 'reality'. The best naturalist or realist drama, of the Garnett–Loach–Allen school for instance, breaks out of this cosy habit by the vigour, clarity, originality and depth of its perceptions of a more comprehensive reality. The best non-naturalist drama, in its very structure *dis*orientates the viewer smack in the middle of the orientation process which television perpetually uses . . . It shows the frame in the picture when most television is busy showing the picture in the frame. I think it is *potentially* the more valuable, therefore, of the two approaches.[58]

More than anywhere, naturalism has become a questionable and much-questioned style in the story documentary. This dramatisation of actuality (which has been called all sorts of things, from dramatised documentary and fictional documentary to docudrama, drama documentary, dramadoc, re-enactment, dramatic reconstruction and so on) does in fact pose problems peculiar to television. In the theatre, the staging of a 'real' situation can never be misread as unmediated unreality. In the cinema the picture is somewhat more ambiguous, admittedly. But on the domestic screen, embedded in a continuous flow of largely non-fictional items, the drama documentary runs the risk of itself being read as non-fiction. There is therefore some force to Paul Ableman's argument when he talks about

the trouble with extreme naturalism. It is self-defeating. If it succeeded perfectly it would cease to exist. The sole result would be that the store of reality would be minutely increased. But the aim of the artists – however it be defined – is certainly *not* marginally to increase the world's store of reality. It is surely to transcend reality by means of a visionary apprehension, and presentation, of the essence of life. It then interacts with reality on a basis of at least equality. It has its own sphere which should be kept distinct. It follows therefore that the goal of the fictional documentary and the goal of art, as it has always been conceived, diverge. No matter how vital it is for all art, even the most surreal or abstract, to incorporate elements of reality which provide indispensable reference points for the contemplating mind, it is equally vital for it not to merge completely with the phenomenological world.[59]

This argument is fairly close to that of Kennedy Martin's article referred to above; but much of the attack on fiction-in-documentary-guise is a political-argument-in-philosophical-guise. If the fate of homeless Cathy has been presented in too documentary a manner, do we resent it (if we do) because we feel that we have been conned about Cathy as a person, which is an essentially aesthetic matter, or that we have been conned about the housing problem, which is very much a political matter? To be sure, fiction should not sail under a false flag. But Gus Macdonald, Head of Features with Granada, claims that worries about confusing, let alone surreptitiously radicalising, the viewers are excessive:

The boundaries between forms may be blurred but because of that they are well patrolled. Television authorities (and viewers) get agitated when drama is mixed with actuality, or fact with opinion, without the proper signposting. Audiences demand to be told the status of the information being offered . . . On the other hand, it would be naive to assume that a sudden revealed 'truth' on television would result in social ferment.[60]

Naive perhaps; but this fear reflex seems to be activated every time the tone of a TV play invites the questioning of official views. While the faulty signposting of fiction may upset the aesthete, the really heavy barrage comes from the noisy spokespersons of the so-called silent majority. *Days of Hope*, to take a conspicuous example, wasn't strictly speaking a story documentary, being so obviously set in the past; it did however, have all the hallmarks of spontaneous unconstructed observation. Letters to the *Radio Times* protested against the serial's portrayal of the Army in the First World War as 'disgusting', 'lamentable tripe' and a 'jolly bad show'. *The Times* devoted a lead editorial to it. Admitting its artistic merit and rejecting the notion that it should be suppressed, the editorial stated,

It is not surprising that such a partisan series has attracted criticism from those who do not regard the advance of socialist revolution in these years, or indeed at any other time, as an unmixed blessing. Indeed the three plays already broadcast have at times positively provoked such a response . . .
As with many television plays the producers of the series have adopted some of the techniques of the documentary to achieve a greater dramatic effect. A danger of confusion in the mind of the viewer can arise.[61]

Even when there is no such danger of stylistic confusion, television drama can easily find itself in the front line of ideological battles. The attack on the so-called permissiveness of the late sixties and the seventies – a relaxation from earlier taboos in which television has not raced ahead of the theatre and the cinema – comes in moral guise, but there may be a more comprehensively authoritarian subtext. Obvious targets are the linked areas of bad language, sex and violence. Much of the artillery is fired off by the National Viewers' and Listeners' Association, a pressure group on the media (not only television but theatre and cinema as well) run by the highly articulate Mrs Whitehouse. The National VALA, according to one of its leaflets, 'believes that Christian values are basic to the health and well-being of our nation. It therefore calls upon the broadcasting authorities to reverse, effectively, the current humanist approach to social, religious and personal issues.'

Public concern with a form of drama that invades the family home is of course perfectly proper. Whether the work of VALA – which according to Stuart Hood 'is best described as representing a brand of right-wing populism'[62] – really aims at a fair balance in television programming is another matter. VALA's attack on a variety of programmes is certainly sweeping. In one of its publications, exception was taken, on the grounds of violence, the exploitation of sex, bad language or blasphemy, to the following programmes, which differ widely in terms of intention or achievement: *Gangsters* (BBC-1), *The Professionals* (London Weekend), *I Claudius* (BBC-2), *Target* (BBC-1), *Hazell* (Thames), *Hawksmoor* (BBC-1) and *The Sweeney* (Thames) – and Dennis Potter's *Pennies from Heaven* (BBC-1), David Mercer's *Flint* (BBC-1) and Barrie Keefe's *Nipper* (BBC-1) as well as his *Champions* (Granada).[63]

Perhaps the most significant target singled out for attack by VALA was Keefe's play *Gotcha* (transmitted on BBC-1 on 12 April 1977). Dealing with attempted and actual violence in a confrontation between an almost pathologically disturbed comprehensive-school boy and two of his teachers, the story was a sustained cry of pain. It could not by any stretch of the imagination be said to be 'exploitative'. If it grated on the viewer's nerves this was inherent in the subject. But when at the end of 1978 the BBC proposed to show the play once again a campaign was mounted to avert this; and indeed the repeat didn't take place. The National VALA was quoted as saying, 'This shows that the BBC takes notice of what the public thinks.' One may doubt whether the public was consulted in any meaningful sense; what is certain is that an important and deeply felt play was kept off the air. Letters appeared in the press in its defence; one of these stated,

it seems to me that the play raises important issues which need 'shocking' incidents to shake off the complacency obstructing constructive discussion.

I fear that Mrs Whitehouse shares this complacency, and that in her campaign as self-appointed moral guardian she is overlooking the true meaning of the play, and, like others perhaps, is seeing only the superficialities of a revolt against established authority.[64]

Possibly even more indicative is the hostile reaction that met the four-part series by Gordon Newman and Tony Garnett, *Law and Order* (BBC-1, April 1978). In a different world from dear old Dock Green, these plays aroused the ire not only of VALA but also of the Prison Officers Association and the Metropolitan Police. It would appear that it was owing to pressure put on the BBC that a repeat contemplated in 1979 was cancelled and that *Law and Order*, for all its success (in terms of viewer response, that is), wasn't sold abroad although there were willing buyers.

Some sort of tug-of-war as to what can and what cannot be shown will always be going on in any broadcasting system anywhere. The precise force and nature of these pulls will of course differ in different circumstances. But it must never be forgotten that the high standing television drama has enjoyed with viewers in this country (and with foreign buyers, too) during the sixties and seventies is due not only to the excellence of production standards but, first and foremost, to the quality of the writing. Television playwriting will flourish best in an atmosphere of freedom both in choice of subject and in matters of style. To narrow the confines within which writers are allowed to work – no matter whether the pressures are those of politics, commerce or organised campaigns – cannot fail to have an adverse effect on the quality of TV drama.

Does that matter in any deep sense? Much of the controversy about the image of the world created by the domestic screen (an image including but not limited to drama) is part of an infinitely older argument about the effect that any spectacle has on actual behaviour. Should the arts show only admirable behaviour? Does the showing of reprehensible behaviour invite imitation? In *The Republic*, Plato suggested that the imitative arts undermined civic virtue, and in Book III he recommended that in his ideal state visiting actors would be anointed with myrrh, have a garland of wool placed on their heads – and after this friendly reception sent packing to keep out their corrupting influence. Puritan opposition to the English theatre during the sixteenth and seventeenth centuries has left its mark, perhaps even to the present day. For a long time the cinema, here and elsewhere, was blamed for all the moral shortcomings of society; the spread of violent and/or licentious behaviour after the First World War was directly attributed to it, and one of the chief functions of censorship in different countries was to prohibit all sexy (more rarely, violent) films, or at any rate to snip out any such sequences from films that were shown. Political censorship reflecting official views was the norm.

The spotlight of attention has shifted from the cinema, no longer regarded as a model for mass behaviour, over to television. Research done into the influence of the cinema on conduct tended to be methodologically crude. Similar research in the sixties and seventies into whether behaviour exhibited on the TV screen – not necessarily confined to drama – does in fact modify behaviour has been more sophisticated. The last word has not been spoken yet; perhaps it never will be. It is extremely difficult to isolate any single stimulus from the whole web of social causation.

Some research (not unchallenged, it's only fair to say) has come to the conclusion that disturbing incidents on the TV screen *may* rub off on behaviour in certain age groups. William Belson argues that *'high exposure to television violence increases the degree to which boys engage in serious violence'*.[65] Similarly, H. J. Eysenck and D. K. B. Nias state that 'the evidence strongly indicates that the portrayal of sex and violence in the media does affect the attitude and behaviour of viewers; that these effects are variable, depending on the details of presentation and the personality of the viewers; and that recommendations for action depend on the person's value system'.[66]

The final point is worth noting. Even if a link between frequent viewing, attitude-formation and real-life content could be proved beyond a shadow of a doubt, which isn't likely because of the complexity of the problem, we are left with decisions that relate to our fundamental beliefs. The question of an intellectually respectable television drama policy is open to debate; it ought to be debated fully and publicly. What is not acceptable is the suggestion that a play can be assessed by a mechanistic totting up of acts of violence or eroticism: so many blows, so many bullets, so many gropes and groans. Even if we concede that it is intrinsically undesirable to show, let us say, acts of sadistic violence (and even here we'd be in deep waters), there is no substitute for a sophisticated sense of dramatic values. An action may be exploitative in one context and entirely valid in another. What must also be rejected is the choking off of the ventilation of public issues; this is one of the most valuable functions that television drama can perform.

Eysenck and Nias are of course right in warning against any simplistic equation of censorious attitudes with standard political alignments when they plead that we should

cease to regard the battle between puritans and libertarians as one between political right and left. There is no meaningful relation between opposing pornography and wishing to lower income tax, or between a belief that the portrayal of violence in the media will cause violence in the streets and dislike of nationalization. In fact, it is obvious that there is far more pornography, obscenity and violence in the media in the capitalist countries than there is in the communist countries.[67]

That is indeed so. But if pressure-group activity against the alleged permissiveness, socio-political as well as sexual, of British television drama springs from the desire to 'reverse . . . the current humanist approach to social, religious and personal issues' the argument inevitably becomes ideological. Authoritarian undertones are clearly detectable in the attacks on some television plays.

Predictions about the future of British TV drama would be hazardous. Inevitably it will be linked with the state of playwriting in all media and in a wider sense with the political, social, economic and spiritual climate in the country. But it will also be influenced, as it has been in the past, by the developing technology of television itself.

We have seen that theories confidently put forward from time to time have tended to be overtaken by events. In the past it may have been necessary to insist on the difference between the television play and other forms of drama; now it is more useful to point out the similarities.

If TV drama in its early days had to emancipate itself from the stage play it nevertheless retains an umbilical link with the theatre. Studio-based drama survives; real time as a performance factor has not been totally eliminated by the techniques of videotape and/or film editing; dialogue may still at times outweigh visual signalling in dramatic importance. Many plays still begin in the theatre and then transfer effectively to the small screen. Thus, Mike Leigh's sharply satirical *Abigail's Party* began its stage career in Hampstead, the fruit of an intensive period of group improvisation by the actors; it proceeded to make a splendidly effective *Play for Today* (3 November 1977), winning its lead Alison Steadman the Best Actress award for the year. *Abigail's Party* felt like a TV play, not the televised version of a stage play.

But the link with film is equally close. Indeed, sometimes it's difficult to draw a clear distinction between films made for the large and those made for the small screen. Broadcasting organisations in a good many countries (e.g. Italy, Austria, the German Federal Republic) will commission films to be televised first and then shown in regular cinemas. In spite of the difference of screen size these films work equally well in either outlet. And cinema films, golden oldies as well as new releases, have become an intrinsic part of TV programming. Are these films TV drama or not? To argue the point is to indulge in metaphysics. Whatever hard-line theorists may assert, the viewing experience is not necessarily all that different.

The close relationship between television and the cinema is shown by the popularity of the spin-off – i.e. one medium borrowing from the other. The situation in Britain makes an interesting contrast to that in the United States, where the traffic tends to go from the large to the small screen. Thus, the American Broadcasting Company's *Nanny and the Professor* was a spin-off from Disney's *Mary Poppins*, and its family serial *Here Come the Brides* was based on the musical *Seven Brides for Seven Brothers*. This reflects the strong position of the American film industry. The reverse is true in this country, where a good many cinema films have been directly inspired by TV drama – e.g. *The Quatermass Experiment* (US title: *The Creeping Unknown*), *Quatermass II* (US title: *Enemy from Space*), *Quatermass and the Pit* (US title: *Five Million Years to Earth*), *Life in Emergency Ward 10, On the Buses, Steptoe and Son, Sweeney, Dad's Army, The Alf Garnett Saga, Porridge* or *Man at the Top*, ultimately based on John Braine's novel *Room at the Top* but more directly on a TV series. From the writer's point of view there are obviously some differences in writing for the two media, the running time of programmes being one and budgeting being another, but the fact remains that they are tending to coalesce more and more.

The real distinguishing mark, then, of the television play is not so much how it is made or transmitted but how it is received, i.e. in the home. It plays to the largest audience possible, but an audience split up into its smallest components; hence its tone of voice is public and private at once. But if we are reluctant to make any predictions about the future technology of recording and transmission, we shouldn't be overconfident either in forecasting reception in years to come. Line standards may alter and result in images with still sharper definition; screens may expand, possibly coming to fill an entire wall; stereoscopy may be a distant prospect. All these innovations would have some bearing on writing.

More relevant perhaps is the exciting prospect – which to some extent is already with us – of the widespread home recording of TV plays. This might be on cassette, disc or some other system. When such a practice has become general the status of TV drama will alter profoundly. It may become a regular thing for viewers to build up their private library of recordings for playback at their own convenience, with cost as the only limiting factor. The commonplace that television is an ephemeral medium will have lost much of its validity.

In these new conditions, drama written for the small screen may well become the principal form of playwriting in Britain – not only in terms of output but also of esteem. Some of this change is already under way. 'Television playwrights', according to Fay Weldon, 'used to aspire to write for the stage, and stage playwrights used to despise television, by virtue of dreadful, debilitating, class-based cultural snobbism. The barriers are now crumbling with remarkable speed, to the enrichment of both theatre and television.'[68]

It will become increasingly self-evident that TV drama merits close study. If it is an imperfect literary art this is a characteristic it shares with playwriting for the stage. In neither case can the words on the page ever be self-sufficient. They cry out for production – to be embodied by actors and supplemented by sounds and images. But with television – in contrast to the theatre – the student will be able to make a rewarding instant and repeated comparison between script and production. There is already a wealth of texts of TV plays available in print. The National Film

Archive has a growing collection of TV drama classics; that, and the increasing number of home recordings, will make television literacy a general fact of life.[69]

It is hoped that the present volume will make a modest contribution to a reassessment of British television drama. Its contributors come from various fields – criticism, teaching and research, writing and production. The range of authors singled out for analysis does not pretend to be exhaustive; it cannot even be representative within the limits of one book. More remains to be said – particularly perhaps in the field of the series and the serial.

If there appears to be some bias towards the single play, this is more a matter of convenience than of dogma: as I have stated before, the longer dramatic forms deserve – sometimes if not always – to be taken seriously. In any case, not all the writers discussed are exclusively single-play authors. Alan Plater has written competent as well as much more than competent series, and Dennis Potter has helped to give significant stature to the serial format.

There is a thread running through all the essays in this volume, however; and that is the shared conviction that television drama matters. It is an important aspect of the culture of today. It merits critical attention.

2   Jim Allen

PAUL MADDEN

THE MAJORITY OF Jim Allen's plays have their roots in a reality directly experienced by the writer, constructed as they are from the working lives of working men, whether miners, navvies or dockers, more often than not politically involved at the raw end of industrial relations in strikes, occupations, and picket lines. They fuse lived experience with Marxist, specifically Trotskyist, beliefs.

In *The Rank and File* (BBC-1, 1971) a wife berates her husband for staying up late when she thought her luck was in. Clumsily he's attempting to type on one finger a news-sheet for his fellow workers who are on strike. The incident comes directly from Allen's own experience and makes you realise that 'the writer knows about it, he's not read about it',[1] to use Allen's words. In the late fifties he started a miners' newspaper with his workmates for the 'rank-and-file' miner called simply *The Miner*. Since he had inspired the paper he was obliged to learn to use the typewriter they had clubbed together to buy on hire-purchase, and to become its editor. The articles he wrote for *The Miner* constituted his first written work. This scene can be paralleled by a score of equally small but significant scenes scattered throughout his work, which possess the authentic tang of life as lived and not merely as imagined (it's difficult not to apply the pejorative here). Two more will suffice as examples. In *The Lump* (BBC-1, 1967) Yorky, a long-standing militant, advises his student comrade to remove his tie before joining a picket line, lest a policeman should be tempted to take hold with dire consequences for the wearer. A shop steward in *The Big Flame* (BBC-1, 1969) squats on a toilet and, pencil in hand, gets through his paperwork in the only office available.

The two exceptions to the above amongst Allen's major plays are *The Talking Head* (London Weekend/Kestrel, 1969) and *A Choice of Evils* (BBC-1, 1977). Both nonetheless offer valuable introductions to the characteristic political preoccupations of his work and are essentially similar, despite their superficially dissimilar subject matter. *The Talking Head* does, however, relate to Allen's own experience of being a professional writer and, what's more, a writer out of step with his television (pay)masters. Mark, an erstwhile radical, who slips the occasional subversive line or scene into the popular drama series he produces, defensively explains to Larry, his top writer, that it is inevitable that political beliefs and ideals will be corrupted to some degree. Larry has thrown a tantrum before the technical crew, actors and 'big brother', the programme controller, and denounced the series as 'crap!'

'Mr Trotsky put his finger on it', Mark points out, 'when he said that unlike the worker, who is merely required to sell his labour-power, and the tension of his muscles, the intellectual has to sacrifice his entire personality, and not just through fear, but through conscientiousness, and as a result he's unable to accept the fact that his professional frock-coat is only a different kind of prison uniform of better cut than ordinary.' These words were strikingly echoed by Tony Garnett (the producer most associated with Allen's work) in an interview in *Theatre Quarterly*. Garnett encouraged Allen to give up writing on *Coronation Street* if he wanted to be a serious writer. 'I don't think you can write a lot of episodes like that, doing things absolutely mechanically and technically. I don't think you get anything for nothing. I don't think you get paid that kind of money for doing that kind of thing without having to give up something of yourself. A man is a whole man. Trotsky wrote a great piece on this, talking about the difference between doing some jobs like, say, being a plumber or an electrician where you can do your job and your relationship with the bourgeoisie is detached, in the sense that you can keep yourself. But if you're in one of the bourgeois professions, like a lawyer or a doctor, or an artist, they really want you, lock, stock and barrel. They want your soul.'[2]

The Talking Head questions whether any radical worth his revolutionary salt can resist becoming absorbed by the bourgeois institution of television and avoid the small compromises becoming the big lie, surrendering too easily to the common illusion that merely being there magically guarantees some revolutionary value. As Larry says, 'The intellectual comes copper on himself.' In a famous attack on naturalism in television drama at

Edinburgh, John McGrath (associated with experimentation in
BBC TV drama, and with the early *Z-Cars*) described why the atmosphere at the BBC in the sixties under the director-generalship
of Hugh Carleton Greene was relatively free: 'And so the artist
could still be an artist, even in front of twenty million people: he
was no real threat to the established order, indeed he made
life more interesting. Within limits, of course . . . The majority
of the staff producers had anyway done a thorough job of
interiorising the values of the ruling class. Every good member
of the English professional class, to which they belong, has a
built-in policeman – *le flic en soi*.'³ The dilemma for the radical (as
it must have been for Allen) is painfully real, not just the loose
change of small-talk amongst the intellectual set exemplified,
for instance, in the discussion group Mark attends. The play
rehearses the classic debate between reformism and revolutionism.

In *The Man Beneath* (1967), which turned up in Rediffusion's
anthology series *The Gamblers*, Leslie Sands, who seems to
specialise in playing socialists of the old school, flinty integrity
uppermost (Yorky in Allen's play *The Lump* and earlier the
engine-driver father in David Mercer's *Where the Difference Begins*), takes the part of an old miner, Martin. Martin stays down
the pit in a protest against its forthcoming closure. His wife
bitterly complains to the Pit Manager, a former workmate of
Martin's whose radicalism has been somewhat tempered by his
position, that 'Nationalisation's made no difference to us.
There's nowt changed, and t' Coal Board just owd gaffer writ
large.' The hopes raised by the return of a Labour Government in
1945 were slowly but surely crushed. Martin himself is disillusioned: '. . . Was all a pack 'er lies . . . An' we swallowed it . . .
Book said fer us ter fight 'em, an' we did . . . Book said organise,
so we went along an' organised, though there were times they
hammered us like pegs into t'ground.' The union can't be relied
upon, they're 'bloody renegades', colluding with management to
betray the workers. All he can do, whilst his workmates obli-
viously carry on working, is to make a one-man protest, in the
event a despairing and futile gesture with tragic and unforeseen
consequences. On paper the play reads sentimentally as it
attempts to evoke Martin's brand of gut socialism fired by the
years of the Depression, struggling against the TV drama cliché.
Down the pit he sings 'The Red Flag' and remembers the day the

mines were nationalised. But intelligent direction would no doubt have rendered it moving.

In *The Talking Head* Larry is the lone voice of protest; Mark, the castrated radical, integrated into management, 'fighting the good fight from his centrally heated office'. Allen puts into Larry's mouth much of the contempt he feels for those controlling programmes, who have by implication sold out. In an interesting parallel autobiographical piece (in *Journey to a Legend and Back*) he reserves if anything, more venom for 'this sick league of frightened men'.[4]

But if Mark has betrayed his ideals, Liz, Mark's wife, and his so-called best friend Larry betray Mark by sleeping together. The requisite going to bed of two of the leading characters has all the elements of a cliché of the television drama Allen despises. As directed, any political discussion between Liz and Larry is undercut by a lingering sexual tension. It *should* be read as an indicator of the shallowness of Larry's radical commitment, especially taken in conjunction with his cutting remarks to the continuity girl about sleeping around because 'with us clever sods, the rules don't apply'. Neatly Munro (the programme controller who can also lay claim to a radical past) offers Larry Mark's job as producer of the prime-time police series to alter and develop as he likes. His acceptance is left open, but it's clearly an offer he can't refuse. Ultimately Larry, like Mark, is in pejorative television jargon a talking head, committed to rhetoric but not to action. The play concludes somewhat melodramatically as Mark exits, back to camera, arms outstretched against an opening lift, assured by Munro he'll make 'the best religious programme since the crucifixion!' Allen's first major play *The Lump* less obviously conjures up a crucifixion image. The camera pans across Yorky's dead body from his left hand across his face down to his right hand. It is difficult to judge whether these images were consciously intended by the writer or should be attributed partly or wholly to direction.

A Choice of Evils apparently hung around for six years before being taken up by *Play for Today* producer Margaret Matheson. Unusually for Allen it is based on a specific historical event – which took place in Rome during the closing stages of the Second World War. Thirty-three German SS men were killed by Italian partisans. As an act of vengeance the Germans rounded up ten Italians for each man killed, picked at random, and executed them 'to encourage the others'. Allen's play focusses on Father Borrelli, a politically active, Marxist-oriented Catholic priest who was amongst the captives, and the attempts by Cardinal Volponi, a former radical comrade, to intercede on his behalf with Pope Pius XII and the Nazis. The dramatic triangle is completed by Maria, Borrelli's girl friend. The play articulates a powerful attack on the Catholic Church which had concluded a Concordat with Adolf Hitler, a notorious accommodation effectively ensuring that the Church turned a blind eye to the Nazis' extermination of the Jews. Allen takes sideswipes at the oppressiveness of the Catholic Church and its unholy alliances elsewhere, as in *The Lump* – the site agent and the union official together visit the local priest, who is only too happy to deter the building-workers from participating in unofficial strike action. Throughout a chilling image persists – of a pope, civilised, withdrawn and contemplative, indifferent to the life-and-death struggles raging outside the Vatican, sitting in a quiet garden engrossed in a book, whilst the rest of the world goes literally to hell. Cardinal Volponi overlooks from a balcony Pope Pius carried aloft and applauded by Vatican functionaries. Borrelli elaborates later on the similarities between Hitler, Stalin and Pius, 'each one omnipotent' and manipulating almost identical power structures. But 'No single person, institution, religion or political party has the right to tell everybody what to think': there unmistakably through Borrelli speak the author and his political mentor Trotsky.

According to Volponi, 'the elite of this world' make all the important decisions – 'And you are its statesman,' replies Borrelli. Cardinal Volponi, like Mark in *The Talking Head*, has become wittingly or not an apologist for an institution which in the name of political expediency defends the very order progressive forces seek to overturn. The Abbot-General pointedly reminds him, '. . . the Church has need of men like you, your Eminence. It would be a tragedy if you allowed it to destroy *your career*' (my italics). Volponi is caught in the same contradiction as Mark (or to a lesser extent the Pit Manager in *The Man Beneath*). He is a heretic who came into the fold, tolerated by the system so long as he's useful.

Borrelli refuses the cynically easy way out, the signing of a piece of paper guaranteeing his freedom but effectively a renunciation of the principles by which he has lived his life. Volponi's revelation of Stalin's deals struck with the West to carve out

specified areas of influence in postwar Europe, thereby abandoning and betraying a host of revolutionary movements, does not
sway him. Borrelli chooses death rather than betrayal, a choice of
evils certainly. But the play more subtly and convincingly
suggests that his choice lies between religion and politics degraded into a choice between two authoritarian systems, Catho-
licism and Stalinism – no choice in fact. *A Choice of Evils* could
almost be *The Talking Head* transposed from the fey parochial
world of television to the historical world of violence and death,
adding real edge to its sustained political debate.

Jim Allen was born in Manchester (where he still lives) in 1926,
the year of the General Strike. His family were Catholic, of Irish
descent; his father was a labourer who could find no work during
the Depression. On the outbreak of war in 1939 he lied about his
age and started work in a wire factory. Four years later he volun-
teered for the army, serving in the occupation forces in Germany.
Whilst he was imprisoned for fighting outside a public house a
fellow prisoner roused his interest in socialism, thus awakening
his political consciousness. Once released he began reading vora-
ciously as he'd never done before. Apart from Marx, he was most
influenced by Jack London, particularly by his book *People of the
Abyss* (from which the protagonist of *The Lump*, Yorky, quotes to
a young student worker). 'Other writers who influenced me were
Upton Sinclair, and John Steinbeck, but London was the big
influence, enough to light up a few corners. He's a man's man in
the romantic sense – he wasn't an academic, but someone who
had experienced everything himself.'[5] It is easy to understand
Jack London's attraction for Allen, who came from a world of
work and was comparatively uneducated.

There followed a succession of jobs, mostly in the building
trade as an unskilled labourer. Later he went to sea as a ship's
fireman. Finally he became a miner for four years. His activities
on his miners' newspaper no doubt led to his being blacklisted
from the mines when he tried to return after recuperating from a
pit accident. So he decided to try his luck once more on the
building sites.

Meanwhile, despite having become a Marxist, he had not
joined the British Communist Party, which was merely a satellite
of Moscow, its intellectuals distorting the truth behind Stalin's
Russia. He explains that he was 'always completely anti-Stalinist
long before it became popular . . . long before the Khrushchev

speech'[6] which violently denounced Stalin's regime. 'I've been chased by Stalinists who sincerely believed that I was an agent of capitalism, I was thrown off a miner's bus once going at a fair old speed.'[7] He was to join the Labour Party, from which he was expelled in 1962 for being a member of a small Trotskyist party, the Socialist Labour League. (This was a forerunner of the Workers' Revolutionary Party.) He also left the SLL for reasons he is unwilling to divulge. But it's not difficult to deduce Allen's distrust of socialist parties essentially petty-bourgeois and elitist in character, remote from the industrial worker at the point of production. 'The only question is one of political leadership and the foundation . . . of a party that will lead the workers to power,' says Eddie, one of the rank-and-file committee concluding *The Rank and File*. 'The biggest problem today', Allen said recently, '. . . is the crisis of leadership.'[8]

When he returned to the building industry, political activity on the left was controlled by the Communist Party. Despite his previously heavy involvement as a political organiser (within the trades unions and in strikes by miners, dockers, tenants etc.) and a desire to emulate his work amongst the miners, his refusal to join the CP ensured his isolation. He thought of trying to earn his living as a writer and wrote a play about a hod-carrier. Granada read it and in 1964 contracted him to write scripts for their twice-weekly saga of the North, *Coronation Street* – an unlikely beginning for television's leading political writer. He worked on the *Street* for eighteen months but inevitably found the demands imposed by a formula soap opera riding high in audience ratings restrictive and accordingly left, breaking his contract. John Finch (later creator of *Family at War* and *Sam*) suggested him to Ken Trodd, then a story editor for the BBC's *Thirty-Minute Theatre*. In this slot his first play was transmitted – *The Hard Word*, a two-hander about the building trade (the 'hard word' is a colloquialism for the sack).

Allen had the idea for his first major play, *The Lump* (1967), whilst he was still contracted to *Coronation Street*, but found Granada uninterested. It was Finch who arranged a meeting with *Wednesday Play* producer Tony Garnett and director Ken Loach who had just made *Cathy Come Home* (BBC, 1966). Allen recalled, 'What I found exciting about their work was the documentary approach to drama that enabled them to throw real people on to the screen in real situations.'[9]

Garnett and Loach flourished whilst Sydney Newman, former producer of ITV's *Armchair Theatre*, was BBC Head of Drama in the Carleton Greene era. At ABC Newman had encouraged new writers to write topical realistic drama about contemporary Britain, but confined within the television studio. Studio TV drama had been largely shaped by a theatrical tradition, whose influence still persisted into the sixties. Garnett and others were impatient with a drama removed from the real world unlike anybody's real experience. 'We're doing art' was the stock response to such criticism. On the other hand, 'We were interested in social forces and the fabric of people's lives and the kind of conflicts that go on particularly at places of work, where people spend quite a lot of their lives. It seemed to be driving us towards actually going out there ourselves.'[10]

The Lump, like *Cathy Come Home*, is a propaganda film, a conscious exposé of social evil. The notorious Lump system, whereby individuals worked as subcontractors responsible for their own tax and insurance, was an all-too-common feature of the building industry. Since workers were usually itinerant (and probably Irish) they were naturally 'on the fiddle', and left themselves open to exploitation by the gaffer, or to exposure. Allen admits that at first he was influenced for the worse by *Coronation Street* (studio-videotaped and produced on relatively small budgets). So on Garnett's advice he altered the first draft freely. According to Jack Gold, its director (whom Garnett had recruited from documentary film), the play nonetheless possesses 'possibly a more conscious dramatic shape, even slightly melodramatic'[11] in contrast to the trailing story-lines of the average television series. It was filmed on location in Middleton and Collyhurst where Allen lived – the local Labour Club serving as the place where Yorky calls a meeting.

Yorky on his own estimation is a militant, who leads a walk-off from the site after being sacked for complaining about safety standards. He is, in his way, a romantic figure fond of quoting Lenin and London, who didn't marry and have children because if you did, you had to toe the (bosses') line and keep your mouth shut. It's a warm but not sentimental portrait, in which there is much of the author. Yorky is contrasted with Mike, a student, a veritable Candide in the harsh world of the building site. The student is a necessary and effective device, through whom the world of the play, alien to the experience of most of its audience, can be mediated. In this sense perhaps the play is stagey.

Its nub is a discussion where Yorky explains to Mike the iniquities of the Lump (serving as a transition to the play's ostensible subject and more significantly his politics). Yorky admits to being a Communist, but not a member of the Communist Party – 'If I were a member of the Communist Party, and someone accused me of plotting revolution, I'd sue them for libel!' Impetuously Mike follows Yorky on to the Lump and finally precipitates a fight between Yorky and Maguire, the ganger, which ends in Yorky's death when a trench collapses.

There doesn't seem to be any particular subtext here. Mike, who refuses to work in the driving rain, is sacked and in a principled stand against the ganger tries to persuade his fellow Lump men to lay down tools against Yorky's advice. For Yorky there are more important jobs to organise elsewhere. It would be too unequivocal an interpretation to apply a conclusion of *The Rank and File*, 'Blind militancy will get us nowhere', but nonetheless this lesson Mike learns. The struggle between Yorky and Maguire in the rain and the mud truly symbolises the brutality of the Lump and (not too fancifully) represents that larger struggle Yorky has conducted all his life on behalf of Labour against Capital, a strong man against stronger foes. Like Ben in the four *Days of Hope* films Mike has been politicised. He does indeed have a 'few gold nuggets' (Yorky's words repeated at the close) to take back home, and so, the author intends, should the play's audience who see through his eyes. But the political impulse of *The Lump* is deflected into a personal drama of individual consciousness, a consequence of its naturalistic form, emphasised by its functional direction.

In subject matter and content *The Lump* belongs with *The Big Flame* (1969) and *The Rank and File* (1971), and to some extent with *In the Heel of the Hunt* (Granada, 1973). Unlike *The Lump*, *The Big Flame* and *The Rank and File* are expressed in terms of collective action, and certainly in the latter this is to the detriment of the drama. Introducing *The Big Flame* in the *Radio Times*, Tony Garnett, its producer, stated that it was set in the future so that no one could have any possible doubt that it was a drama and not a documentary. This was a reference to fears voiced within the BBC management and elsewhere that audiences failed to distinguish whether such realist works were dramas or documentaries – over the years the controversy has dogged most of Garnett's productions up to *Law and Order* (BBC, 1978). They have consistently adopted a style which has been confused with the techniques and conventions of the standard television documentary. It is in fact and of necessity a piece of artifice. In another context Garnett has stated that the BBC wanted actors to look like actors. Loach and Garnett deliberately cast unknowns, some of them 'real people', in order to reinforce the veracity of their productions. On the whole the controversy over fiction or fact is sterile, serving to mask an attack on the political content of such works.

Of this set of plays *The Big Flame* is the most interesting, politically and dramatically. It takes place in the wake of the Devlin Report on the docks advocating the decasualisation of labour and poses a hypothesis, the take-over of the docks in the port of Liverpool by its workers – a decasualisation of the employers, that is. If the play has a central figure it is Jack Regan, a 'militant' and self-styled Trotskyist, who is brought in by the rank-and-file committee to advise on the running of the strike. He proposes that the docks should be occupied; he's learnt from experience that the political initiative gained by a strike is soon dissipated. 'When we had the ball at our feet, we didn't know what to do.' He's honest enough to admit that 'There'll be no revolution, but you'll have lit a bonfire.' The play predated the wave of factory sit-ins and work-ins of the early seventies, proof if it were needed of Allen's close involvement with his subject matter. As in *The Lump*, men are seen to take action themselves, outside of such orthodox political mechanisms as their trade union. They are in fact slandered by the union as an organised conspiracy, a predictable and all-too-familiar reaction. Inevitably the occupation is betrayed, the army and police move into the docks, and the 'ringleaders' are arraigned.

In its aesthetic strategies *The Big Flame* is more sophisticated than *The Lump*. Like Allen's other work it is essentially a realist drama. Nonetheless it retains Brechtian elements, particularly in its use of voice-overs to comment on the action (amongst them the author himself) which play a 'consciously interpretative role', according to Raymond Williams.[12] The abandoning of an exclusive emphasis on the individual protagonist, a convention of naturalism, allows Allen some freedom of form, whilst the play incorporates the progressive by injecting an element of 'what if . . .' into its realist structure. The overall message of the play is encapsulated in 'the Ballad of Joe Hill', the song of the American Wobblies, sung by a docker – Joe Hill may have been killed, but he didn't die. Despite the defeat of the occupation, the death of a docker and the imprisonment of its leaders, the fight will continue, workers will take their destinies into their own hands, and that almost mystical feeling Jack Regan tries to describe in court will come again.

The Rank and File is a thinly disguised version of the strike at Pilkington's Glass Works in St Helens (virtually a company-owned town). It is prefaced by these words: 'A film based principally on events that took place in Lancashire in the spring of 1970'. Allen was invited to speak with the strikers and took along a copy of The Big Flame to show them. After the screening, an old man asked why he didn't do a play about the glass-workers. The old man showed him his back 'lacerated with molten glass'[13] and explained that he'd worked fifty years and then been sacked. As Allen says, 'He'd got me by the bollocks, hadn't he?'[14] The Rank and File recalls the story in a scene where a striker, humbly wanting his job back, is re-employed without his pension rights despite long service. The play was commissioned by a sympathetic producer at Granada. Granada withdrew the commission, perhaps under some local pressure, and the BBC picked up the play, stipulating, however, that names were changed and the location shifted to Stoke on Trent.

Wage irregularities provided the impetus for the strike, but it rapidly turned into a strike against general grievances, the first in a hundred years. As in The Big Flame Allen focusses on the Rank and File Strike Committee who effectively ran the strike in defiance of their union executive. Allen obviously finds the subject congenial and is able to apply his characteristic political analysis to the events – workers take action only to be betrayed by those who supposedly represent their interests: trade-union officials and TUC leaders. Allen himself appears in the play to brand them 'handpicked Judas goats'. Guarantees of no victimisation after a return to work are proved worthless.

The play seems to have been written in some haste and in essentials replicates The Big Flame. But inevitably Allen is too restricted by its basis in real events. As the events of the strike accumulate – mass meetings, a confrontation with the police – the drama becomes shapeless. Allen's thesis, integral to the fiction of The Big Flame, here seems imposed from without. Unconvincing parallels are drawn with the situation of workers in Hitler's Germany and Mussolini's Italy arising from a topical reference to the Industrial Relations Bill. The play closes self-consciously on a quote from Trotsky voiced over stills of children that 'life is beautiful, that the future generation cleanses of all the oppression, violence and evil and enjoy it to the full' [sic]. It's innocuous enough, but by all accounts Allen and director Ken Loach worked hard to persuade the BBC not to excise it. Allen's own verdict on *The Rank and File* was that it was probably 'too didactic . . . a lantern lecture'.[15]

It may seem so far that Allen's plays are dull indeed, political tracts masquerading as drama. But this would seriously understate their tremendous humour, exuberance and vitality, expressed most vividly in the crowded pub and club scenes with which his work abounds. As he has said himself, he hasn't known a strike yet where there hasn't been at least one booze-up in a pub. It's here that the improvisation methods favoured by a director like Ken Loach score. Loach improvises within the script, but improvisation 'lifts' the work, creating the illusion of reality that the characters of the drama are people of flesh and blood, not evanescent phantoms.

This quality is missing from *In the Heel of the Hunt* (1973). It is the only full-length play by Jim Allen produced by Granada, apart from three editions of *Crown Court*, the formula drama series. *The Extremist* (Granada, 1975) typically features a militant building-worker who is accused of conspiracy to intimidate men to stop work and of causing an explosion to damage property; in *Those in Peril* (Granada, 1976) a trawler-captain is accused of causing the death of a deck-hand; *Tell the Truth and Shame the Devil* (Granada, 1976) takes the case of two teenagers accused of a vicious assault. Allen blames himself for the failure of *In the Heel of the Hunt*. He remembers visiting its location only once, whilst *Days of Hope* was shooting. The play concerns the itinerant workers who form building gangs and interweaves two narrative strands – the story of a girl from a family of tinkers compelled to live with another tinker as man and wife, and that of Sean, a factory worker who comes to work on the building sites. Sean is young and inexperienced (like Mike in *The Lump*) with left-wing sympathies but little commitment. There is some ambiguity about whether he has come to replace Dugan, a Communist Party organiser, who is arrested by the police. But to all intents and purposes politics are absent from the play. The plot is not fully developed, and the weak theme is not helped by some lifeless direction.

Three thirty-minute plays by Allen were transmitted during this early period of his work. *The Pub Fighter* (Rediffusion, 1968) is a sharp, effective piece, not without pathos. A pub fighter from the Yorkshire coalfields, whose wife has run away with a local tycoon, is challenged by a younger professional the tycoon has hired. Despite near-defeat, he wins through and as a final gesture rejects his wife's plea to take her back. It's a play about pride and the keeping of integrity. *Walt, King of the Dumper* (BBC-2, 1971), directed by Jack Gold, is also about integrity, and in this sense both plays relate to Allen's other work. Superficially it is an enjoyable comedy about a dumper-driver. Walt puts on a fine acrobatic display for an attractive woman who watches him at work, precariously steering his dumper and singing 'Raindrops Keep Falling on My Head'. At first sight the lady appears to reciprocate his feelings, but the idyll ends when his boss turns up and promptly beds her. But Walt has the last laugh – to the horror of his boss and his obsequious workmates he refills the hole they've dug and calmly walks off the job, his own man to the end. *The Punchy and the Fairy* (BBC-2, 1973) is a conversational two-hander, set on board ship between two men who have had a homosexual relationship – a sad, sordid, claustrophobic tale.

Days of Hope (1975) is Allen's most sustained and ambitious work to date, a series of four dramas which cover ten crucial years in modern British history – 1916, the period of the Great War, through to 1926, the year of the General Strike. Allen and his collaborators Ken Loach and Tony Garnett did not intend that *Days of Hope* should be just another historical costume drama, a popular staple of television schedules. 'Our motive for going into the past', stated Garnett 'is not to escape the present: we go into the past to draw lessons from it. History is contemporary.'[16] In its way *Days of Hope* is a family saga, but a saga with a difference, where political ideas are filtered through the changing circumstances of the family, principally Philip, Sarah his wife, and Ben her younger brother, during the decade.

In 1916 Philip is a conscientious objector, a Christian Socialist, whereas Ben is anxious to join up and see some action. Throughout the films the waning radicalism of Philip is contrasted with the burgeoning revolutionism of Ben. It's as if Allen were expos-

2 *A wartime scene from the first episode of Jim Allen's four-part serial* Days of
Hope, *shown on BBC-1 in September–October 1975.*

ing the roots of reformism as typified by Mark in *The Talking Head*
and of revolutionism, represented by Father Borrelli in *A Choice of
Evils*. Philip is arrested and finally sent out to the front, Sarah,
who supports his views wholeheartedly, begins work for the
No-Conscription Fellowship. Meanwhile Ben has joined up and

is posted to Ireland because of unrest there. His experiences in Ireland, coupled with the miners' lock-out of 1921 when troops were brought in, convince Ben he should desert. Ben is instrumental in encouraging the miners to stand up against the local mine-owner, which leads to inevitable confrontation with police and army.

At the beginning of the third film Ben is serving a three-year prison sentence. In a significant exchange the chaplain likens society to his watch – it has 'a grand design' with which no one should tamper except within the established order of things, in political terms through the ballot box. Ben deliberately drops the watch – 'if them wheels and spring are already set, and if we're not allowed to touch 'em, perhaps the only thing to do is to scrap the lot and start all over again'. It is an effective if slightly glib indication of Ben's conversion to revolution as a means of changing society, and his subsequent joining of the Communist Party comes as no surprise. Philip has become a Labour MP in the first Labour Government, sponsored by the Transport and General Workers Union (the General Secretary of which was the virulently anti-Communist Ernest Bevin). Allen catches well the idealism of the time and the heady enthusiasm for a new dawn of social change. But Philip's idealism is rudely shattered when he learns with incredulity of emergency plans, laid during the Tories' term of office, to deal with any General Strike or emergency resulting from trade union actions, which have been secretly passed on to the Labour Government.

It is an omen of the betrayal to come in the fourth part, the betrayal of the General Strike by union leaders, the Labour Party and the Communist Party. Much of the film covers the closet negotiations of TUC leaders with Prime Minister Stanley Baldwin and his cabinet, from which necessarily the fictional characters stand apart. Sarah and Ben have been involved in setting up the Councils of Action, local self-help groups to cope with the effects of the strike. Rifts are beginning to appear between Sarah and Philip, who wants her to resign from the Council of Action. Ben has become progressively disillusioned with the role of the Communist Party in the strike.

Undoubtedly some of Allen's best work is in *Days of Hope* (and incidentally Ken Loach's too). All four films are crammed with memorable scenes – the girl forced to sing an Irish rebel song amidst jeering British soldiers; the booby-trapping of a soldier by a ten-year-old boy (with its contemporary parallels with the troubles in Northern Ireland); the miners' visit to the house of the coal-owner who condescends to feed them; the House of Commons reception for a Russian delegation, which the miners 'gatecrash'. The first two films, *1916 – Joining Up* and *1921*, where Allen has consciously striven to dramatise the experiences of fictional characters within real events, are the most successful. The real events begin to overwhelm the fictional elements in *1924* and *1926 – General Strike*, particularly in the latter's account of the failure of the strike. Allen feels that in the fourth film he'd 'stayed too close to the documentary evidence, but . . . was afraid of being picked up on accuracy',[17] the sort of historical nitpicking he described in a *Tonight* discussion following the series. This highlights a paradox of political dramas such as Allen's employing strategies associated with naturalism. The political content of the work is frequently marginalised by debate on the accuracy of (period) detail.

Allen offers an alternative version of the failure of the strike to received versions, a straightforwardly Trotskyist interpretation (primarily from the perspective of Ben) which is on occasion too simple and too blunt. Trotsky referred to 'the treacherous liquidation of the General Strike' in Britain in his book *The Revolution Betrayed* about the larger betrayal of the Russian Revolution.[18] Ben and Sarah are the vehicles for the message of the play – revolutionaries, they stand for the working class which has been betrayed by its leaders and by social democrats like Philip, who failed to grasp the potential of the strike.

Television fiction, dominated by the naturalistic aesthetic, performs much the same function as the naturalistic fiction of the late nineteenth century. It was fiction that above all reproduced the appearance of reality in accurate and authentic detail. For Allen and Garnett the (political) content of the work is of prime importance. Naturalism as a form is transparent, drawing little attention to itself, and thus, so it is thought, content is made paramount. Allen believes that 'it is the content that any serious writer should concern himself with'.[19] But according to John McGrath, 'The excitements now are not about the form of the drama, but about its content; with no realisation that it distorts what the writer is trying to say, contains it within safe limits.'[20] Content, Allen would say, determines form; McGrath argues that the form, i.e. bourgeois naturalism, is actually inimical to the 'political' content: the naturalistic trappings do render *Days of Hope* conventionally at one level as a costume drama, whatever the intentions of its makers.

Attacks on naturalism, however, leave out of account the way an audience perceives a particular television fiction, i.e. within the context of other fictions and within its experience of the real world. Certainly its very transparency and familiarity enable a work to be read easily by an audience. Some critics have identified this accessibility as a weakness of the form with respect to political drama and film, since, they allege, it presents the audience with a conclusion it is obliged to accept or reject (according to prejudice) as in *The Rank and File* or less starkly *Days of Hope*. Ken Loach said referring to *Days of Hope* that 'I think many people react against something which speaks to you sternly from the screen and tells you what you must think. So we've tried to make films which will communicate in a narrative way, which will share experiences with the audience, and in which the audience will come to the same conclusion that we've come to.'[21]

The issue is raised with equal acuteness by *The Spongers* (BBC-1, 1978), at the time of writing the most recent Allen play to be transmitted, and winner of the Italia Prize. There is a perceptible shift of emphasis in *Days of Hope* from organised politics to the politics of community action based on the individual. But even this politics is absent from *The Spongers* in its story of Pauline and her family of four children (including a mongol daughter) deserted by her husband, ironically the spongers of the title, pitted against an uncaring system. 'Set against the tinsel backcloth of Jubilee year, a time of high unemployment and public spending cuts, *The Spongers* is a grim parable of the 70's welfare state, in which the legacy of its founding socialism appears to be a bureaucracy concerned with balancing budgets.'[22] The impetus for the play came from the lurid exaggerated stories in the popular press about social-security scroungers.

Like *Cathy Come Home*, *The Spongers* is a shocking and powerful tragedy (Pauline eventually kills herself and the children) which, of all his plays, drew, Allen says, the best response from viewers. Unlike *Cathy*, his script is more consciously even-handed in its treatment of state officials who are just doing their job whether obstructing or helping Pauline – the social worker is seen to be powerless. There are no villains. The most significant line in the play is the judgement passed by a neighbour, 'She had no right to do it – she should have stuck it out like the rest of us, instead of letting them get one over on her.' In a review, I wrote somewhat harshly that 'this oblique appeal to a defiant class solidarity is whistling in the dark, unable to compete with the immediately preceding images of death . . . Such tragedies are well authenticated. But here the viewer, confined within the narrative of a "true" story, inherits an overwhelming sense of despair, the mind-numbing impotence traditionally induced by television's surfeit of bad news.'[23]

Allen's achievement is to reproduce faithfully the experience of a victim seldom available so directly, faced by a complex bureaucratic network, who can find no one to blame but herself. Criticised for not leaving an escape for Pauline from her despair, Allen replied, 'There was a temptation, but if I had accepted it, it would have been artificial, because people in their exposed position, when they are at their weakest and most defenceless, they don't walk out with flags flying and say we'll live another day. Part of their tragedy is that they don't know the way out themselves.'[24] Undoubtedly Pauline's experience corresponds to that of the larger part of the play's audience to whom the remote politics of Westminster, however discredited, represent the only politics of change.

In a series of plays currently in production based on the Langley estate (where *The Spongers* was set) Jim Allen rights the balance by focussing on a whole community's organised resistance to the consequences of political decisions exemplified by rent increases and evictions. His future work promises to prove as provocative as ever as it sites politics amongst ordinary people and their potential capacity to transform their everyday lives.

Appendix

Television plays transmitted

	Coronation Street	Granada

Episodes of 6.1, 8.2, 8.3, 22.3, 14.4, 5.5, 17.5, 21.6, 12.7, 11.8, 23.8, 18.10, 17.11, 15.12. 1965; 12.1, 21.2, 30.3, 18.4, 6.6, 29.6, 25.7, 8.8, 22.8, 12.9, 26.9, 16.11, 12.12. 1966; 4.1, 30.1, 20.2, 22.3, 19.4, 15.5, 5.6, 19.7. 1966

15.6.66	*The Hard Word*	BBC-2 *Thirty-Minute Theatre*
1.2.67	*The Lump*	BBC-1 *Wednesday Play*
7.12.67	*The Man Beneath*	Rediffusion *The Gamblers*

27.2.68	*The Pub Fighter*	Rediffusion *Half-Hour Story*
19.2.69	*The Big Flame*	BBC-1 *Wednesday Play*
30.8.69	*The Talking Head*	LWT/Kestrel *Saturday Night Theatre*
20.5.71	*The Rank and File*	BBC-1
20.9.71	*Walt, King of the Dumper*	BBC-2 *Thirty-Minute Theatre*
10.1.73	*The Punchy and the Fairy*	BBC-2 *Thirty-Minute Theatre*
16.12.73	*In the Heel of the Hunt*	Granada
11.9.75– 2.10.75	*Days of Hope*	BBC-1
3.12.75	*The Extremist*	Granada *Crown Court*
25.2.76	*Tell the Truth and Shame the Devil*	Granada *Crown Court*
13.10.76	*Those in Peril*	Granada *Crown Court*
19.4.77	*A Choice of Evils*	BBC-1 *Play for Today*
24.1.78	*The Spongers*	BBC-1 *Play for Today*

Television plays not yet produced

The Stolen Republic (1977–8). Two television films about the rise of Nazism in Germany after the First World War
The Commune (1978-9). Two television films set on a council estate about the inhabitants taking over the running of the estate

Filmscript not yet produced

The Rising (1974). Feature-film script about Ireland from 1916 to the twenties

Interviews

'Jim Allen Meets His Critics' (edited transcript from *Tonight* programme), *The Listener*, 94, 2,427 (9 October 1975)
'The Day the Scroungers Loafed No More', *Socialist Challenge*, no. 31 (2 February 1978)

Criticism

Gordon Burn, 'What Jack Gold Thinks About "Angry Jim" and His New Play', *Radio Times*, 192, 2,497 (18–24 September 1971), 6
D. A. N. Jones, 'Citrine on *Days of Hope*', *The Listener*, 94, 2,427 (9 October 1975), 458–9
Colin McArthur, '*Days of Hope*', *Screen*, 16, 4 (1975) (under 'Film Culture'), 139–44
Colin MacCabe, '*Days of Hope* – A Response to Colin McArthur', *Screen*, 17, 1 (1976) (under 'Film Culture'), 98–101

Bart Mills, *'Days of Hope* – Going to Extremes', *The Listener*, 94, 2, 423 (11 September 1975), 337–8.

Máire Messenger, 'Imitating Life', *Radio Times*, 218, 2,828 (21–27 January 1978), 4–5

3   Trevor Griffiths

EDWARD BRAUN

No TELEVISION DRAMATIST today is more articulate than Trevor Griffiths in his appreciation of the multiple hazards of confronting anyone wishing to exploit the medium as a means of raising the audience's political consciousness. Yet equally, no other writer has expressed such confidence in the possibility of this aim. In the preface to the Faber edition of *Through the Night, and Such Impossibilities*, Griffiths quotes Raymond Williams in support of his conviction:

The 'telly glued' masses do not exist; they are the bad fiction of our second-rate social analysts. What the masses, old or new, might do is anybody's guess. But the actual men and women, under permanent kinds of difficulty, will observe and learn, and I do not think that in the long run they will be anybody's windfall.[1]

This belief in the vitality and political awareness of the British working class is a major theme that runs through practically all Griffiths' plays. Equally, it is his main reason for choosing television as his principal medium. Earlier in the same preface he writes,

while at its most secure [theatre] offers the writer a greater degree of control than any other medium over the production of his work, it is incapable, as a social institution, of reaching, let alone *mobilising*, large popular audiences, at least in what is more and more desperately re- ferred to as the Free World. Success in the theatre can confer fame, prestige, wealth, critical acclaim and a place in literature, but all of them will be pickled in a sort of class aspic. To write only for the theatre is to watch from the covered stand; you stay dry but there's a pitch dividing you from another possible, and possibly decisive, action on the terraces.[2]

Thus, although by 1979 Griffiths' theatrical output totalled five full-length plays[3] and four shorter works,[4] he had already reached the point where, as he told me in an interview in May 1979, he saw writing for the stage largely as the necessary means of sustaining a reputation which would enhance his bargaining power when dealing with television.[5] At that time his *Comedians* was still playing throughout the United States and Canada, but it had been written over four years earlier and Griffiths had no further theatrical work in view.[6] On the other hand, his adaptation of *Comedians* was scheduled for transmission by the BBC in autumn 1979, and he had recently completed a version of D. H. Lawrence's novel *Sons and Lovers* which was shortly to go into production for ATV.

Most of Griffiths' early work was written for the stage, notably *Sam, Sam* in 1968–9 and *Occupations* in 1970. But unlike the many young writers recruited by television from the theatre, Griffiths worked initially in television, being employed from 1965 by BBC Leeds as a Further Education Officer. During that time, he not only developed a general understanding of the structures of control in broadcasting but also gained practical experience by directing a discussion series called *Something to Say* with people such as Richard Hoggart, Brian Jackson, E. P. Thompson and a studio audience of teachers in adult education.

Although, as Griffiths acknowledges, he knew little at this time about 'how to initiate television plays', his earliest surviving dramatic work, *The Love Maniac*, was, in fact, commissioned for television by Tony Garnett's company, Kestrel Productions. Written in 1967, it was bought by Garnett but never produced for want of a ninety-minute slot. Later, it was adapted for radio and broadcast in December 1971 under the title *Jake's Brigade*. Two years before that, BBC radio had broadcast *The Big House*, a sixty-minute play derived from an actual case of unfair dismissal of a militant worker in an engineering company. In 1971–2, his final year with the BBC, Griffiths wrote seventeen half-hour parts for the Granada Television series *Adam Smith*, using the pseudonym 'Ben Rae' to circumvent the BBC staff regulation which forbade work for a rival company.

The previous year (following the London première in October 1971 of *Occupations* by the RSC at The Place) the BBC had commissioned Griffiths to contribute a play to the series *The Edwardians*. Entitled *Such Impossibilities*, it deals with the role of the labour leader, Tom Mann, in the Liverpool transport workers' strike of 1911. Griffiths envisaged it as a corrective to the view of history conveyed by the rest of the series, which featured such personalities as E. Nesbit, the Countess of Warwick, Marie Lloyd, Baden-Powell, Rolls and Royce, and Lloyd George. At the same time, he had an eye to the play's bearing on the worsening state of industrial relations under the Heath Government. The aims of *Such Impossibilities*, Griffiths writes, were 'to restore, however tinily, an important but suppressed area of our collective history, to enlarge our "usable past" and connect it with a lived present; and to celebrate a victory'.[7]

Having accepted Griffiths' detailed preliminary outline, the series producer, Mark Shivas, was uneasy over the completed script and wished to discuss alterations. This Griffiths refused to consider, so Shivas rejected the play altogether, giving high production costs as the reason. Certainly, with its large cast and considerable use of film locations, *Such Impossibilities* could not have been made cheaply, but probably no less of a deterrent for Shivas was the play's disquieting conclusion that 'Political and industrial action must at all times be inspired by revolutionary principles.'[8] The loss is regrettable, for with its vivid portrayal of the powerful central figure of Tom Mann and the rapid unfolding of the strike's drama against the Liverpool background, the text gives promise of compelling television. It is understandable that early in 1979, following a rehearsed reading at The Warehouse, Griffiths should have resisted an invitation from the Royal Shakespeare Company to adapt *Such Impossibilities* for the theatre, for it would have been a denial of the play's true medium.

Thus, Griffiths failed to disrupt the BBC's affectionate projection of Edwardian England, but it was a lesson well learnt, and further opportunities for intervention in 'the consciousness industry' were soon to present themselves. Whatever damage Griffiths' reputation may have suffered from the rejection of *Such Impossibilities* was more than repaired by John Dexter's production at the National Theatre in December 1973 of *The Party*, with Laurence Olivier in the role of the veteran Trotskyite, John Tagg. In the original version (it was rewritten by Griffiths for a touring production by David Hare in 1974), the play was somewhat cumbersome in structure, equipped with a needlessly opulent setting and overloaded with a number of merely emblematic minor characters. But even so it demonstrated the dramatic power of articulate political debate in which one side is pitted against the other, with equal conviction, leaving the spectator to form his own synthesis from the dialectic presented. Griffiths had adumbrated this form earlier both in *Sam, Sam* (completed

1969), in the characters of the brothers Sam One and Sam Two, and in *Occupations*, with Gramsci, the passionate advocate of comradely love, forced by the abortive Italian revolution of 1920 to concede the need for the ruthless organisation exemplified by the Soviet agent Kabak. The danger in both these plays is that the audience may see the two characters as representing an either/or choice, whereas with *The Party* the clear invitation is to pursue the argument in one's own mind and seek a fusion of ideas. In Griffiths' next play for television, *All Good Men*, there is a similar presentation of alternatives.

Whereas *Such Impossibilities* was commissioned to fit into the context of a series with all the preconceptions that that implies on the part of the producer, *All Good Men* (or *History*, as it was originally titled) was the product of a set of restrictions altogether different but no less a part of what the television dramatist may have to contend with. In the interview with me cited above Trevor Griffiths recalled that in summer 1973 he was invited at short notice by the BBC *Play for Today* script editor, Ann Scott, to write a seventy-five-minute play to replace one that had failed to materialise. The budget was to be limited and the setting to comprise a multiroom studio set, with no allowance for filming. The opportunity of a platform to talk to the large audience commanded by *Play for Today* overruled any objections that Griffiths might have felt to writing to order; within a few days he had conceived the possibility of a script, and within six weeks it was written. However, Griffiths' problems did not end there: *All Good Men* was scheduled for transmission on 31 January 1974, but because of the restrictions on electricity supply caused by the current miners' strike all television programmes were subject to a curfew of 10.30 p.m. In consequence, it was necessary to cut the original text from a running time of seventy-five to sixty-three minutes, losing the greater part of the opening scene.[9] It was a sacrifice that Griffiths was prepared to make, given the relevance to the miners' present position of the play's central figure, Lord Waite, and his secret betrayal of the miners in the General Strike of 1926. Having already required his audience to focus on sophisticated ideological debate in both *Occupations* and *The Party*, Griffiths was encouraged further at the time of writing *All Good Men* by his own reaction to Eric Rohmer's film *Ma Nuit chez Maude*, in which the audience's expectations of amorous adventure are confounded when three people who meet in Clermont-

Ferrand spend a long time in elaborate discussion of Pascal's theory of probability. 'I was thrilled by talk, by the fact that people could actually talk and yet still hold interest. It was a belief I'd had for some time.'[10]

In *All Good Men* the action centres on the preparations for an 'in-depth' interview of Edward Waite, retiring Labour MP, ex-miners' leader and cabinet minister, and soon to be elevated to the peerage. On the eve of the interview, Lord Waite celebrates his seventy-first birthday with his daughter Maria, an art teacher in a comprehensive school, his son William, a research graduate in politics at Manchester University, and Richard Massingham, the ex-public-school television interviewer. Ostensibly to re-hearse the forthcoming interview, William challenges his father to justify the record of the Labour Party in office over the past fifty years. This Waite does in a flow of impatient rhetoric, a shade too familiar in tone to be wholly convincing and subtly undercut by inflections and mannerisms that allude to George Brown, Lord Robens and, particularly with the cunningly deployed pipe (never smoked, as we later learn), Harold Wilson. Yet it remains a powerful and sincere display, and seemingly, enough to crush William particularly, as he says, 'Look. You're old. And you're ill. And you're my father. There's no way I can win. I asked my question, you answered it.' For Griffiths has taken care to invest the situation with a more urgent excitement: first, we have seen Waite a few days earlier suffer a mild heart attack, so we know that now he may be in danger of collapse; secondly, William is not just any chance left-wing adversary, but his own son, and a reflection of the young working-class idealist that he himself may once have been. Much of William's resentment towards his father springs ironically from the fact that he has been given the chances Waite never had; early in his life the family had moved from a dingy two-up, two-down in his Beswick constituency to 'Didsbury, four bedrooms, attics, cellars, gardens, playschools, parks . . .' – and on to this sequestered property in Surrey, where the worst problem is the squirrels attacking the yew-trees. Wil-liam is objecting both to his own and to his father's deracination, and by analogy to the Labour Party leadership's loss of touch with true working-class origins and aspirations.

Goaded by his father's patronising scorn, William resumes the attack and gives his version of Labour's achievements: not a social revolution, but 'a minimal social adjustment'. The debate reaches a climax of acrimony when son challenges father on his conduct during the General Strike, and thus we arrive at the true motive behind William's original challenge: in the course of his research he has gained access to confidential Miners' Union files, which have revealed that Waite opposed the strike in Union District Executive voting from start to finish, and then acted as vice-chairman of the committee to agree pay reductions and redundancies – a fact that Waite has been careful to exclude from his autobiography. There is no defence, and Waite can only align himself with Beatrice Webb's view of the General Strike as 'a proletarian distemper that had to run its course'. For good measure, he reveals his acceptance of a peerage to William, and retires to bed, apparently discredited. Yet an uneasiness persists: as Waite has already remarked, William has set up the exposure of his father in Massingham's honour, and he now reveals that he has had photocopies made of the incriminating minutes for use in the forthcoming interview. For his part, Massingham is probably planning a hatchet job on Lord Waite in any case, so they emerge as an unappealing alliance, and William is not much redeemed by his contempt for Massingham's phoney objectivity, his claim to be 'simply the film camera, the tape recorder, the lighting man'. His collusion with the derided 'media man' is not unlike Kabak's deal with Fiat in *Occupations*.

The closing scene shows the first take of the interview in the conservatory, with Massingham immediately broaching the question of Waite's view of the General Strike. As Waite starts to reply, his lips move soundlessly and the image is bright, washed out, like a pallid waxwork. The camera pulls back and cranes up to show him alone in a deserted space, draped in his baronet's robes. The credits roll, to the strains of 'There'll Always Be an England', as though sounding a requiem for a whole era of Labour government.

Yet even if the play has persuaded one to question the shabby pragmatism of Labour in office, the alternative represented by William of high-minded social revolution has a certain dogmatic certitude about it that is no closer to working-class humanity. Whether the audience can find any alternative between these two extremes is doubtful: whereas Waite's daughter, Maria, is shrewd, warm, uncompromised and equally a product of the same family background, she remains in terms of political alternatives a peripheral figure, merely suggesting qualities that her father and brother have lost sight of. But if Griffiths does not present a solution, it is perhaps because in the early 1970s he could see none within the spectrum of British socialism, only qualities that endure and might yet be translated into action: the working-class faith is there, but in fragmented form.

Briefly reviewing *All Good Men* in *New Statesman*, Dennis Potter acknowledged 'some of the sharpest, most telling and intelligent speeches ever heard on television' and noted the 'truly stupendous performance from Jack Shepherd as the young radical, eyes sliding off centre in the search for thought, face blanched with earnestness, fingers extending like talons with the wiry tautness of argument'. Yet, at the same time, he complained that the play 'was only about what it was about . . . People are more than, or other than their opinions, so any play which deliberately confines itself to lengthy exchanges of familiar ideas, however well-phrased and passionate, is in perpetual danger of collapsing into itself.'[11]

This criticism seems to me to misread Griffiths' dramatic purpose entirely: the central point of *All Good Men* is that Waite is very much other than his opinions, and this we discover as his beliefs and actions are revealed. Whereas it may be common enough knowledge that Labour ministers are, for the most part, something other than 'men of the people' (a fact that has become a good deal more apparent in the aftermath of the Wilson resignation), yet television is still deployed constantly to reassure us that they remain precisely that. The very fact of locating Waite in a setting of Home Counties ease is enough to set him at an ironic distance from his Manchester back-to-back origins. Not only that: William and Maria are the children of his first, presumably working-class, marriage; but he has a second, estranged wife from higher up the social scale. Early in the play (Scene 3), when he suffers his heart attack over a solitary dinner, we hear in voice-over his recollection of the mocking, contemptuous words of the second wife as he engages in some guilty sexual activity with her. The words follow directly on snatches from past events: Chamberlain's 'peace with honour', Attlee in 1945, Bevin's 'naked into the conference chamber', Gaitskell's 'we will fight, fight and fight again'. The whole passage becomes associated with a sense of inner guilt, which seems to precipitate the heart attack. Given the taunts of his wife, the idea conveyed is that of inadequacy, in sex as well as in government, born of a sense of class inferiority. This is confirmed later when William berates Labour leaders for their need to be thought of as 'responsible' men.

Possibly the first indication of Waite's subconscious guilt is too fleeting to lodge in the viewer's mind, the voices-over too confusing; but there is no doubt that Griffiths is trying in *All Good Men* to reach far deeper into the Labour Party's collective psyche than Dennis Potter was able to grasp. It was an exploration that was to reach far deeper two years later with the greater scope afforded by the eleven-part series *Bill Brand*, where fundamentally the concerns were the same as those of *All Good Men*.

Although Waite and parliamentary Labourism are the centre of the play's focus and Massingham, the Wykehamist interviewer, only, as Griffiths put it to me, 'a way of seeing refractions of the reality of that life through the institutionalised television process',[12] the action still serves to demystify for the viewer the image-forming process of the personality interview. In achieving this, Griffiths was undoubtedly helped by his inside knowledge of the methods employed by television in the shaping of its audience's consciousness.

Griffiths regards *All Good Men* as essentially his first television play; it was his first opportunity to learn about play-making, as opposed to discovering the means of access and control and the securing of equal rights for the author alongside director and producer, which had been his principal gains from the *Adam Smith* series. As regards the creative side of production, Griffiths readily acknowledges the support of Ann Scott as script editor and above all, of Michael Lindsay-Hogg, a director he has worked with regularly since *All Good Men*. Certainly, the direction was notable for its discretion and for the judicious use of reaction shots, in particular of Frances de la Tour as Maria, the one unambiguous moral reference point in the play.

The audience figure for *All Good Men* was low for *Play for Today*: only about four million, though apparently the reaction index was high. The critical response was slight, but this was as likely an indication of the critics' prior assessment of Griffiths as a TV playwright as it was a measure of the production's intrinsic worth. Such was undoubtedly the case three months later when Griffiths' next work, *Absolute Beginners*, was transmitted virtually unannounced within the unlikely context of the *Fall of Eagles* series. Previewing the week ahead, *Time Out* advised its readers,

'Do not be tempted to watch this Griffiths play, despite the fact that his last offering, about working-class betrayal during the General Strike by a Labour Life Peer to be, was a powerful political play. This is about 1903 and Lenin, but in the nostalgic *Fall of Eagles* series. There are better things on BBC2.'[13] The *Time Out* critic could never have viewed *Absolute Beginners* before writing this, and he grossly underestimated Griffiths' strategic acumen. Certainly *Fall of Eagles* as a series was a nostalgic grand tour of the last years of Europe's remaining autocratic dynasties, the Habsburgs, the Hohenzollerns and the Romanovs, inspired, says Griffiths, by the sentiment 'How lonely it must have been for these great people. The twilight of an age. If only they'd had the liberal good sense to see what was coming, they could have averted the holocaust, and crucially the holocaust of October 1917.'[14] In fact, the original series outline envisaged an episode called *Time-Bomb in London* which would deal with the 1903 London Congress of the Russian Social Democratic Party and the crucial split which led to the emergence of the Bolsheviks. When Stuart Burge took over as series producer, this was one of the episodes that remained to be written, and he offered it to Griffiths with the promise of total authorial autonomy. Griffiths readily accepted, reasoning,

Here was an opportunity to write a play about a very serious event in socialist and revolutionary history pretty well unimpeded, with a fair amount of resource, and most important, lodged in a series which was going to be contemptibly popular. I mean, whatever Stuart did at this late stage, this was a series which was one sugar-coating after another, and I sensed that to put a bitter pill inside that sugar-coating would actually get it swallowed, and tasted and used quite extensively.[15]

'Quite extensively' is an understatement: not only was the series repeated twice by BBC, but it has sold abroad to more than sixty countries, making it probably one of the half-dozen most popular series the BBC has ever made. Yet in terms of political complexity and density of argument, *Absolute Beginners* makes no concessions whatsoever to what is derisively termed 'popular taste'. After a brief introductory scene at Tsar Nicholas's Summer Palace, in which Minister of the Interior Von Plehve briefs the Tsar on the measures required to quell revolutionary agitation, the action moves to the Bloomsbury flat of Lenin and Krupskaya. By rapid stages the conflict is established between Martov and Zasulich, the advocates of a revolution based on the ideals of human brotherhood, and Lenin, ruthlessly set on forging a dedicated vanguard leadership. In between stand Krupskaya, torn between loyalty to Lenin and respect for the ideas and feelings of their old friends and comrades, and the young Trotsky, flamboyant, opportunistic and prepared to back the winning side. In the distance is Plekhanov, the father of Russian Marxism, living in serene émigré retreat in Geneva, but ready to back Lenin.

As he had done in earlier plays, Griffiths establishes the personal–political dichotomy, using an authentic incident at an *Iskra* editorial board meeting when Lenin refuses the demands of Martov and Zasulich to accept proof of gross immoral conduct by the agent Bauman as reason for his expulsion from the party. According to Lenin's rigid revolutionary code, Bauman's value as an agent overrides all personal misdemeanours. The irreconcilable conflict is isolated in the following exchange:

MARTOV [*losing control*]. You can't separate private from public like that, can't you see it man! We are what we *do* . . . you, me, Bauman, all of us. Party morality is more than just loyalty to the party . . . it's the highest level of ethical consciousness yet afforded the human species . . .

LENIN. Metaphysics, Julius. Another time, perhaps, we may speculate. Just now we're trying to make the revolution *possible*.
[*Silence. Martov, disturbed, thrown, shivering a little, unused to being in conflict with Lenin*][16]

Importantly, the conflict is seen to be not merely one of viewpoints, but personal and emotional. By this stage, the close affection between Lenin and Martov is well established. Dramatic tension arises from the fact that Lenin will sacrifice this intimacy if need be, but Martov only with the deepest pain, and this has its profound political as well as personal meaning.

When Griffiths wrote *Occupations* he could allow himself a certain freedom to compress historical events and even to invent a major character such as Kabak, the Soviet agent,[17] together with his countess mistress, in order to give life to the antithesis to Gramsci's political beliefs. In *Absolute Beginners*, whilst seeking to explore similar issues, he was much more tightly bound by history, and there is nothing of significance in the script that cannot be traced back to an authentic source. The problem for Griffiths was that, apart from Lunacharsky's *Revolutionary Silhouettes* and Krupskaya's memoirs of Lenin (written under the constricting circumstances of the Soviet period), there is little information about the major revolutionary figures as *people*, since historians tend to portray them in terms of absolutes to correspond to their own particular version of events. As Griffiths puts it, 'None of them said much about Lenin's gut.'[18] So what he did was to take what anecdotal detail there was and transform it into images and incidents which are significant yet realistic in terms of human behaviour.

Lenin's refusal to entertain the complaint against Bauman is one example; another is his delirious resistance to the agony of shingles, which suggests his determination to surmount all human frailty. Similarly, our first sight of him in the play is as he completes fifty press-ups before breakfast. Conversely, when first we see Martov, he is in impassioned debate with anarchists in a pub by the British Museum, and he is 'thin, smallish, bearded, untidy; papers and pamphlets bulge from his person'. Lenin, by contrast, is seen at this point against the background of the British Museum; 'He carries a roll of galleys under his left arm; stares sombrely at the entrance of the pub across the way.'[19] In other words, Martov, for all his likeness to Lenin, is an émigré, 'Dilettante, intellectual. Unreliable'. He epitomises the weaknesses that Lenin seeks to purge from the party organisation. Similarly Georges Plekhanov is first encountered in his home in Geneva; his study is 'Large, expensive, tastefully and expensively got out. Double doors join to the next room. A view of the mountains from the window. The room is full of books and "objects".' It is evident that he belongs to the theoretical past of Russian Marxism, but not to its revolutionary activist future. The key contrasting image of Lenin is at the London Congress: at the crucial stage of the debate he is seen backed by an impressive semicircle of 'hard men'.

Yet the character is far from monolithic: I have mentioned the attack of shingles, and there are the moments of intimacy with Krupskaya, when she feeds him bread and milk on his sickbed, shyly offers herself at night, quietly defies him to console Zasulich. Then there is the final ironic impression after the awkward farewells have been exchanged by the conference delegates over Karl Marx's grave in Highgate: Lenin and Krupskaya 'Turn, walk off towards the gate, two simple bourgeois on a Sunday morning stroll'[20] – cutting abruptly to Tsar Nicholas shooting crows in the park at Tsarskoe Selo to the ominous opening bars of Shostakovich's Fourth Symphony. What comes across is perhaps more predetermined than Griffiths intends, partly because one cannot help superimposing on the action what one knows of subsequent historical events, but also because the play as transmitted ran fifty minutes compared with the eighty plus of Griffiths' original text.[21] In consequence, some depth is lost, specifically from the relationship between Krupskaya and Zasulich, from the portrayal of Bauman (and the justification for Lenin's retention of him), and above all from the depiction of Tsarist absolutism in the opening scene, designed to motivate Lenin's ruthless aim of 'a party built like a fist, like a brain balled'.

Deprived of this early view of the barbarism and total lack of scruple in Nicholas's police state, the viewer is in danger of concluding that the London Congress was where Russian Communism lost its soul and set itself on the course that led to the thirties terror. Nothing could be further from Griffiths' intentions: what he was seeking to pose was the classic dilemma of ends and means in terms of human, as well as political, behaviour.

Nor did he consent to compromise with the conventional demands of a popular series: there is no simplification of the interfactional debate within the ranks of the Social Democrats, and indeed the viewer is as hard put as Martov himself to keep pace with Lenin's manoeuvres in the final stages. However, the broad lines of conflict are clear enough, and the personal tragedy of the brave Vera Zasulich deeply moving at the end. In an interview with *Theatre Quarterly* in 1976, Griffiths said, 'In TV one is up against the notion that the audience is soft-headed, that the material must be pre-digested and so on. I contest and contend that the whole time, and I won't have any script-editors working on my work finding knotty and difficult bits, and cutting them off, and getting the thing down until it's a story and nothing else.'[22] Without doubt, *Absolute Beginners* suffered no such simplification, even though, thanks to time pressures, it is the only production to date in which Griffiths has had no part in the final edit – and here the director, Gareth Davies, must be given due credit. If anything, the effect of the cuts in the script was to make it *more* difficult to assimilate.

Much the same thing happened with *Occupations* when it was transmitted by Granada in September 1974, four months after *Absolute Beginners*: the two-hour theatre text was pruned to achieve a running time of seventy-eight minutes. Griffiths was prepared to make the sacrifice in order to reach the wider audience, but in this case much of the play's power, particularly in the scenes with the Turin workers, was lost.

In addition to having three plays produced on television in 1974, Trevor Griffiths completed the writing of two more: the first, *Comedians*, was staged by Richard Eyre at the Nottingham Playhouse on 20 February 1975, transferring subsequently to the National Theatre at the Old Vic, and the following year to Wyndham's Theatre; the second was another television play, *Through the Night*, which had to wait a year before it was transmitted by the BBC (2 December 1975).

Originally, *Through the Night* arose out of a commission from Granada for a play based on an experimental prison in Sheffield. Griffiths' interest in this subject was overtaken by his reaction to a diary that his wife, a social worker, had kept when she was admitted to hospital for a biopsy operation on a lump in her breast and came round to discover that the breast had been removed. Out of this recorded experience and Griffiths' own reaction to it there emerged a rapidly written script, called originally *Maiming of Parts*, and submitted to Granada as *Through the Night*. Granada's response was swift: the play's focus was hard to locate, it would cost a lot, and they didn't want to do it. Angered by this rejection, Griffiths next sent the text to Ann Scott, script editor at the BBC. Deeply disturbed personally by it, she was eventually persuaded by a doctor friend that the horror of the subject must not be ducked, and agreed to produce the play. Similarly, Michael Lindsay-Hogg needed to overcome his physical aversion to the content before he could agree to direct. There were further obstacles to be met: in particular, Griffiths recalls pressure from above to cast a star in the role of the cancer victim in order that the audience might thereby have the reassurance that she would not die. Also Griffiths and Lindsay-Hogg determined to resist the customary convention of shooting documentary-style drama in authentic settings, preferring to concentrate their resources on strong casting, elaborate studio sets and lighting.

The experience of Christine Potts, a working-class mother in the play, follows closely that of Jan Griffiths. Diagnosed initially as a non-urgent, low-cancer risk, she is admitted for a biopsy after a three-week delay, signs an open consent-form when drowsy with anaesthetic in case the operation reveals 'anything, well, nasty', as the house surgeon puts it. The operation follows, and a malignant tumour is discovered:

> [*The Registrar teases out a sliver of flesh, scraping it into a small round plastic container.*]
> REGISTRAR [*OOV*]. Path lab, nurse. Oh and phone Doctor Mount, tell him we might have something for his mice in an hour or so . . .
> [*CU Christine, in repose*]
> STOURTON [*OOV*]. How old is she?
> [*Pan round the table. Return to CU Christine. C.U. Pearce*]
> PEARCE [*OOV*]. Twenty-nine.[23]

Christine recovers to find her breast amputated, but is given no explanation beyond what her diffident husband, Joe, is granted by the Ward Sister: 'Well, she said when they opened you up it were nasty tissue and there were some sort of infection, so the specialist decided you'd be better off without' – plus a vague and frightening reference to 'more tests and that'.[24]

When Stourton, the surgeon, makes his ward round, we share Christine's point of view of the muttered conference at the bottom of the bed and her confusion at the barely audible exchanges. Of the surgeon, she gets no more than a sight in half-profile 'as though [he were] shy or embarrassed'. Later, Chatterjee, the Indian nurse who attends to her dressing, can only admire the 'excellent wound' and marvel at Stourton's skill. Finally, in depression Christine seeks night-time sanctuary in a lavatory cubicle and is persuaded to emerge only by the intervention of the friendly and unkempt houseman, Dr Pearce. Over cocoa in his room she finally extracts an explanation by a great effort of will;[25] she learns that a malignant tumour has been removed and finds the courage to put the question 'What are the chances?' The chances, it seems, are good, but await confirmation from the tests she is to undergo. 'But from now on [says Pearce] you live every day for keeps. The rest of us may continue to cherish the illusion that we're immortal. You know you're not.' Christine now has the strength to face her scar, even to joke about it to the scandalised Chatterjee: 'What did he do it with, a bottle?' The play ends with her joining in an anarchic drink-up in the ward organised by Mrs Scully, a regular visitor to the operating theatre, to which the scant remains of her stomach testify.

Whereas in *All Good Men* Griffiths interpolated a critique of the celebrity interview and the sham of the 'objective' presenter, and conceived *Absolute Beginners* partly as a terse corrective to the fond nostalgia of the *Fall of Eagles* series, *Through the Night* was calculated to cut across expectations born of the more predictable examples of the television hospital genre. As Peter Lennon observed in *The Sunday Times*,

> There was an interesting contrast here with the hospital series *Angels* (BBC-1), which in the relatively inessential details of hospital routine is authentic enough. But the nurses in *Angels* consider that they are rising adequately to a final crisis in a man's life by giving his hand an encouraging squeeze to help him to oblivion. In Griffiths' play, finely served as usual by Michael Lindsay-Hogg's direction, life is more oppressively complicated, intractable and only temporarily reassuring.[26]

The contrast is pointed out by something Pearce says to Christine in his room about the surgeon's remoteness from his patients:

> Mr. Stourton's a good man. He is just . . . not used, not equipped to deal with you as a person. The gap is too great. [*Pause*] And there's something else. The reason he can't speak to you, look at you, after the operation is that for him you represent a failure, even when the operation is a success. Because each time we use surgery we fail, medicine fails, the system fails, and he knows it, and he bears the guilt.[27]

In essence, the same point has already been signalled to the viewer by the uneasy detachment of the surgeon and his entourage during the ward round; the nurses' nursery talk to the patients ('We're going to take you for a nice wee ride down to the theatre') serves to preserve the same defensive distance. The extreme of impersonality is conveyed by the pathologist, Mount, who falls with voracity on his fifty grammes of infected tissue. Griffiths wished to go much further by including the horrific image of the amputated breast dumped casually into a waste-bin, but this was resisted in production. The point he is making, I think, is that the medical profession allows the necessary scientific detachment of its treatment of the patient's *parts* to extend to its care of the *whole* individual, leaving him or her adrift in ignorance and fear.[28] Quoting Hippocrates, Pearce says to Christine,

> 'For whoever does not reach the capacity of the common people and fails to make them listen to him, misses his mark.' Well, we're all missing the mark, Mrs. Potts. And we need to be told. Not just doctors and nurses, but administrators and office men and boards of management and civil servants and politicians and the whole dank crew that sail this miserable craft through the night.[29]

Thus the play's broader political implications are indicated, and the continuity with Griffiths' other work emerges: as Gramsci had said, the army not only can, but *must* be loved.

In the course of production, the script was extensively revised, particularly in response to solicited medical opinion. As Griffiths said to me, Scene 36 between Christine and Pearce 'bears all the torsions of organised BBC advice'. Specifically, he was confronted with the moral obligation to ensure that the play did not deter women from referring lumps in their breasts to their doctors, advice he could hardly ignore, but not relevant to the main argument about the way patients are treated when they are in hospital.[30]

Immediately following the screening on BBC-1 on 2 December 1975, watched by an estimated audience of over eleven million people, the Corporation's duty officer logged close to a hundred phone calls, the producer's office and the *Radio Times* received many letters, and Griffiths personally some 180. Marjorie Proops in the *Sunday Mirror* opened her columns to readers with experience of mastectomy treatment and received over 1,800 letters in ten days.[31] Thus the play loosened the taboo on the most feared of diseases – though not for the *Observer* critic who wrote, 'I found this week's episode of *The Nearly Man* by Arthur Hopcraft sufficient excuse for not watching *Through the Night* (BBC-1), a Trevor Griffiths play about breast cancer which I lacked the nerve to face.'[32]

As Griffiths says, *Through the Night* is, without question, his best-known piece. He also regarded it in 1979 as the high point so far of his collaboration with Michael Lindsay-Hogg. One can see why: the studio settings yielded nothing in authenticity, whilst, time and again, the camera and lighting made telling comments within the naturalistic context, frequently adopting (again in contrast to conventional hospital drama practice) the patient's viewpoint. There was the opening examination in out-patients, with Mrs Potts, uncovered and in distant isolation beyond the backs of the doctors in close-up; there was the arrival and departure of friends and relatives at visiting time through a sequence of glass doors and past the ward sister's office that kept the inmates well segregated from the outside world; there was the corridor ceiling seen by Christine from the trolley through advancing sedation on her 'wee ride' to the operating theatre. None of the shots was technically obtrusive, but all of them underscored rather than merely registered the experience. The acting throughout, with Alison Steadman as Christine and Jack Shepherd as Dr Pearce, served only to bear out Griffiths' contention that naturalism is the form most adjacent to the television audience and hence presents least obstacles to the full assimilation of a complex argument. Between Alison Steadman and Thelma Whiteley as the decent but remote house surgeon, Dr Seal, a wealth of meaning was conveyed even by the following simple exchange:

SEAL. How long ago was it we saw you?
CHRISTINE. Just coming up to three weeks, doctor.
SEAL. Yes. [*Still feeling Christine's breast*] Still no pain?
CHRISTINE. No.
SEAL. Good. Yes. Good. [*She feels again under the armpit.*] Is it about the same size would you say?
CHRISTINE. No. I think it's a bit bigger.[33]

Only in the nocturnal scene between Christine and Pearce discussed above did the weight of the rhetoric seem to put strain on the context – for all Jack Shepherd's skill in making intricate concepts sound like newly coined thoughts. Here, 'the torsions of organised BBC advice' seemed actually to be contorting the natural speech rhythms and demanding the impossible of Shepherd; yet still he managed to retrieve credibility with the concluding line 'Do you know something? My mother's proud of me. [*He laughs drily.*] Wow . . .'

Whereas, in terms of public response at least, *Through the Night* has been Trevor Griffiths' most successful play, *Bill Brand* (1976) remains an unequalled example of television drama as a form of extended political dialogue, surpassing even the controversial *Days of Hope*, broadcast by the BBC a year earlier. The first episode of *Bill Brand*, which went out on Thames Television at the peak time of 9–10 p.m. on 7 June 1976, attracted an audience of ten million, and over the following ten Mondays the figure held at seven to eight million. Subsequently, the series was repeated in the early-afternoon slot, thereby reaching a largely different audience.

In an interview in *The Leveller*, Griffiths recalls that the original idea for *Bill Brand* came to him on the Election night in March 1974 when Labour were narrowly returned to government.[34] The actual writing process occupied him for a full two years after that, extending well into the production period. For the first and only time, Griffiths worked with an independent producer, Stella

Richman, who remained executive producer when the series was sold to Thames Television.[35] In consequence, Griffiths enjoyed unprecedented control over the means of production, although Jeremy Isaacs, Thames Controller of Programmes, was to become a firm champion of the series. Even so, production was fraught with problems: first, it was only after a confrontation with a full assembly of writer, directors and actors that Thames agreed to let the series go out at prime time, though not, as originally hoped, in the spring; then, the budget was so far overspent after the completion of the sixth episode that Griffiths was faced with the demand to shoot the remaining seven entirely in studio. Griffiths preferred to maintain the established standard by reducing the series by two episodes, thus necessitating extensive rewriting and the sacrifice of certain themes planned for greater expansion.

Finally, when production plans for *Bill Brand* were already far advanced, Granada announced their intention to screen *The Nearly Man*, a series arising out of a single play by Arthur Hopcraft, which, like *Bill Brand*, featured a Labour MP, albeit right-of-centre. The resemblance between the two series ended there: as the MP Christopher Price wrote in *The Listener*, 'Hopcraft took a snapshot: Griffiths has tried to portray a political odyssey.'[36] Not surprisingly perhaps, the network controllers were loath to contemplate a second series about a Labour politician, particularly given the poor impact that *The Nearly Man* had made. Furthermore, overseas companies who had already committed themselves to purchasing the Hopcraft series refused to consider *Bill Brand*.

Griffiths spells out his objectives:

What I was trying to say throughout the series was that the traditions of the labour movement were inadequate to take the struggle further, and that we had to discover new traditions or revive even older ones. And that we had to seek connective tissue between electoral party politics, which still has a mystifying mass appeal, and extra-parliamentary socialist activity.[37]

How did Griffiths set about achieving these objectives? Brand (played by Jack Shepherd) is introduced in the opening episode, the bye-election in 'Leighley', a Manchester suburb, at which he is elected to parliament. Ex-International Socialist and liberal studies teacher at the local tech, he describes his political stance in an interview for local radio:

I am a socialist of the sort that Bernard Levin and his trail-blazing claque would describe as reactionary. I actually believe in public ownership and exchange. I actually believe in workers' control over work, community control over the environment. I actually believe that the real wealth of any society is its people – all of them, not just the well-off, the educated and the crafty, which I suppose makes me a democrat too. (Episode 1, Act 2)[38]

Brand's struggle to maintain these principles in the face of parliamentary and constituency pressures during his first year at Westminster at the same time as he copes with the conflicting demands of his private life, furnishes the basis for the series. The crises Brand gets involved in all closely resemble events of recent history, or, at times, of history yet to be made: massive redundancies in the textile industry followed by non-union work-ins; the struggle for party leadership when a Wilsonian prime minister resigns mid-term;[39] a 'Further Prevention of Terrorism Bill', designed to extend the police's power of detention; secret deals with union leaders leading to the cancellation of nationalisation plans and the curbing of wage demands.

Through all this Brand becomes inevitably involved in skirmishes with the whips' office, Tribune Group (here 'Journal Group') debates, censure motions by his constituency party, the compositing of conference resolutions, the procedural wrangles and frivolous badinage of select committee meetings. It is here that the series was at its most revelatory, showing, as Dick Taverne, the breakaway Social Democrat MP, wrote in *New Statesman*, 'the weaknesses of Parliament and above all the silliness and the humbug and the cant'.[40] Other MPs announced themselves less impressed, and the Tribune Group as a whole seemed to Griffiths to be hell-bent on discrediting the series from the start.[41] But what came across to the general viewer was highly credible – even the punch-up in select committee when Brand floored an obstreperous Tory.

As with all his other work for television, Griffiths chose in *Bill Brand* to restrict himself to the prevailing realistic mode of television drama, partly in order to avoid creating needless stylistic barriers which might obstruct the flow of a complex argument between him and his audience, partly in order to facilitate direct comparisons between his and other versions of reality available on television, partly to avoid using characters as mere attitudes, which might undermine the overall sense of truth. In the *Leveller* interview he says,

I try to occupy the space of all the people I'm talking about. I have actually met almost nobody who goes around saying to people, 'Well, the trouble with me is I'm a total shit. I tell lies all the time, and all I'm about is self-advancement; I don't give a fuck for anybody.' People don't seem to operate that way.[42]

There are instances in *Bill Brand* where the need for compression seems to override this principle, but it is only some of the secondary parliamentary characters who suffer. For the most part, Griffiths does manage 'to occupy the space' of those he is talking about. Three examples demonstrate the point: John Venables, the donnish, right-wing prime minister; David Last, the Foot/Benn Hampstead intellectual left-winger whom Venables defeats in the final leadership ballot; and Cedric Maddocks, the long-serving chief whip.

John Venables is contrasted with his predecessor, Arthur Watson, sketched in brilliantly within the single Blackpool Conference episode (and realised with light-footed cunning by Arthur Lowe). Whereas Watson, like Harold Wilson, is 'a cork among stones' with 'a dazzling absence of belief', Venables is in the Crosland/Jenkins line of revisionists, prepared to give his opponents a courteous hearing, yet believing passionately in the Labour Party as 'a consortium, an alliance of necessary and fruitful contradictions expressive of the whole of a society, not just of a segment or a class' (Episode 5, Act 3).[43]

In the course of a summer seminar at Oxford Griffiths gives Venables's reasonableness free rein, but only, one notes, to have it undercut successively by Brand's scornful quotation from Crosland's *The Future of Socialism* and a shot of a redundant textiles factory in Leighley. Similarly, the ostensibly civilised logic of his 'New Deal' when he becomes prime minister is wholly discredited for the viewer by his brutal rejection of the loyal but overprincipled chief whip.

David Last is the means whereby Griffiths is able plausibly to bring Brand rapidly into contact with the Government at ministerial level; Last pursues Brand as his next PPS, for, as he says, 'If I can't take you with me, where the hell do I think I'm going anyway?' Late at night in the Midland Hotel, Manchester, and after a lot of whisky, Brand gives Last his candid view of him: 'I read your book on Morris when I was seventeen, your book on Tom Mann a bit later. Always seen you as in a tradition, a fixity, part of an earlier great refusal. Now there's nobody where you were – and there's nobody where you are' (4.2). Last's reply is that refusal alone is not enough: 'I'm sixty suddenly. Thirty years like a week, all of it touchable, bound together by what? By a sort of rhetoric: air on air. Not enough I thought. It doesn't ever just happen. It has to be made, and it has to be led' (4.2).

But far from promoting Last as the best alternative, Griffiths is often at pains to discredit him – notably by depicting the positive glee with which he engages in surreptitious party manoeuvring. If Bill and the viewer are ultimately persuaded by Last, then it is in full knowledge of his deficiencies – in spite of them, in fact, and because of the sheer passion and conviction generated by the man. The appeal may be emotional, but at least it is to *socialist* emotions and recognisably a part of the same tradition that unites all those of the left throughout the series.

Cedric Maddocks, the chief whip, is no less a part of that tradition: an ex-docker from the East End, whose father helped to organise 'the big one', the docks strike of 1889. When Venables becomes prime minister, Maddocks baulks at mobilising all-party support for the revisionist 'New Deal', and is summarily discarded. Up to that point he has seemed a likeable parliamentary fixture, with a sneaking regard for Bill, but a machine-man for all that. Now, as he prepares reluctantly to move to the House of Lords, he gives Bill the benefit of his experience:

You won't see it, Bill, but we've changed this country. *We* have changed it. In 1931 – in that year we could have just phfft! Finished! Gone under. But we didn't: we got our heads down, and we stuck, and we were ready in '45; and we changed this country: coal, railways, road-transport, electricity, gas, steel, N.H.S., education, social welfare. But we could have gone under, not stuck . . . You've got to love this Party. You're in it, of it, but you don't love it – not family. (11.2)

The words echo Lord Waite's apologia for the Labour Party in *All Good Men*; but they are unadorned with his oratorical flourishes, they command respect – Bill's and ours. Cedric Maddocks is part both of the tradition and of the reality that has to be worked with. Short of revolutions, politics are, in Maddocks's words, 'give and take, here and there, come and go'. There can be no absolutes – as Brand discovers yet again when during the 'Fight for Work' campaign he encounters Willie Moores, the formidable 'Allied

and General Workers Union' leader at TUC headquarters. He
suggests that Moores may have done a deal with the government. Moores replies with vehemence,

I've been a socialist since I was eleven. Where I come from, the Rhondda,
they put it in the tea. When I was seventeen my dad and me packed a
bag, we took a train, a boat, and then a train again. Three days it took – to
Spain see. Two years fighting Franco's fascists. I came back on my own.
Now I didn't fight, and he didn't die, so that I could come back and
betray my own class, O.K.? (10.2)

His words are moving, unanswerable – but Bill replies by asking
disingenuously if the plans for dock nationalisation still stand: it
is Moores who is silenced, and he leaves glowering, without a
word. The point is underscored as the camera pans from him to
rest briefly on a portrait of Lord Citrine in peer's robes. Moores is
discredited yet the memory of his passionate and sincere outburst persists: another contradiction that has to be faced.

At constituency level, too, Brand has to learn to accept the
compromises of everyday politics: the case of a woman denied an
abortion cannot be publicly pursued in a constituency with
23,000 Catholics, most of them Labour voters; a Trades Council
engagement must be cancelled for the sake of a fund-raising
wine-and-cheese party organised by the 'Heaton Moor crowd',
the right wing of the party, whose support and votes Brand still
needs; faced with a possible snap election in the autumn, 'the
wild man of Leighley' must restore confidence by opening fêtes,
judging beauty contests and joining in Wolf Cub sponsored runs.
But there is no compromising of principles amongst the hard core
of constituency party workers, only a rigid sense of reality. As
Albert Stead, the veteran Party and Union Regional Secretary,
advises Bill, 'You've got to stay in touch. You can't run all the
time.' And, quoting Gorky, he puts the question 'Is this the
rabble on which we are to build a revolution?', to which the
answer is 'Yes, comrade, it is: they're all you've got' (8.1).

It was at constituency level that Griffiths could draw on his
personal experience of Labour Party membership, and it furnishes one of the key relationships of the series, that of Bill and
his agent, Alf Jowett. Brand is answerable to Jowett for his voting
at Westminster, his public utterances, his image in the press, his
conduct in the constituency, even the irregularities of his private
life: anything that might affect his chances of remaining an MP.

Jowett is pragmatic, abrasively critical, but immovably socialist. When, in the final episode, Bill is contemplating voting against the Venables government in a vote of confidence, Alf supports him:

We have had these buggers leading us before. They're like dry rot. Clear 'em out of one area, and they creep in somewhere else. They can't win, because reality's not on their side. They think capitalism's like a coat of paint, like a veneer, and underneath is the structure. And it isn't: capitalism is the structure, the reality. And it splits us up, sets us against each other in classes, in thought, in life-style, in aspirations and all the rest of it. But it breeds resistance in every worker who goes down the road, in every tenant who's evicted, in every man and woman denied the chance to be human (11.3)

Thus, with Albert Stead and others, Jowett embodies the continuity of struggle and belief within the Labour movement, a continuity emphasised when Bill's unemployed brother, Eddie, shakes off his earlier apathy, joins the Fight for Work movement, and marches alongside Albert Stead.

Standing to the other side of Bill, and in virtual opposition to Alf Jowett, is Bill's mistress, Alex Ferguson. It is not only that she threatens to undermine the image Bill presents to the electorate, but, more important, she embodies the world of alternative politics that he has left behind, but which still conditions his responses. Moreover, her independent, feminist view of sexual politics implies a radical critique of the power structures that Bill, in becoming an MP, appears to endorse, and which now threaten their relationship. Add to this Bill's tendency to revert to the male-dominant role of his Northern, working-class conditioning, and one has a nexus of ideas so complex as to be incapable of proper development within this series. In fact, as Trevor Griffiths concedes, the Bill–Alex relationship is properly a series in itself. A further problem was the impossibility of depicting their sexual relationship with the explicitness that Griffiths required to convey their powerful mutual attraction. The one scene of their lovemaking that was shown was by normal television standards highly explicit, but, in Griffiths' judgement, merely risible. Even though the relationship had greatly deepened by the time it ended in Episode 8, it remained problematic, and the correlation between sexuality and politics never became sufficiently clear – a criticism I have already made of *All Good Men*.

One would not expect the final episode of *Bill Brand* to offer conclusions; as Griffiths said in an interview in *The Times Educational Supplement*, 'I'll probably never complete a play in the formal sense. It has to be open at the end: people have to make choices, because if you're not making choices, you're not actually living.'[44] Hence, it is acceptable that we see Brand at the end still skirmishing with the whips' office and stubbornly invoking the ringing phrases of the party manifesto which others have conveniently forgotten. Any resolution of his ambivalent position at Westminster would be a falsification of the real-life truth. But one argument is affirmed without qualification, an argument that has run through the entire series and, for that matter, through every play that Griffiths has written before it: if socialism comes, it will come from nowhere but the working class. In the final episode (entitled 'It Is the People Who Create'), Bill houses an agitprop theatre group for the weekend, whilst they give a performance at the Leighley Labour Club. Discussing their ludicrous débâcle there, one of the actors says, 'If you're going to make connections, raise consciousness, you've got to start where people are actually at, not from some notional point in the middle of your own middle-class guilt-ridden hang-ups' (11.3). Bill Brand readily acknowledges the point – and so does Trevor Griffiths, never losing sight of it in his plays. That is the reason why, more than any of his contemporaries in television, he can be described as a socialist realist – socialist realist, that is, in the broad tradition of Gorky, O'Casey, Sholokhov, Steinbeck and Brecht, aiming, as Lukács says, 'to describe the forces working towards socialism *from the inside* . . . to locate those human qualities which make for the creation of a new social order'.[45]

Appendix

Television plays transmitted

1972	*Adam Smith* (17 episodes)	Granada
15.6.73	*The Silver Mask* (Episode in series *Between the Wars*)	London Weekend
31.1.74	*All Good Men*	BBC-1 *Play for Today*
19.4.74	*Absolute Beginners* (Episode 6 in series *Fall of Eagles*)	BBC-2
1.9.74	*Occupations*	Granada *Sunday Night Theatre*

12.7.75	*Don't Make Waves* (written with Snoo Wilson; Episode 7 in series *Eleventh Hour*)	BBC
2.12.75	*Through the Night*	BBC-1 *Play for Today*
7.6.76–16.8.76	*Bill Brand*	Thames
29.10.79	*Comedians*	BBC-1 *Play for Today*

Plays published

(For Griffiths' published TV plays, see Appendix 1.)
Sam, Sam, Plays and Players, April 1972
Occupations and The Big House, London: Calder & Boyars, 1972
Lay By (with others), London: Calder & Boyars, 1972
The Party, London: Faber, 1974
Comedians, London: Faber, 1976
Apricots and Thermidor, London: Pluto Press, 1978

Translation

Anton Chekhov, *The Cherry Orchard* (a new version from a translation by Helen Rappaport with author's preface), London: Pluto Press, 1978

Other plays produced

The Wages of Thin (1969)
Jake's Brigade (radio, 1971)
Gun (1973)

Other writings

Tip's Lot (juvenile), London: Macmillan, 1972

Interviews

Andrews, N., 'A Play Postscript', *Plays and Players*, April 1972, pp. 82–3
Ansorge, P., 'Current Concerns' (also with David Hare), *Plays and Players*, July 1974, pp. 18–22
Croall, J., 'From Home to House', *The Times Educational Supplement*, 25 June 1976, pp. 18–19
Hayman, R., 'Trevor Griffiths – Attacking from the Inside', *The Times*, 15 December 1973, p. 9
Itzin, C. and S. Trussler, 'Transforming the Husk of Capitalism', *Theatre Quarterly*, 6, 22 (1976), 25–46
Silburn, P., 'Gambit Interview', *Gambit*, 8, 29, pp. 30–6
Taylor, G. and N. Gray, 'Brand of the Recent Future', *Streetlife*, 1, 11 (1976), 22–3
Thomas, N., 'Trevor and Bill – On Putting Politics Before News at Ten', *The Leveller*, no. 1 (1976), 12–13
Tynan, K., 'Party Piece', *The Sunday Times*, 16 December 1973, pp. 82–7

Criticism etc.

Barnes, M., 'The Plain Face of Politics', *The Sunday Times*, 8 August 1976, p. 27

'Good Television – but How Many MP's Are Bill Brands?' (unsigned), *The Economist*, 14 August 1976, p. 26

Gould, T., 'One Brand of Hero', *New Society*, 5 August 1976, p. 300

Hay, M., 'Theatre Checklist No. 9: Trevor Griffiths', *Theatrefacts*, no. 9 (1976), 2–8

Hunt, A., 'A Theatre of Ideas', *New Society*, 16 January 1975, pp. 138–40 (repr. in P. Barker (ed.), *Arts in Society*, London, 1977)

Lennon, P., 'The People Speak', *The Sunday Times*, 7 December 1975, p. 39

Marsden, P., 'Bill Banned', *Socialist Worker*, 21 August 1976, p. 11

Morris, J., 'Reviews: Bill Brand', *Red Letters*, no. 3 (1976), 14

Potter, D., 'Prickly Pair', *New Statesman*, 8 February 1974, p. 198

Price, C., 'Haggard Odysseus', *The Listener*, 22 July 1976, p. 85

Prince, P., 'Soft Centre', *New Statesman*, 12 December 1975, p. 766

Tariq Ali, 'Bill Brand', *Red Weekly*, 3 June 1976

Taverne, D., 'Bill Brand and I', *New Statesman*, 30 July 1976, pp. 140–1

Williamson, A., 'Bill Brand – Monosyllabic Melodrama', *The Tribune*, 30 July 1976

Winston, B., 'Public and Private Medicine', *The Listener*, 11 December 1975, p. 798

Wolff, J., 'Bill Brand, Trevor Griffiths, and the Debate about Political Theatre', *Red Letters*, no. 8 (1976), 56–61

Wolff, J., S. Ryan, J. McGuigan and D. McKiernan, 'Problems of Radical Drama: the Plays and Productions of Trevor Griffiths', *Literature, Society and the Sociology of Literature* (Colchester: University of Essex, 1977), pp. 133–53

4 David Mercer

KHALID EL MUBARAK MUSTAFA

THIS ESSAY WILL discuss David Mercer's contribution to the development of TV drama. It will be divided into two parts, the first of which deals with Mercer's introduction to the medium through his trilogy, *The Generations*. The second part examines one of the best examples of his most mature TV plays – *In Two Minds*. The choice of plays was influenced not only by the desire to cover various stages of Mercer's career; it was also intended to highlight the two predominant themes in his work: madness and politics.

1

It is perhaps ironical that the play which introduced David Mercer to TV was originally written for the stage.[1] We have his own word for that.[2] A close study of the text of the play will also support this statement. There is, moreover, every indication that he was in the first stages of learning and perfecting his craft as a writer.

The first scene of *Where the Difference Begins*, preceded by a short telecine clip introducing the old railway worker Wilf Crowther, is a very good example of the opening scene of a stage play. It brings in all the major characters: Richard, Wilf, Gillian, Edgar, Margaret and Beatie, and it announces all the major themes of the play. An imminent death in the family[3] is the reason for the get-together. Wilf, looking at Gillian's bulging stomach, asks when she and Richard will be getting married. This gives Richard the chance to introduce the other theme to us.

RICHARD. As soon as the divorce is final. It should be through in about a month.[4]

Edgar and his wife Margaret arrive and immediately the rift between the two brothers is apparent. Edgar is enraged by Gillian's presence and reacts angrily.

EDGAR. I told you when Janet started the divorce I'd no intention of meeting your new girl friend.[5]

This is in contrast to the friendly if low-key reaction of the father, who is after all the one best entitled to be narrow-minded and intolerant.

We see how a brief scene is made to work very hard by introducing all the major characters and all the major themes of the play.[6] It is left up to the words to shift us in space. What could be termed 'verbal flashbacks' give us, for example, as much information as possible about Wilf's entire working life: that is, he's due to retire in six months after forty years of what he calls 'hard labour'; and that instead of a pension he gets a gold watch from 'Sir Brian' of British Railways. According to Aunt Beatie, he's proud and stubborn and has fought hard for the education of his two sons who now live far away in London – unlike her own, none of whom 'lives more than ten minutes walk away'. His wife is dying in the room upstairs, and he is deeply disappointed by the strained relationship between his two sons. When Edgar starts the quarrel about Gillian's presence, Wilf bursts out: 'What the bladder of lard's going on in here? Are you fratching afore you've gotten into t'house?'[7]

The use of an upstairs room (which we don't see until later) for the dying mother was probably dictated by the basic theatrical rule of requiring as little space and demanding as few sets as possible.

This assumption is supported by the fact that Mercer, rewriting for the camera and consequently relieved of the problem of immobility, inserted a short silent scene (involving an additional set) of Mrs Crowther dying in bed immediately after the end of Scene 1, as well as adding the telecine opening of the play showing Wilf at his engine – so that the first scene is flanked at both ends by two silent camera-inspired sequences. There are other elements in the first scene which work equally well for stage and television, notably the contrast in appearance and language between Wilf and Beatie on the one hand and the 'visitors' from London on the other. Set side by side on the page they look like two different languages.

GILLIAN. . . . . Aunt Beatie said she left you some dinner in the oven. Shall I put it out?

WILF. I don't know as I feel like eating owt love, thank you. It'd nobut
stick in me gullet . . .[8]

Later, commenting on Richard's painting hung on the wall, he
tells her, '. . . I've never seen flowers like them in nature, mesen.
Yon looks like summat t'cat's thrown up.'[9] Clearly the first scene
is an example of writing for the stage.

The rest of the play is solid talk; it relies heavily on language, on
words, with the characters made to 'talk out their predicaments'
as David Storey quite rightly summed it up.[10]

As the action unfolds it becomes clear that Wilf had lost his two
sons before (physically) losing his wife. Education has helped
them to cross the class barrier and become people with whom he
cannot identify. The two are not equally 'lost', however: Richard,
the younger son, is a radical as far as his politics are concerned.
The personal and political conflict between him and his elder
brother provides fuel for the play's fires.

As far as the form is concerned the pattern is dictated by the
first scene. The third scene, for example, carries on with the
argument about the rights and wrongs of bringing Gillian along
and about the way Edgar looks at the working classes through a
middle-class viewfinder. This sort of scene is better for reading
than for acting; it is so static that even in a theatre it is bound to
create problems of devising grouping and movement for the
actors. It culminates in Edgar's commentary on his father's kind
of socialism: '. . . You don't think my father thought he was
bringing up two future intellectuals for the Labour Party, do you?
It was *brass*! Anyway, the kind of socialism he went in for, it's as
dead as the dodo.'[11]

It is Edgar who, several scenes later, ends the muted but
powerful confrontation between them.

EDGAR. I'm going out for a bit. I love my Dad. As much as you do. But he
was wrong.
   [*Edgar goes out. Richard follows and shouts after him from the door.*]
RICHARD. That's where the difference begins.[12]

The way the following scene is linked to this last sentence is a
good example not only of competent writing but of writing that
offers several options to a perceptive director. The word 'begins'
ends one sentence. The next scene opens with the word 'station'.
It might seem an obvious link in the text, a station being a point of
end as well as beginning; but it is bound to be much more subtle

in production as a relationship between the verbal and the visual. Another vital point is the contrast between the visual hustle and bustle of the station with the entirely verbal tone of the end of the previous scene: slow sound works as a contrast to fast-moving picture.

Scene 13 itself, which, in a telecine insert, opens with the station, balances the quick sharp exchanges of dialogue with the excited movement of the visual action.

> *Scene 13*
> *Station, afternoon of the same day.*
> [*Richard runs up the slope into the forecourt of the station, looking at his watch. He gets a platform ticket from the machine. The train arrives and as he runs up the steps of the footbridge, people from the train come across the bridge towards him. He pushes through them and sees Janet. She is conventionally well-dressed – a smart, good-looking woman.*]
> JANET. I'm glad you came to meet me.
> RICHARD [*taking her suitcase*]. You shouldn't be here.
> JANET. How is your mother?
> RICHARD. She died last night.
> JANET. Oh –
> RICHARD. Look, Janet. You can't come to the house.
> JANET. Why not?
> RICHARD. Let's go to the buffet. We've got to talk.[13]

The verbal refrain which includes the title of the play is an old and proven theatrical ploy which Mercer puts to clever use. The word 'difference' is used for the first time by Richard when he tells his father about the two differing views, his own and his brother's. 'You know dad, Edgar and I have opposite views on just about everything. Only his fit the world as he sees it and mine fit the world as I'd like to see it. That's a big difference.'[14]

Contrast is used throughout the play. Two examples will illustrate this.

Gillian was clever enough, once she was alone with Wilf, to steer the conversation towards his plans for the future and eventually towards every man's most cherished topic: his work. He is sufficiently relaxed to tell her about the light side of it.

> WILF. Well, when you take an engine back you have to fill a report card in, if there's owt wrong with it, for t'fitters. I always put summat down as'll give them food for thought, like. Take this one last week. Reight shook us insides up it did. So I put on t'card; this engine has square wheels and oval axle boxes. You should've seen t'foreman's face.
> [*They both laugh. Beatie comes in from the stairs door. She is crying.*]

BEATIE. You'd best go up now Wilf lad.
  [*Wilf gets up. He is suddenly very old and tired. He stops to look at the two women by the fire side as he goes out.*][15]

The relaxed mood culminating in laughter contrasts sharply with Beatie's crying and the sad mood this generates.

Another scene-to-scene link which makes contrasting use of the verbal and the visual is to be found at the end of Scene 3 and the beginning of Scene 4. Edgar speaks of his father's socialism.

  . . . Anyway, the kind of socialism he went in for, it's as dead as the dodo.

  Scene 4
  [*Wilf closes his wife's eyes. He crosses her hands on her breast. He stands up, looks down at her. He looks at the framed photograph on the chest of drawers – of two men at an open-air bookstall with posters – 'Join the Left Book Club'. Again he looks at his wife's face – and then back to the photograph.*][16]

We move from the verbal mention of death in connection with Wilf's kind of socialism to a silent scene showing an actual death – and the father looking at a photograph that illustrates an aspect of his socialism.[17]

A reference to autobiographical aspects would help to complete the picture. According to David Mercer, his own father was a train driver[18] (like Wilf), his elder brother a scientist (like Edgar). He himself studied painting and hoped to make his career as a painter, worked as a supply teacher and had an experience of divorce (like Richard).

It is also worth noting that the play opens and closes with Wilf. The opening is a silent telecine insert of him at the cabin window of his cab. The time is established as late afternoon (death of the day) and the season as winter (death of the year). This gloomy tone is confirmed by the death of the mother later on in the play.

The other bracket encasing the play is Wilf's last speech, which, though gloomy all through, ends with a bright note calling for hope and optimism.

WILF [*he looks at Gillian as if appealing to her, nodding over his shoulder at Richard*]. He says last night as being a husband and father's all he's capable on, like. [*Pause*] Well, that mun be a start – mun't it?
  [*Gillian looks up at him. Close-up of Wilf and Gillian*]
                              END[19]

He speaks of a 'start', meaning a fresh start. The close-up is of him and Gillian, who represents a new start for the collapsing marriage and who – because she's pregnant – stands for the general promise of a new life (a new start after the mother's death).

Thus we see that David Mercer's first play bears the marks of its initial conception as a stage play, notably in the presentation of characters and main themes in the first scene, as well as in its use of verbal flashbacks in place of visual mobility in space and time. Nevertheless the text of the play provides evidence of skilful writing, especially in the subtle handling of contrast and inter-scenic as well as trans-scenic verbal and visual rhythms.

The play is very ambitious in that it shatters the myth that television drama should steer clear of public and political issues. A *Times* reviewer spotted this when he considered that *Where the Difference Begins*, despite several weaknesses, 'draws into its domestic problems tensions of personality and a sense of the world today usually excluded from a genre that squares the domestic problem with the boredom of a stale marriage or the spiritual growing pains of the adolescent'.[20]

The play also contains some pointers towards Mercer's future preoccupations.

The dialogue between Richard and Edgar after Wilf and Margaret leave them offers an example. Edgar expresses his surprise at the reason for which his wife Margaret defends Richard.

RICHARD. Maybe she's taken a look at you and come out of the anaesthetic.
EDGAR. And just what do you mean by that?
RICHARD [*both angry and tired*]. Oh, Edgar! You still haven't caught on, have you? You're still wondering what the fuss is all about. It's family life chum.[21]

This idea of family life is developed later in a series of plays. Mercer significantly chose the words *Family Life* as a title for the film version of his play about schizophrenia, *In Two Minds*.[22]

All these positive aspects do not conceal the fact that the play also contains evidence of inexperience like heavy polemical 'talking out' of characters' dilemmas and the aborting of dramatically promising situations. It says something for Mercer's later development that it was he who described this play as 'one of the dreariest plays ever written by me or anyone else for that matter'.[23] Even if we allow for some exaggeration and a degree of self-baiting, the remark certainly has a lot of truth in it.

The director's contribution added some fine nuances which gave a lift to the play and added visual comments to the action. Wilf is grief-stricken in the room where his wife lies dead: a shot through the window shows his face, and trickling rainwater gives the impression of tears. Another example is the CND badge worn by Richard in a house in which there is 'war' on more than one front. The theme of 'the difference' is underlined by a shot of the mantelpiece clock in the middle, with Wilf and Richard on either side. Another shot shows Wilf between his two sons. The clock (time) is also linked with the newspaper *The Times* which indicates Edgar's change of class.

The promise shown in this play bears more fruit in the next play in the trilogy.

2

After *Where the Difference Begins*, the BBC made a more or less open offer to David Mercer agreeing to do whatever he cared to write. The result was his first play specially written for TV. As might be expected, *A Climate of Fear* provides a unique opportunity to detect the changes in style, mainly in terms of the increased awareness of the medium and the gradual shedding of a beginner's weaknesses.[24]

The first interesting point to note is the piecemeal release of information. Instead of a crowded first scene which gives away too much, like the first scene of *Where the Difference Begins*, this play starts with a short court scene where Colin is sentenced to three months in prison following a 'non-violent protest against nuclear weapons and policies'.[25] The scene generates enough interest to hold our attention; but it says very little about what actually happened. What was the 'action' in question? What sort of people are the accused (and condemned)? What are their occupations? Which one of these characters before the court will be followed up and developed – all three, two or one?

A significant awareness of the medium is evident in the opening scenic directions: 'Colin Waring, George and Ray are in the dock. The Magistrate and Court Officials are heard but not seen.' Part of the scene is deliberately masked from the viewer, whose viewpoint can only be that of the camera. On stage the viewer's eye would be free to roam and concentrate on whichever object it might choose. There is no way of getting rid of irrelevant space, and the most a writer or director can hope for is to direct attention, by force of action, to this or that part of the stage area. Nothing guarantees that a member of the audience won't choose to look at the loose shoelace of a minor character intentionally tucked by the director into an obscure corner of the stage. In TV drama there is a foolproof method of dictating what the viewer is allowed to see and what he should not see. Selection is made for him.

Awareness of the medium is further shown in the imaginative use of the cut – not as in *Where the Difference Begins* to shift from one location to another (e.g. from Wilf in the cab to Wilf coming up the street), but in breaking up a scene into several parts and moving from one to another. On stage, a naturalistic production of a party scene would require the different groups to freeze and/or keep quiet and subdued in order to focus attention on the group which is doing the talking; and while the audience hear them, they would be expected to pretend that the other groups on stage can't catch what they are saying. The party is at Clive Edgerton's house, lively and crowded with chattering people. Mrs Rawson gossips about her au pair girl:

[*Mrs. Rawson, trying to light her cigarette, flicks her lighter as she speaks.*]
MRS. RAWSON. I caught her standing over Nina's milk with a cigarette in her mouth this morning. We had a blazing row but her English is appalling. You know I'm sure she's pregnant. She has an Indian –
[*Someone lights her cigarette.*]

CUT TO:
[*Edgerton stubbing his cigarette in ashtray on piano. He takes a drink to Frieda. Frances and Leonard are with Mrs. Wyman and Brian Bell. Frances watches them contemptuously.*][26]

A deft shift is taking place here as if from one scene to another with several linking points. Mrs Rawson's attempt to light her cigarette implies that the cigarette is in her mouth. She is speaking about a cigarette in the au pair girl's mouth. She mentions a 'blazing row' and we see a *flame* as someone lights her cigarette. Here we have two cases of the visual versus the verbal. Cigarettes carry us to the next group because the cut is from the lighting of Mrs Rawson's cigarette to the stubbing out of Edgerton's cigarette.

While the second group is discussing Cuba, Brian – hoping to avoid a clash between Frances and Mrs Wyman, the American woman – splits the group by offering to introduce Leonard and his daughter Frances to someone else. A pan of the camera is made necessary without its being specifically mentioned in the text. Mrs Wyman has just said that Castro was still shooting people.

BRIAN. I know. It's terrible. May I just introduce you to [*They move away towards the other groups.*]
LEONARD. Can't you give it a rest? Just for once?
FRANCES. These people don't care about anything – [27]

The fact that their conversation continues while they're moving away indicates that the camera leaves the group and follows them.

Scenes 9 and 10 provide another example of skilful dramatic writing. Scene 9 takes place in Leonard and Frieda's bedroom while Scene 10 takes place in the prison cell in which Colin is kept. The dialogue between Leonard and Frieda shows Frieda's growing realisation of the gulf that separates her from Leonard and a deep feeling of disappointment at the sort of life she was trapped into leading.

FRIEDA. You love me – and inside love, I'm starved. I have a nice house – and inside the house I'm frightened. We have friends – neighbours – and among them I'm appalled by them. I love you – and inside *that* love there's hysteria because I want to live before I die. I want love to nourish life. But it doesn't. [*Pause. Speaks suddenly and sharply*] It makes a cow out of a woman![28]

The argument is carried on, and about one page and several lines after the above-quoted speech Leonard falls asleep while Frieda is speaking. The description of her hand at that moment equates the physical groping with the earlier psychological one when she was speaking: 'Her hand gropes in the darkness. Slowly, she withdraws it.' The action of Frieda's hand ends the scene – only to be followed by 'Scene 10. A Prison Cell',[29] which implies an analogy with the bedroom as a sort of marital prison. An added dimension is the presence in the cell of Colin, who is himself a result of the bedroom prison. The prison theme is confirmed when, towards the end of the tenth scene, Colin speaks of his father to Ray, one of his two cell-mates: 'He won't just come here to see me. He'll come for the satisfaction of knowing that he acted magnanimously. He won't be a father. I won't be a son. We're trapped, him and me.'[30]

The last scene but one – Scene 13 – provides an example of a more adventurous use of telecine, compared to the conservative, straightforward use of it at the opening of the previous play. The telecine insert in this play is not silent: it is a BBC newsreel clip with Bertrand Russell speaking.

His speech is interrupted by a telecine insert of onlookers on a traffic island, followed by a cut back to the demonstrators marching. This in turn is followed by yet another cut back to telecine to show us Frieda walking, seeing Colin, Frances, Tom and Peter as they sit, and joining them. Another cut follows to the newsreel film to show demonstrators being carried into police vans, and again the newsreel film is not silent.

[*John Tidmarsh interviews George Clark.*]
TIDMARSH. Would you say that this demonstration has been a failure?
CLARK. No. As far as the demonstrators were concerned – an absolute triumph . . .[31]

An important confirmation of the claim that the telecine is used more ambitiously here is to be found in its relationship to that part of the scene which precedes it. It provides a contrast of preoccupations: Rawson, their neighbour, has called to complain about Frances roaring down the street on her scooter late at night. After the complaint has been heard, both men become 'anxious to deny that there has been anything wrong'.[32] In the process Leonard makes his own contribution in exposing the pettiness of his private concerns.

LEONARD. I can't stand being on bad terms with people next door. By the way, have you seen what Morley's dog's done to my young currant bushes? The little beggar's got in and rooted half of them up. I must say they want to –
[*Frieda gets up and hurries over to Leonard. She is obviously distressed.*][33]

Frieda then asks for the car keys, says she is going to London and 'goes out and slams the door'. The last word of the scene is Leonard's call: 'Frieda –' Immediately there is a cut into telecine. Bertrand Russell is speaking: 'I doubt if many of those here present today realise the very considerable likelihood of a nuclear war within the next few months . . .'[34] A sharp contrast is intended and realised here between the commonplace and almost banal preoccupations and worries of the Rawsons and Leonard on the one hand and those of Bertrand Russell and the demonstrators on the other. Frieda leaves one group and joins the other. It is worth noting that Rawson complains about the noise of the scooter while Russell refers to another twentieth-century invention: the bomb. Rawson says the scooter disrupts his wife's sleep, while Russell's speech is clearly intended to wake people up to the danger of war; he also refers to death, which is a kind of sleep.

Freed by the BBC from the necessity of making his plays more attractive to producers by keeping the numbers of the cast down to a minimum, David Mercer indulges himself in his second play by using a much longer cast list than in his first.

So we see that in his first play specially conceived in television terms Mercer shows more awareness of and sensitivity to the medium. The promise of *Where the Difference Begins* has already been partially fulfilled.

3

The following discussion of the third play in Mercer's trilogy, *The Birth of a Private Man*, proposes to seek further proof of the continuing perfection of his writing techniques. The play shows his efforts to achieve what John Huston referred to as 'the time balance between words and action',[35] which when conceived by a writer means that 'dialogue and camera set-up are not at war', the aim being to 'seek a certain word and a certain set-up to carry a certain idea. Sometimes one single word is enough for this, or even complete silence, if the image is right.'[36]

The opening telecine sequence helps to make the point. The theatrically influenced presentation of major characters in the first scene of *Where the Difference Begins* is reversed. In that play the characters were introduced talking. However, when the four major characters are introduced in this play, none of them utters a word. The scene is set in a cemetery and speaks for itself. It starts with 'A cemetery on the outskirts of an industrial town in Yorkshire. Winter. A coffin lies in its open grave . . .' A colliery brass band is playing; earth is thrown on the coffin, and then Frieda, Peter and Frances walk away, with Colin hurrying to join them. During the whole busy scene only one sentence is spoken – a miner clasps Peter's hand and says, 'You've brought your dad home, then –'[37] This one sentence dots the i's and crosses the t's in the whole scene. Peter Driffield's father is dead; and Frieda, Frances and Colin have come with Peter for the burial. A lot could have been said, but it would have been superfluous. The picture alone was sufficiently eloquent.

Scenes 6, 7, 8 and 9 illustrate another aspect of David Mercer's craftsmanship, viz. his awareness of the fluidity of television space. He shifts the scene from location to location quite freely; but not unnecessarily. Scene 6 takes place in a transport café; Colin is with the drivers. He walks away from them to a telephone in the passage and rings up Frieda. The next scene shows Frieda picking up the telephone in her flat in London. Scene 8 brings us back to Colin on the phone, and Scene 9 is in Colin's bedsitter in Pimlico. Scene 10 is in Frieda's Earl's Court flat where Jurek, a Pole who is to marry Frances, is introduced to the play. The next three scenes take place in Warsaw, while the last scenes of the play take us to locations as diverse as the East German–Polish border, Warsaw, a night club in West Berlin and finally the Berlin Wall. Of the three plays in the trilogy this last one is the freest in the use of space.

The next interesting point is yet another advance in Mercer's use of film. In Scene 12 – 'Viewing Theatre in a Warsaw Film Studio' – a film-within-the-play is being shown: a silent flashback into the Second World War history of Warsaw – its destruction by Nazi planes, the 1944 uprising and the rebuilt new Warsaw.

Apart from tying up with the tragedy of Jurek's sister, the film-within-the-play gives a time dimension which is quite essential in establishing the Continental locations to which the action of the play has shifted.

On the whole, the play marks an even greater command of the medium on Mercer's part. *The Birth of a Private Man* is a mature work of art – totally unpredictable and written in a way that would not work equally well on a stage.

Although not planned as a trilogy – at least not when the first play was conceived and written – the three plays hang together and complement each other, not only in the broad lines of the plot but in some minute details which act like nails hammered in at specific points to hold together some large boards. The most centrally situated one relates to Colin.

In *Where the Difference Begins*, Richard (Colin in the following two plays) tells his father Wilf, '. . . I'm tired. I'm so tired that being an adequate husband and father is about as much as I can reasonably expect of myself now. [*Pause*]'[38] His father refers to this in the closing speech of the play.

WILF [*he looks at Gillian as if appealing to her, nodding over his shoulder at Richard*]. He says last night as being a husband and father's all he's capable on, like. [*Pause*] Well, that mun be a start – munt it?[39]

Richard is tired of political involvements and considers becoming a 'private man'. His CND activities are, however, highly thought of by Margaret, Edgar's wife. She tells her husband, '. . . You sneer at Richard and the people that go on the bomb marches, but you're a *smaller* man for not even entertaining the idea.'[40]

In the second play, *A Climate of Fear*, Colin, who wears Richard's mantle, returns to the theme of a private man's contribution. In the prison visiting room he tells his father, Leonard, '. . . What have you done? Built a house and put a wife and children in it – put your gifts as a scientist into weapons of mass murder – isn't there something inconsistent there? Brick on brick and seeds in the garden and your children growing into a man and a woman. What for? To burn? To incinerate? Is *that* your example?'[41] Later in the play Colin becomes 'tired' and makes it known before the march: '. . . God, I wish I could break a leg or something. I don't want to go through it all again.'[42]

The third play, *The Birth of a Private Man*, contains references which link it with the two previous plays. Colin wants peace – not CND Peace with a capital P but Linda's kind of peace: '. . . It would be strange, wouldn't it? To stop agitating. Turn your back on everything. Watch your wife grow pregnant, take a job, furnish a flat, keep your head well down . . . in a world you believe the *public* men will destroy.'[43] This ties in with what Colin said to his father in the second play; Colin is now moving into a position which is basically similar to the one he attacked his father for in that play. It also ties in with what Richard expressed in the first play about the role of an adequate husband and father being the ultimate he could hope to achieve – because he was so 'tired'. The idea of being tired is to be found in the third play when Jurek tells Colin, 'I am as exhausted as you are! . . . But I prefer to live!'[44]

At the end of the second play, *A Climate of Fear*, Colin comments on his and Frieda's arrest, on an allegedly impartial law and on the divisions of society by saying, 'Wait till you come to the doubletalk – both sides are right, according to their values. And supposing we don't choose to die for any of the bastards.'[45] This speech fits in neatly with Colin's words at the Wall when he shouts, at the end of *The Birth of a Private Man*, '[*shouting over the crossfire*] A man, damn you all. Damn you on both sides. Your statesmanship . . . your deceit . . . your contempt –'[46] In the one play the reference is to two sides *within* a society; in the other it is to the two main ideologies confronting each other in Berlin.

Colin's position at the Wall caught in the crossfire is used to recall the trap or prison theme which pervades the second play: 'A searchlight comes on. There is wild firing across the wall now, in which Colin is trapped.'[47]

Lastly, the title of the third play in the trilogy, *The Birth of a Private Man*, could arguably be seen as an alternative title to the trilogy as a whole: *The Generations, or The Birth of a Private Man.* Frances changes and becomes a Communist; Frieda moves left politically and, in her private life, divorces Leonard; but at the heart of the three plays is the gradual change in Richard/Colin and his tragic end. This is not only a political comment. It is in human terms of a much deeper significance. It refers to the choices men try to make in circumstances which are larger and overwhelmingly more powerful than they are.

The trilogy ends the first phase of Mercer's creative contribution to the art of the television play. It is, however, also a stepping stone to the next, equally significant, stage.

4

Is there anything which is not, technically speaking, an assault? Birth. School. Work. Sex. Life. Consciousness. Death – [48]

I shall now attempt to show how, in his television play *In Two Minds*, David Mercer applied his mature talent and skills to tackle a problem rooted in the very fabric of society. In the process, he once again refuted the widely held misconception that the television play is by definition and nature a second-rate and hastily conceived and executed example of sloppy workmanship, and he established the involvement of television drama with such pioneering thinkers as R. D. Laing. In so doing he went one step ahead of the British theatre, which has always been suspicious of theory and philosophy and which has eschewed cross-fertilisation with intellectual currents in the manner common enough on the Continent, especially in France.[49]

In Two Minds is constructed with the aid of scaffoldings which are variants of the word 'view'. It is presented in the form of successive interviews: with Kate; with the family (internal views); with people outside the family (external views); with the other Kate, the 'voice' (interior view). Thus camera directions are built into the text so that the words 'point of view' refer not only to a camera angle but to a way of interpretation.

The interviews made long takes necessary. The rhythm of Scene 12 became so slow that when the film version of the play was made, this was one of the scenes which had some action injected into them: that part of the scene in which the knife incident is related is turned into action and movement, thus accelerating the rhythm. The narration of the incident started as follows:

MRS. WINTER. She was mistaken in one thing. There was no row. No recriminations. We behaved as if she wasn't there. [*Pause*] I put the breakfast on the table. She was looking from one to the other. She couldn't get over it, that we weren't *angry*! [*Pause*] I gave her the bread and the knife, to cut some. She's cutting the slices, and crying over it. [*Pause*] Well it was up to her to say the first word. And when she did, it gave me a chill I can tell you.
VOICE. What was that?
MRS. WINTER. She said: 'You got rid of my baby' –
WINTER. And she takes the breadknife and goes for Dolly –
MRS. WINTER. What happened actually, she threw it at me.
VOICE. She missed you completely, though –
MRS. WINTER. Well, it fell on the floor in front of me.[50]

The same goes for the eleventh scene during which 'Kate sits very still in a canvas chair with her hands folded in her lap.'[51] She continues like that for the whole scene reacting to the doctor's questions, or rather to the doctor's voice's questions. The slowness of the rhythm is underlined by the fact that one of the slowest parts of the scene comes at its end. After more than two pages of dialogue during which only one character is seen, sitting, Kate, in one of the longest speeches of the scene, relates the incident when she was locked out. '. . . Well. I got back very late this night, it was about two o'clock. And the door was locked. She put her head out of the bedroom window and said I could do what I liked – she wasn't going to let me in. [*Pause*] I got in an awful temper and went off . . .'[52] This part of the scene, too, was turned into action and movement in the film version.

Another aspect of Mercer's writing technique is the strand of duality which runs through the play. It derives from the title and in turn illuminates it.

(i) *The play as a whole* is in two minds; it does two different things at the same time. It's both a work of fiction and a rearrangement of factual or factually based material. (This is a point which I shall enlarge upon presently.)

(ii) *Kate* is in two minds. We see two Kates. One is introduced in the very first scene. '. . . She is in her twenties – a rather rough, plain face, but she could be very attractive.'[53] The other Kate is best described by herself in one of her 'normal' and articulate moods. She tells the doctor, 'I seem to myself like a piece of machinery. All the bits whirring and ticking, but it's not me. It's a *thing*. And I'm outside this machine. Only the "I" that's outside, it's not a person either. [*She laughs.*]'[54]

(iii) *The medical treatment* is in two minds – there are two alternatives, two approaches in dealing with Kate's condition. We have the established and accepted institutional approach and the investigating doctor's approach.

(iv) A further aspect of duality is that we know of *two boy friends* Kate has had, Jake and Peter.

(v) Yet another aspect of duality in the play is the fact that Kate is one of *two sisters*, the other one being Mary. 'My sister Mary got her own flat, and a job. She works as a secretary. [*Pause*] She ran away from here when she was seventeen . . . [*Pause*] *She* got away!'[55]

(vi) Another aspect of duality – the most obvious and the most deadly – is *Kate's parents*, centre of their nuclear family. The closer they come, the sharper – like a pair of pliers – is their bite on the object at the other end of their joint attention.

(vii) The last aspect of duality is that Mercer's *In Two Minds* is a television play about a mentally disturbed young girl called Kate. But the scene-within-the-play, Scene 6, is a description of part of a rehearsal of a television play (in which we have no dialogue relating to Kate's 'case').

> *Int. rehearsal room.*
> *A Director and two actors – Jake Morrison and Annie Rowan are working on a scene.*
> *The actors are sitting on chairs facing each other. The Director stands watching them.*[56]

But we have an idea of the content of the scene being rehearsed when Jake Morrison talks to the investigating doctor in the pub.

JAKE. What do you think of the play then?
  [*Pause*]
VOICE. It's about Kate, isn't it?
JAKE. She was the author's bird for two or three months . . .[57]

This is a positive indication, albeit an oblique one, that the scene was taken from the television play *In Two Minds*.

The earlier discussion of David Mercer's *The Birth of a Private Man* shows that his preoccupation with mental instability preceded his reading of R. D. Laing's books – if we accept as correct his statement that it was after writing *A Suitable Case for Treatment* that he began to read Laing.[58] His own experience of a nervous breakdown in 1957 and the psychoanalysis which followed for months on end must have been both a source of information and a cause of interest in the field.

It was, however, the playwright Dennis Potter who first revealed that, as far as *In Two Minds* was concerned, other factors than merely deep interest and personal experience were at work. Writing in the *New Statesman*, he said, 'David Mercer was probably being sensible when he rather shiftily insisted on *Late Night Line-up* that his terrifying drama *In Two Minds* (The Wednesday Play) was not based on or written to support any particular psychiatric theory . . . But if Mercer's denial was understandable, it was in my opinion rather less than honest.'[59]

He then expressed the view that the play was based on R. D. Laing's theories and revealed that Laing and his colleague David Cooper had actually received a fee from the BBC in connection with the play.

Almost six years after that *Late Night Line-Up* programme David Mercer, when interviewed by *Theatre Quarterly*, had a significantly different statement to make. Asked whether Laing co-operated in the writing of *In Two Minds*, he replied,

He was official consultant on it . . . It was a completely invented piece, by the way, it wasn't a Laing case-history – though it had all the characteristics of one. Laing was in any case ethically prevented from giving me access to his files . . . I invented every single word and I didn't even know, when I was writing, that it was going to be given a documentary treatment by Ken Loach.[60]

But this again is apparently not the whole truth and nothing but the truth. David Mercer is not necessarily being 'less than honest'. He might have immersed himself in Laing's work so much and so deeply that, by the time he came to write the play, his memory unintentionally fed his pen with Laingian material.

This much is certain:

(i) There seems to be a way round the ethical ban on access to case-history material. When names are either omitted or changed beyond recognition and when no other details are provided that might lead to identification of the patient in question, such material may be published for the whole world to read and consider.

Volume 1 of R. D. Laing and A. Esterson's book *Sanity, Madness and the Family* is subtitled *Families of Schizophrenics* and consists of analyses and excerpts from interviews with eleven families. It is a source of material for Mercer's play. The preface thanks patients and members of their families for consenting to be studied and permitting the result of the study to be published. It asserts that every care has been taken to 'preserve the anonymity of all persons involved'.[61]

(ii) The embryo of some of the dialogue and situations can be traced mainly to this book by Laing and Esterson. A family referred to in *Sanity, Madness and the Family* as 'the Churches' had a daughter who was diagnosed as a schizophrenic. The conclusion drawn about the pattern of her relationship with her parents, especially the mother, is formulated as follows:

A constantly repeated sequence is that Claire makes a statement and her mother invalidates it by saying:
  (i) She does not really mean what she says, or
  (ii) She is saying this because she is ill, or
  (iii) She cannot remember or know what she feels or felt, or
  (iv) She is not justified in saying this.
Then Mrs. Church follows with a statement that unintentionally validates what Claire has said . . .[62]

This is in fact almost identical with the pattern of the relationship between Kate and her parents, especially her mother:

KATE. I don't want to go to the doctor –
MRS. WINTER. It was your idea –
KATE. *You* suggested it!
MRS. WINTER. *I* said: maybe you ought to see the doctor. And you agreed. If you hadn't agreed, then we wouldn't be – would we?[63]

Kate makes a statement, her mother invalidates it by suggesting that Kate is contradicting herself or changing her mind; she then confirms that the suggestion was actually hers. The scene ends with Kate agreeing to go to the doctor's.

The abortion provides another example. Mrs Winter's attitude was that Kate didn't know what she wanted: 'She didn't want it. She *said* she wanted it. [*Pause*] But I knew different.'[64]

When visiting Kate in hospital, her parents discuss the chair incident with her – she allegedly held a chair and scared the nurse. The discussion demonstrates the mother's attitude that

(i) Kate was not Kate when she did it. In other words she didn't mean to do what she did.

(ii) When Kate swears, it isn't she that's swearing. She only does it because she isn't well.

(iii) When Kate apologises for calling her mother 'a bloody liar!' the apology is accepted because Kate didn't mean what she said anyway. The discussion runs as follows:

MRS. WINTER. The little girl *I* brought up wouldn't have . . . well, you know, with the chair. Can't you see what a strain you put on people? If you didn't know you were doing these things . . . if you said *that* . . . well I'm sure we'd all understand.

KATE. What would that prove?

MRS. WINTER. It . . . doesn't it show lovey that you're not *my* Katie when you go round doing things like that? D'you see?
[*Pause*]

KATE. Whose bloody Katie am I then?
[*Pause*]

MRS. WINTER. That's another thing. [*Pause*] The swearing. The bad language. [*Pause*] I've . . . I believe you use some awful language . . . to the staff . . . and they know it isn't you of course. But they're entitled to your respect, same as me and your father.

KATE. You and Dad use swear words.

MRS. WINTER. *Everbody* uses an oath now and then. It's not quite the same thing. I know you . . . such expressions couldn't pass your lips when you're well, only –

KATE. You're a bloody liar!
[*The Winters exchange sympathetic looks, contriving to seem outraged at the same time.*]

WINTER. Kate –

KATE. I'm sorry. [*Pause*] Sorry Mum –

MRS. WINTER. It's all right darling. I know you didn't mean it.[65]

In David Mercer's play, Kate makes the acquaintance of a young male patient. She doesn't speak to him first; but she is nevertheless the one who makes the first move by going to where he is painting and stopping quite near. Throughout the scene, Kate is portrayed as the bolder, the more daring, of the two. It is she who suggests going for a walk.

KATE. Have you finished your painting?

YOUNG MAN. Nearly.

KATE. Shall we go for a bit of a walk?

YOUNG MAN. A walk?
  [*Pause*]
KATE. Yes. Anything wrong with that?[66]

And later on:

KATE. What if we did do something?
  [*Pause*]
YOUNG MAN. Is that what you're after?
KATE. No. But I'm asking. Is it any of their business?[67]

This scene immediately comes to mind when we read about the Fields in Laing and Esterson's book:

Mother saw June at the hospital gate with a young male patient called Robin.

MOTHER. Well – for instance tonight June at the gate with Robin; well that's all right, arm-in-arm – not arm-in-arm – June takes Robin's arm, Robin doesn't take hers [*laughs heartily*] – and he was just as anxious for June to come with us.
JUNE. You half dragged me there, didn't you?[68]

Another interview in Laing and Esterson's book, this time with the Golds, reminds one of scenes in *In Two Minds*. The interviewer, just as in the play, is asking questions about the early childhood of their Ruth:

Your wife has described her relationship with Ruth in the early days as close. How could you describe *your* relationship with her?
FATHER. Well, not as close as my wife. Naturally a girl and her mother – [69]

Mr Winter in Mercer's play is not as close to Kate as her mother.

VOICE. You mean Mrs. Winter prevented you?
WINTER. Prevented? Dolly wouldn't prevent nobody doing nothing! It's not in her nature. No. It's more like . . . well, she's Katie's *mother* after all. Isn't she?[70]

Another aspect of Kate's early childhood was her being an ideal child. She tells the investigating doctor, '. . . Mum says I was perfect when I was little . . .'[71] Mrs Winter confirms this when interviewed: 'She was as near perfect as a little girl could be! . . . We never had a minute's trouble with her . . .'[72] Ruth's parents in Laing and Esterson's book say something similar about their daughter.

MOTHER. A very considerate child always.
FATHER. She was, yes.

MOTHER. A very respectful child and never a moment's anxiety with her.

Ruth has one other thing in common with Kate. She has quarrels with her parents about drinking. Her parents, like the Winters, contradict themselves when speaking to the doctor. Ruth's parents say:

MOTHER. . . . And for a young girl to sit and drink all evening –
FATHER. Well she doesn't drink a lot.
MOTHER. No, but when she's not well she's confused and she doesn't know what she's doing, so she probably does have more drink than she really would –
INTERVIEWER. I'm sorry – I thought you said before that she doesn't drink very much.
MOTHER.
FATHER. She doesn't.[73]

The investigating doctor in Mercer's play encounters a similar situation.

VOICE. So then. Kate drinks, Mrs. Winter?
MRS. WINTER. Well. Not what you could call drink.
VOICE. But your husband says she drinks . . . Does she get drunk?
MRS. WINTER. *Drunk*? Our Katie? What's Gerry been saying to you? What I mean – are we trying to get it all out in the open or aren't we?
VOICE. So Katie drinks, but she doesn't get drunk?
MRS. WINTER. I think I can say we've brought that girl up to know how to behave. But she goes in these pubs, you know. With all sorts. Talks to them. It's her illness.

Later in the same interview the investigating doctor asks if her husband goes to the pub.

MRS. WINTER. He's a man and he's entitled to his drink if he wants one. [*Pause*] He has his drink, and that's that.
VOICE. But he doesn't get drunk?
MRS. WINTER. *Nobody* in this house gets drunk, doctor.
VOICE. Including Kate?
MRS. WINTER. *Nobody* . . .[74]

Another point in common between Kate and Ruth is that they are both either being denounced for associating with 'beatniks' or accused of looking like 'beatniks'. Kate says to the investigating doctor, 'Do you like my hair? I like it long. My mother says I should have it cut. Says I look like a beatnik.'[75]

Ruth's mother, on the other hand, told the doctor, '. . . When she's been ill she's brought people home that she normally wouldn't tolerate, you know, these beatniks.' One of the conclusions reached from a study of the relationships between Ruth and her parents is that their attitudes are sometimes contradictory: '. . . oscillating between implicit expressions of disapproval and explicit avowals of approval'.[76]

In Kate's case, her mother doesn't approve of giving her a key to the door; but she insists that she approves. Kate describes the situation to the investigating doctor:

VOICE. You haven't got a key of your own, then?
KATE. Oh, she offered me one. But she said I didn't need it. What did I want to bother with a key for? She'd never lock the door before I came in, and she trusted me she said – to come home at a reasonable time. [*Pause*] I think she was right. It's right to trust somebody.[77]

Mrs Winter herself leaves no doubt at all that she treats Kate as a responsible adult. When interviewed about the locking-out incident which resulted from the fact that Kate didn't have a key of her own, she tells the investigating doctor –

MRS. WINTER. . . . How did *we* know where she'd been?
    [*Pause*]
VOICE (*neutrally*). But you didn't ask her.
MRS. WINTER. I didn't have time, did I? She'd gone, when I came down. Off. In a temper. [*Pause*] She's a grown girl and her life's her own, but . . .[78]

In another scene, Kate tells her parents when they visit her in hospital, 'There's this big machine . . . at the centre of the earth, and it controls everybody. Me, you, *her* . . . all of us . . .'[79]

R. D. Laing uses the idea of the machine to express the way the 'group' operates and exerts control by arranging itself 'in patterns, strata, assuming and assigning different powers, functions, roles, rights, obligations and so on . . . The group becomes a machine – and it is forgotten that it is a man-made machine in which the machine is the very big men who make it.'[80]

This is not far removed from one of the most controversial of R. D. Laing's assertions:

There is no such 'condition' as 'schizophrenia', but the label is a social fact and the social fact a *political event*. This political event, occurring in the civic order of society, imposes definitions and consequences on the labelled person. It is a social prescription that rationalizes a set of social actions whereby the labelled person is annexed by others, who are legally sanctioned, medically empowered, and morally obliged to become responsible for the person labelled. The person labelled is inaugurated not only into a role, but into a career of patient, by the concerted action of a coalition ('conspiracy') of family, G.P., mental health officer, psychiatrists, nurses, psychiatric social workers, and often fellow patients.[81]

All the participants in the conspiracy against Kate are shown to have contributed their share in annexing her and inaugurating her into a career as a patient.

WINTER. If you don't co-operate with these people – after all they're doing their best . . . well you could be in here for ever.

   [*Pause. Kate suddenly looks her mother straight in the face.*]

KATE. I sometimes think – if I *do* co-operate, *that's* how I'll be in here for ever.[82]

The evidence of the quotations above from R. D. Laing's books shows that David Mercer owes more than just the general idea of *In Two Minds* to the psychiatrist's theories. His assertion that he invented every single word of the story is only partly true.

At the end of the play, the director shows an ECT session, with the students not wholly accepting the lecturer's views.

The play has – understandably – stirred up a hornet's nest. It would take a good many pages to enumerate reactions of anger and outrage. A representative example is Anthony Burgess's outburst in *The Listener*.[83] Burgess was annoyed by what he described as the failure of the play to suggest a solution after successfully arousing concern about Kate. In that sense the play was, for him, 'worse than pornography, for pornography offers, if not discharge in itself, at least a signpost pointing to discharge . . .' He goes on to describe the play as 'a dangerous hybrid' and to stress that this effect was easy to contrive but that 'art is more difficult'.

The whole *Wednesday Play* department comes under fire as being encouraged by the 'misguided' and wholly devoted to anti-art. The play had merely confirmed the suspicions he had had before watching it, for he states at the very beginning of his review that it was 'as I expected, not a play at all'. Burgess did have some kind words to say about the production – 'it was superbly done; it had the inarticulacy of true life; it was better than art because it was so real . . .' and also 'brilliant, yes, brilliant'.

The medical profession was also disturbed by the play. Dr William Sargant, Head of the Department of Psychological Medicine, St Thomas's Hospital, contributed a letter to a lively correspondence in *The Times* about the play in which he stated, 'the patient portrayed was unrecognizable as a typical schizophrenic. Furthermore the treatment given in the particular mental hospital shown in the play does not happen these days except in a very limited number of hospitals.'[84]

The fact that the play obviously disturbed and provoked a lot of people is, in a way, a measure of its success.

The discussion of the trilogy *The Generations* and the play *In Two Minds* has shown some of the development of David Mercer as a television playwright. In all, his plays are a powerful argument for considering a television drama as a work of art, as an honest, agonising search and questioning that demands an effort from viewers and readers if it is to be fully understood and appreciated. Mercer's plays are of such a compelling standard that even the most virulent attack, like that of Anthony Burgess, is forced to concede their excellence.

Appendix

Television plays transmitted

15.12.61	*Where the Difference Begins*	BBC
22.2.62	*A Climate of Fear*	BBC
21.10.62	*A Suitable Case for Treatment*	BBC
12.2.63	*The Buried Man*	ATV
8.3.63	*The Birth of a Private Man*	BBC
17.3.63	*For Tea on Sunday*	BBC
29.12.63	*A Way of Living*	ABC
2.6.65	*And Did Those Feet?*	BBC-2
1.3.67	*In Two Minds*	BBC-1 *Wednesday Play*
21.1.68	*The Parachute*	BBC-1 *Play of the Month*
11.4.68	*Let's Murder Vivaldi*	BBC-1
27.11.68	*On the Eve of Publication*	BBC-1 *Wednesday Play*
4.3.70	*The Cellar and the Almond Tree*	BBC-1
13.5.70	*Emma's Time*	BBC-1
27.11.72	*The Bankrupt*	BBC-1
22.2.73	*You and Me and Him*	BBC-2
6.5.73	*An Afternoon at the Festival*	Yorkshire
12.12.73	*Barbara of the House of Grebe* (based on Thomas Hardy; Episode 6 in series *Wessex Tales*)	BBC-2

3 Shooting the Chandelier *by David Mercer, shown on BBC-2 as* Play of the Week *on 26 October 1977, with Denholm Elliott as Semyon (foreground), Alun Armstrong as Brodovich and Doris Hare as Milena.*

22.9.74	*The Arcata Promise*	Yorkshire *Sunday Night Theatre*
10.12.74	*Find Me*	BBC-1 *Omnibus*
11.4.76	*Huggy Bear*	Yorkshire
14.8.77	*A Superstition*	Yorkshire
26.10.77	*Shooting the Chandelier*	BBC-2
23.4.78	*The Ragazza*	Yorkshire

Plays published

(For Mercer's published TV plays, see Appendix 1.)

The Governor's Lady, radio version, *Stand*, 6, 1 (Spring 1962); stage version, London: Methuen, 1968

Ride A Cock Horse, London: Calder & Boyars, 1966

Belcher's Luck, London: Calder & Boyars, 1967

Flint, London: Methuen, 1970

After Haggerty, London: Methuen, 1970

Duck Song, London: Methuen, 1974

The Monster of Karlovy Vary, and Then and Now, London: Eyre Methuen, 1979

Short stories published

'Huggy Bear', *Stand*, 4, 2 (Summer 1960)

'Positivist', *Stand*, 4, 3 (Autumn 1960)

'Folie à Deux', *Stand*, 4, 4 (Winter 1960)

'The Long Crawl through Time', in: *New Writing III*, London: Calder, 1965

Films scripted

1965 *Morgan* (film version of *A Suitable Case for Treatment*)

1966 *Ninety Degrees in the Shade* (English dialogue)

1970 *Family Life* (film version of *In Two Minds*)

1973 *A Doll's House* (film version of Ibsen's play)

1977 *Providence*

Interviews, articles, letters to the press

David Mercer with Lewis Greifer and Arthur Swinson, 'What Television Has Meant in the Development of Drama in Britain', *Journal of the Society of Film and Television Arts*, 13 (Autumn 1963)

David Mercer, 'Style in Drama: Playwright's Postscript', *Contrast*, 3, 3 (Spring 1964), 158

'An Open Letter to Harold Wilson', *Peace News*, February 1965

'David Mercer Talks to John Russell Taylor', *Plays and Players*, April 1965, 24, 45

'David Mercer on Why He Writes the Plays He Does', *The Times*, 27 July 1966, p. 6

David Mercer with Roger Manvell, 'The Meaning of Censorship: A Discussion', *Journal of the Society of Film and Television Arts*, 25 (Autumn 1966)

David Mercer, 'David Mercer and the Man Among the Ruins: Interview with Bert Baker', *Morning Star*, 17 November 1966, p. 2

'Portrait of a Playwright: Interview with Gay Search', *Radio Times*, 4 April 1968

'David Mercer Talking to Penelope Mortimer', *Evening Standard*, 17 November 1968, p. 7

'The Drama of Talking Heads: Interview with Stacey Waddy', *Guardian*, 25 November 1968

'Out of the Air: A Words Man', *The Listener*, 19 December, p. 825 (extract from a talk given on *Woman's Hour*)

'Interview with Sonia Copeland', *The Sunday Times*, 20 April 1969

'Mercer Unmarxed', letter to *The Listener*, 28 May 1970

'Interview with Joan Bakewell', in: Joan Bakewell and Nicholas Garnham, *The New Priesthood*, London: Penguin Press, 1970, pp. 84–6

'Cases for Treatment: Interview with Ronald Hayman', *The Times*, 14 February 1970

'Women Are People Too, in a Way . . . : Interview with Helena Matheopoulos', *Vanity Fair*, March 1971, p. 68

'Interview with Geoffrey Reeves on Political Theatre in Britain', *Gambit*, 20 (1971), 75–86

'Interview with Giles Gordon', in: *Behind the Scenes: Theatre and Film Interviews from the Transatlantic Review*, ed. Joseph McCrindle, London: Pitman, 1971, pp. 88–98

'Mercer and the Slag Heap Myth: Interview with John Sandilands', *Radio Times*, 23 November 1972, pp. 9, 11

'Birth of a Playwriting Man: Interview with Francis Jarman and the Editors of *Theatre Quarterly*', *Theatre Quarterly*, 3, 9 (January–March 1973), 43–55

'Interview with Ronald Hayman', in Hayman, *Playback 2*, London: Davis-Poynter, 1973, pp. 122–44

'Interview with Paul Madden', in Madden, *Complete Programme Notes for a Season of British Television Drama 1959–73, Held at the National Film Theatre 11th–24th October 1976*, London: British Film Institute, 1976 (discussions of *Where the Difference Begins* and *And Did Those Feet?*)

'Interview with Ronald Hayman', *Plays and Players*, November 1978, pp. 10–11

Criticism

A. Burgess, Review of *In Two Minds*, *The Listener*, 9 March 1967

C. W. E. Bigsby, 'David Mercer', in: *Contemporary Dramatists*, ed. James Vinson, London: St James Press, 1977, pp. 534–7

S. Clayton, Review of *Emma's Time*, *The Daily Telegraph*, 14 May 1970

Ronald Hayman, *British Theatre since 1955: A Reassessment*, Oxford: University Press, 1979

D. A. N. Jones, 'British Playwrights', *The Listener*, 8 August 1968

Alan Lovell, 'Television Playwright – David Mercer', *Contrast*, 2, 4 (Summer 1963)

Don Taylor, 'The Gorboduc Stage', *Contrast*, 3, 3 (Spring 1964)
'David Mercer and Television Drama', appendix to Mercer's *The Generations*, London: Calder, 1964, pp. 236–82

John Russell Taylor, *The Second Wave: British Drama for the Seventies*, London: Methuen, 1971, pp. 36–58

T. C. Worsley, *Television: The Ephemeral Art*, London: Alan Ross, 1970 (reviews of *And Did Those Feet?* (pp. 32–4), *The Parachute* (pp. 46–7), *In Two Minds* (pp. 64–5) and *Let's Murder Vivaldi* (pp. 214–17))

See also articles in *Plays and Players*, April 1965, p. 24, and May 1970, pp. 48–50, and *The Stage and Television Today*, 6 February 1975, p. 14

Bibliographies

Theatre Quarterly, 3, 9 (January–March 1973), 55–7, 90 (Mercer's stage and TV plays listed); 3, 12 (October–December 1973), 86–7 (additional information and corrections)

Francis Jarman, *The Quality of Mercer: Bibliography of Writings by and About David Mercer*, Brighton: Smoothie Publications, 1974

5   Peter Nichols

BRIAN MILLER

PETER NICHOLS HAS often been thought of as essentially an autobiographical playwright. His television plays are assumed to come straight and undistilled from his own life. Perhaps it is his concentration upon family and domestic subjects, the parallels to be drawn between characters in different plays, the high degree of naturalism in the dialogue and ease of characterisation suggesting 'slice of life' that reinforce this view. Nichols isn't, some might say, a true dramatist at all but a human tape-recorder, albeit a highly accurate and selective one. In some ways, then, it is a pity that so many of his TV plays are not only immediately appealing but memorable. Combine this too-appealing talent with the ephemerality of television, on which nothing of lasting value is ever produced anyway, and one has that strange phenomenon, the plays of a playwright which should be forgotten but which persistently refuse to *be* forgotten, despite a writing style declaring them to be obviously unartistic in a medium known to be strictly for instant mass consumption. It just isn't right.

Anyone who takes the trouble to study the plays of Peter Nichols will certainly be able to create a coherent biographical mosaic. Nichols Man's father was a salesman: lower middle class (*Daddy Kiss It Better*), right wing, pompous but not unendearing (*Forget-Me-Not Lane, When the Wind Blows*); his mother, wholly unintellectual, a warm family woman inclined towards smothering her son and cosseting him even into manhood (*A Day in the Death of Joe Egg, When the Wind Blows, Hearts and Flowers*), and of Bristol origin (*Forget-Me-Not Lane, Hearts and Flowers, The Gorge*). Nichols Man was born too late for the war, too soon for affluence and taking advantage of the Pill, a product of Austerity, National Service (*Ben Again, When the Wind Blows, Privates on Parade*) and Art School (*The Reception*) or some such functional education. As a young London bachelor (*Ben Spray, Ben Again*) he taught for

110

a while (*The Big Boys, The Common*), but being restless he ended up doing nothing-jobs, park attendant and cinema commissionaire (the *Ben* plays). In love with a sexy, glamorous girl who gave him the slip, he settled for the not-so-attractive but maturer woman who provides emotional stability (the *Ben* plays, *The Reception*), though occasionally he meets one fleetingly who makes him regret his choice (*The Brick Umbrella, Hearts and Flowers* for a variation thereof). The early years of marriage, with constant babies arriving and messing, see-saw between sensual fulfilment and bitter recrimination (*The Brick Umbrella, The Reception, When the Wind Blows, Daddy Kiss It Better* and *Hearts and Flowers*), but in the end he settles down to middle-class affluence, though his crying babies are now adolescent sophisticates (*Chez Nous*), and he even mixes in upper-middle-class activities (*The Common*). A successful brother appears in *Hearts and Flowers*, a media man jaded by the occupational hazards of instant success, but one suspects that the two brothers are double aspects of Nichols Man: the modest-living, fraught family man eventually becoming what he sees as a rather glibber success, finding the metamorphosis claustrophobic in a new way. Generally speaking, Nichols Man is never happier than when he is worried, self-pitying, envious or grouchy, depending on which age he happens to be. He does give the impression of being the individual at odds with every manifestation of life's Seven Ages as presented by Britain in the mid-twentieth century. Throughout, his constant enemy has been a latent infantilism (the legacy of the cosseting mum?), the product of a world which won't let him grow up, yet demands a nimble maturity from him at every turn.

Is there any other playwright out of whose plays one could construct such a cohesive biography, inaccurate in points of detail relating to specific plays, perhaps, but remarkably consistent? It certainly adds to the charge that Nichols is essentially merely a transparent writer of his own and his family's life, perhaps just sitting down and writing out in play form what happened that day.

I hope to show that this is a flagrant injustice to one of the most conscious builders of structures among contemporary playwrights for television.

Peter Nichols started off by writing TV plays, and other scripts, for a living, and in all had produced, between 1959 and 1973, some fifteen plays for the medium. (A new series of plays, five in all and currently entitled *Mixed Feelings*, is to be mounted by the BBC, at the time of writing, in 1980.) By 1965, with some financial freedom afforded by his first venture into filmwriting, plus the success of *Joe Egg* on the stage, Nichols's television output began to thin out, though his finest work for the medium was yet to appear. In published interviews Nichols has stated his frustrations with television over the years, the lack of public recognition from or permanency in the medium, the excessive naturalism which prevents a true style from being recognised. The stage by comparison has brought him critical recognition, more money, and above all the means by which he can convey self-evident stylistic intentions to the audience. Certainly no one could deny that many of his stage plays are innovative. Yet Nichols *has* returned to television from time to time, and I suspect something more complex here, a love–hate relationship with the medium.

Peter Nichols grew from being a servant of television into being its master, and his unique structural skill in this medium, which reached its major peak with *Hearts and Flowers* (1970), has developed that medium beyond what it was before he took to writing for it and learning from it. How galling it must be, for one who has used television itself to innovate for television, to be considered by many to be a merely artless autobiographer when writing in that form!

In order to begin to put all this into perspective, let us take a selection of Nichols's plays, considering only those written for television, going back to 1959, when Nichols might very well have written autobiographically as an unformed novice. If there is any truth to the charge that his plays are merely unstructured autobiography, it must surely be most strongly verified from plays of this period of his career.

Let us look at one of his earliest plays, *Promenade*, produced by Granada TV in 1959.

Nicky, twenty-four, and Tricia, nineteen, are two cool and sophisticated offspring of a wealthy former stage star. Tricia has a crush on a labourer called Andrew and wants to marry him, which Nicky resents. Andrew is part of the Crowd, a group of young 1950s trendies clustered around Nicky and Tricia, living a sort of ersatz bohemia in defiance of Britain's iron rules about class. Tricia doesn't necessarily want Andrew to know about her designs. In a way, they are a daydream and perhaps will not survive her father's anticipated objections to the match. When Andrew comes round, we have this exchange:

TRICIA. Hello, mate. [*She kisses Andrew.*]
NICKY. He was right.
ANDREW. What's this with me?
NICKY. She's been talking to the Major about you . . .
TRICIA. Drop it, Nicky . . .
NICKY. And marriage and everything . . .
TRICIA. Your hair's sticking up at the back! [*This stops him for a moment and he twists before the looking-glass.*][1]

In a few lines, we have Tricia's desire to ingratiate herself with the lower-class Andrew, Andrew's sharp and suspicious query suggesting he may be being used, Nicky's resentment and narcissism, and the revelation of Tricia's designs. There is no self-indulgent novice at work here: this is taut writing taken almost to its extreme. Notice a small but telling use of visual action to convey character instantly.

Nicky, meanwhile, has been playing around with Rhonda, also somewhat below him in social or material status. She tells him she's pregnant by him, whereupon he tries to get her to have an abortion. He admits that he's a cold fish, but that's life, isn't it?

NICKY. I didn't force you, or anything.
RHONDA [*hardly audible*]. No.
NICKY. And it's not as though I was the first.[2]

The two agree that they couldn't make a marriage, and they are reconciled, without Nicky being committed to any course of action – which he seems to realise:

NICKY. Shall I speak to this doctor, then?
RHONDA. No. I spoke to mine this morning.
NICKY. But yours says . . .
RHONDA. Mine says – we're safe. It was a scare, but it's over and there's nothing.
NICKY. No danger?
RHONDA. Nothing.
NICKY. Is it certain?
RHONDA. Yes.
NICKY. And you knew, but you let me go on thinking . . .
RHONDA. I wanted to know for sure if there was any hope with you. Don't worry. I could never have carried it through.
NICKY. And don't worry either, dear. I'd never marry on a scare.
RHONDA. I know that now.[3]

A neat and quietly devastating dramatic twist, since the viewer up to then had no more knowledge than Nicky and, if a man, perhaps found himself relieved and then just as suddenly judged. Andrew, meanwhile, becomes fed up with the phoniness of Tricia and the Crowd and strikes up an acquaintance with Rhonda. They opt to leave the triviality of the Promenade where the Crowd hangs out for a more meaningful life together. Nicky meets Lotte, a sexy German (and forerunner of another delectably wayward Teuton, Heidi, in Peter Nichols's latest semi-autobiographical series for BBC television, *Mixed Feelings*), and after sex with her he is found showering, as if to cleanse himself of physical contact. Tricia too is alone, and we leave them to their cool isolation.

Promenade is not only marked by brevity and realism in the writing but by a fully satisfactory plot-structure: a parallel set of couples, one – brother and sister – of shallowness and narcissism, the other – Andrew and Rhonda – of more realism and maturity. The plot engineers the bringing together of the right two in the end, leaving the other two to deserve each other in their barrenness. There is nothing artless or inchoate about this very early and highly skilful play.

There is, one feels, a brilliance here which could take any turning, for fine as it is, *Promenade* is not quite yet what one would call vintage Nichols. For that we must turn to another Granada play, of 1960, *Ben Spray*, in some ways Nichols's seminal early work for television.

Ben is a sacked former teacher of a language school, down-at-heel and living with his flatmate Dave. The one thing he has to look forward to is his date:

BEN. I'll have a job by Monday. First things first. I must be smooth, very smooth tonight. When I take this girl into a bar, the heads all turn. She could take her pick, and she chose me. Why? I'm more smooth than any of them.
DAVE. That's all she knows.[4]

In fact it is a dream and a delusion, as we discover when we eavesdrop upon the girl in question, Pat, talking to *her* flatmate Louise, about him. For it is clear that she intends to ditch him. Louise takes a note from Pat to Ben at the rendezvous. They strike up an acquaintance, during which Ben tries propositioning the sexy waitress for consolation or bravado in the face of his rejection by Pat. Or is it simply that he's off on another fantasy? Louise takes him to her uncle's fireworks party, for it is Guy Fawkes Night. There he meets, among others, Louise's pompous young cousin, Geoff:

GEOFF. Do I know you? Geoffrey Stone of Peterhouse.
BEN. Ben Spray of Gravesend.
GEOFF. Are you a Tab man?
BEN. No, strictly flute. I sometimes double on alpenhorn.
GEOFF. The answer would seem to be no. I meant are you at Cambridge?
BEN. Oh, no. I've been, of course, for a day trip.
GEOFF. Like it?
BEN. Liked the place, hated the people.[5]

Ben is at his best with the one-liner, but it doesn't get him far with Louise's family. More or less rejected by the party, he goes upstairs and meets the little girl of the house, who is in bed. Her mother comes in, and, mistaking Ben's intentions towards the child (he is only sharing with her his own inclination towards stories and fantasies), has him driven from the house. Later, Louise wangles him a job as a cinema commissionaire, wearing, he imagines, a bottle-green uniform with epaulettes and decorations. This launches him into a tall story from his past, but Dave no longer bothers to listen to him.

Ben Spray is a play about immaturity, specifically in men. Whereas the shallow immaturity of Nicky and Tricia was a kind of function in the plot, the immaturity of Ben is the springboard for the play itself. Indeed, the play is a series of leaps up and down on this board of immaturity. It shows a shift in Nichols towards working outwards from character rather than applying characters to fit a plot. If it has a weakness, it is that some of the dialogue is not wholly suited to the new approach but seems almost too brief and direct. It is by no means a perfect play, but it is a major step forward.

Concentrating on immaturity in this period, but without Ben Spray, Nichols – in *The Big Boys* of 1961 – creates an Irish music master at a London Junior School, Larry Argent, possibly in the belief that the kind of fantasy and feyness he was seeking to portray could best be caught on the Celtic fringe. It is the only instance I know of in his TV plays where an Irishman or Celt of any kind is a protagonist. The play begins with Argent spellbinding his little audience with the tale of Theseus and the Minotaur. He completes his tale, and the bell rings. He is someone who, like

Ben Spray, is at ease with children and cultivating their fantasies but – like Nicky – switches off when the bell rings or the lovemaking is over, left to himself, to revert back into himself. He is, in fact, having an affair with Jenny, the wife of a fellow master, Driver. Driver is ex-Indian Army and a muscular, cold-showers type who terrorises the kids. On the eve of the school Christmas pageant Driver discovers them talking intimately about their affair. There is a confrontation, during which Driver gets as good as he dishes out:

JENNY. You must see, our life had become – I don't know – a timetable, a terrible bore.
DRIVER. Thank you.
JENNY. Stop being dignified. It's past that – it's time to *understand*.
DRIVER. I understand. D'you think I don't? Hah! You think I don't.
   [*He walks in a semi-circle. Rubbing his hands together. He is dressing them down like truant children.*]⁶

For all his stridency, it is a blow beneath the belt, though he drives home a good point about Argent being a womaniser, which unnerves Jenny. The pageant intrudes, and Driver goes back briskly to organise – more in his element. As it gets under way, one of the little boys, Alan, is so frightened of going on that he swallows mistletoe berries to make himself ill. Driver comes upon him:

DRIVER. Now you listen to me, Alan. You've got to learn not to take everything to heart. Other people are just as frightened as you. Even the teachers.
   [*Alan looks at him as much as to say 'Even you?'*]
That's true. [. . .] Well, then! You never hear about teachers eating mistletoe, do you?
ALAN. No sir.
DRIVER. Or having fried toadstools with their dinner?
   [*Alan laughs.*]
No. Well, then. Someone has to do these things. What if I hadn't found you and forced you to bring up the mistletoe? What if you'd been ill? Who'd have played your part? Nobody knows your words. And what would your Dad have said? And your Mum? And Mr. Argent? They'll all be looking for you. Come on, we'd better get back.⁷

Alan goes on and is a resounding success, as is the pageant itself. The head publicly thanks Driver, who is not in the hall. He has gone into an empty classroom, to think. But Larry, for whom playing with other people's emotions is a harmless diversion, like telling stories, tells Jenny it's time to pack it in. He himself is off to

Ireland to go on tour as a pianist with a singer. With no illusions now, Driver realises he has to work hard to win Jenny back, and tells her so. Jenny realises she will have to put the charming but flighty Larry down to experience.

And so we see another variation on the theme of 'the one that got away'; this time the charming creature is a man. *The Big Boys* is perhaps Nichols's first successfully integrated TV play. It reads like the small gem of a short story by, say, William Trevor. In structure it is an almost perfect symmetry, the parallel study of two men. The first is Larry Argent: virile in the sensual connotation of the word, easy and successful with women but ultimately undependable. The second is Driver: sexually almost impotent, perhaps, long since sacrificing his love-life to the demands of duty, but masculine in his sense of responsibility, his resolution in adversity, his determination to soldier on and make the best of things. In a sophisticated confrontation Driver is out of his depth, confused, blustering. But give him a problem, such as putting the stuffing back into little Alan, and his positive virtues are evident. What would Argent have done with a tearful boy? Probably packed him off home to get him out of his hair and then obtained another boy to read the part. Not so Driver. With greater understanding he knows that this is one of life's character-building experiences, one the boy must have if he is to grow to be a man. Without bullying, but without offering a hanky to cry into, he skilfully draws Alan out so that the boy is positively looking forward to going on; he imparts manliness to one who will be a man himself one day. Beside this, the kind of masculinity represented by Argent looks shallow and cheap, though at the outset he was the more likeable. The play is a positive step forward in that the dramatic situations are richer: the spectacle of the demoralised Driver having to bail a little boy out of his own demoralisation lifts the play right out of the ordinary.

The next two plays I wish to consider illustrate for me a contrast in Nichols between his worst and his best. *The Heart of the Country* of 1963 is about Frank and Fay, a couple not wholly decided upon marriage, who go to live in the country with a number of other middle-class refugees from city life. But life there, with its futile round of mirthless celebration and wife-swapping, is no more innocent or 'nearer to nature' than life anywhere else. Fay leaves Frank because she feels he's been too dependent upon her (again, the theme of male immaturity), though we had been led to believe, with Frank, that it was Fay who was the dependent one, hesitating over his insistent proposals of marriage through lack of self-confidence. With some skill Nichols shows us that this is the reverse of the truth: Frank proposes marriage not from strength but from weakness and need, and Fay fears he will drain her. Frank is disillusioned by country living, which he sees either as lotus-eating escapism or desecration of nature for personal profit (his 'friends' are more or less divided between the two). At the end he says, 'The heart of this country's paralysed between dreams and destruction. I'd like to find a way of living here without joining either . . .'[8] He packs his bags and returns to the city, a lonely bachelor once more.

Perhaps because it is not a comedy (and Nichols at this stage in his development seems sentimental, solemnly pompous and self-pitying without comedy), I must confess to finding this a dull, lifeless play, dependent too much upon a lethargic situation and not enough upon action or story.

With *The Reception*, produced in 1961, we take on a very different kettle of fish. Indeed, we are pitched into comedy right from the start. Colin and Jill are expecting the wedding-party from her sister Betty's marriage at any moment. But let Nichols tell it for himself:

> [*A sudden ring of the doorbell*]
> COLIN [*whispers*]. I thought so!
> [*He runs out, through the hall and into the lounge while Jill grabs a paper bag from the table. Jill comes from the kitchen and stands by the front door on a chair, takes a handful of confetti and prepares to throw. The wedding march thunders from the loudspeaker in full stereo. Colin runs back, stands on opposite side of the door. Jill mimes one–two–three and they open the door to reveal Mr. and Mrs. Sutherland Senior (Charles and Flora).*]
> COLIN. Oh!
> [*He runs off, back to the lounge.*]
> JILL. Is it Mr. and Mrs. Sutherland?
> CHARLES. What?
> JILL. Mr. and Mrs. Sutherland?
> CHARLES. Yes, that's right.
> JILL. Come in then. Sorry about the . . .
> CHARLES. You're the bride's sister, aren't you?
> JILL. Yes, I'm – [*The music stops. They drop their voices.*] Jill.
> BOTH. How d'you do?
> CHARLES. I suppose we're the first guests?
> JILL. Yes. Are the others on the way?
> CHARLES. I imagine so.

FLORA. We didn't go to the Registry Office.

JILL. Oh . . .

CHARLES. We were so late starting, and I thought we'd better come straight here, as it was on our way.[9]

Thus introductions are made to the groom's rather stiff and aloof parents. The contrast with the bride's parents couldn't be greater:

GEORGE. . . . . They must make a tidy packet between them down there. I mean, there was another lot waiting to go in straightaway . . . proper assembly line job.

ROSE. We gonna stand here in the hall all day, George? Let's get either in or out, shall we?[10]

And so to the arrival of all the party, including the inevitable Coleridge-quoting uncle ('The Bridegroom's doors are opened wide, and I am next of kin') and other relations, including Betty's other sister, the sophisticated Flit. The party is soon under way with that rich blend of the raw with the polished which Nichols captures so well in his family gatherings (as he was to demonstrate again so beautifully in *Hearts and Flowers*), when – uninvited and unexpected – an old flame of the bride's from art school, Bif Wilder, arrives. He has come without his wife Lena (he says) because of lack of a babysitter, but when he presents Betty with his wedding-gift, and it turns out to be a semi-nude portrait he once painted of her, his motive in coming takes on a somewhat darker aspect. Indeed, her suspicions are confirmed when he makes a pass at her in the bedroom; she scratches his face and runs off. Bif doesn't join the party; instead he has the sulks in the bedroom. When Flora, the groom's mother, comes in (and here is another of those richly ironic moments which Nichols makes such good use of: her confrontation with the bride's portrait) Bif mischievously tells her that Betty and her son Lewis had to get married quickly because Betty is pregnant by another man. Stunned, Flora rushes away to tell her husband. While the party is busy playing charades George and Rose get wind of the rumour, and there is a scene, indeed a brawl, for though Lewis the groom manages to control himself, George is less able to when Bif admits it was just mischief on his part. Lewis and Betty leave the reception without anyone knowing. Later, on the train, Lewis persuades Betty not to worry about anything her father thinks any more, anything from the past, and not to go back, but to stick with him and the future. Bif tries to console himself with Flit, but he is seen leaving her flat after what looks to have been more or less a failed adultery. We leave the story with an image of Betty resting her head on Lewis's shoulder on the train and Lewis smiling to himself.

Like *The Big Boys* this has the feeling of a finely wrought short story about it, in structure a high point in Nichols's television achievement.

A short-story writer proper can write a story about something or someone he knows comparatively little about through the use of allusive literary devices. The dramatist writing in effect a dramatised short story needs much greater intimate knowledge of his raw materials, a firmer grasp of character and milieu, or he cannot even write the dialogue. Peter Nichols is a true short-story writer in television form, but being a dramatist he must take his materials from where he can find them; his being an honest dramatist means those he knows most surely. Thus he may use the same raw materials over and over again and rework them several times in different ways. As one studies these plays, one begins to see that Peter Nichols is not a purely 'autobiographical' writer at all, that the similarity of milieus and their possible reflection of his real life have nothing to do with autobiography as deliberate self-revelation and self-projection.

Another major play, *When the Wind Blows* of 1965, shows Nichols reaching out for something new. The wind here is certainly blowing up for a storm. The play exudes pressure. We are now firmly in the land of nappies and babies and the claustrophobia this induces in modern man. No other playwright has come so fully to grips with the idiocies of domestic life. Q is a lecturer and thereby disposed towards articulation. He is also a modern man who wants to share his enthusiasms with his wife. Here he is reading a sycophantic newspaper review to her in the kitchen:

> [*Sits at kitchen table while clatter of cake-tins grows*]
>
> Q. Here is one of our alleged music critics dealing with the latest record from Hairy Brute and the Barbary Apes. [*To Becky*] Play more quietly dear. [*Reads*] 'It represents a profoundly exciting attempt to render the enervated torch song in terms of modern folk art –'
>
> [*Rattle of tins intolerable, Q shouting to make himself heard*]
> Ta!
>
> [*Takes away tins. Scream from Becky*]
>
> NORMA. She was playing. You can't do that.
>
> Q. I couldn't hear myself speak. [*Takes ballpoint pen from pocket*] There.
>
> BECKY. Ta! [. . .]

NORMA. Becky be a good girl, finish that drop of custard. [*She hands Becky a dish.*] Give her a spoon, Q.[11]

The pressure they both feel in this noisy environment finally explodes in a row about his mother.

Q. . . . But if you think I'm going to stand here doing nothing while you insult her up and down hill –

NORMA. Yes, I think you *are* going to stand there doing nothing! [*Both shouting*]

Q. Oh, that's brilliant! A plus –
    [*Becky wails.*]

NORMA. Shut up, you've frightened Becky, shouting like that. She thinks we're rowing. [*Kneels to Becky*] Dada's only joking, love. Smile at her, show her you're only joking.
    [*Q smiles. Wailing goes on. Norma gives cake-tins to Becky. Wailing stops. Clattering begins. With a choked growl rising to a roar, Q leaves the room.*][12]

Later, in his room by himself, Q can at last monopolise his own conversation.

Eventually Q and Norma pile the children into the car for a visit to Q's parents. After considerable chat there is a heated argument which brings out the old animosities: Q's lower-middle-class father resenting the angry-young-manism of his son, Q resenting the father's right-wing views of life, Norma resenting Q's mother's cosseting of her son, Albert the father resenting the way life with Evelyn the mother has bound him to the side of a woman without a thought in her head from one day to the next. This family purgation ended, the two men are fresh and resolved: the young man to return to the warmth of his marital bed, the old man to finally untie the apron-strings and leave his wife for good.

This is far from being merely a semi-autobiographical slice-of-life play. Indeed, so intricate and controlled is it that there is scarcely space to unravel its patterns. Consider the brilliant first scene, with Q arguing with Norma over his own mother's attitude to him at exactly the same time that he is deeply resenting Norma's protective attitude towards Becky. Both mothers protect or have protected their offspring from the resentments of both fathers. The scarcely concealed distaste for his own children as rivals for his wife's attention is but the resentment of his father towards him carried to the next generation. And just as Q and Norma seek and ultimately find fulfilment together in the midst of the uncertain clamour of their younger marriage, so Albert finds in the peace and stability of old age the resolution to break up his marriage. The play is a highly organised pattern, the more remarkable for coming so effortlessly out of the characters. And this is made possible by Nichols once again being able, or almost able, to allow his characters to be themselves the plot. Plot here is not external to character, nor is the play character without plot: it is character as the motive force of the story itself, because the characters are mothers and wives and fathers and children and husbands: i.e. they exist simultaneously as individuals and as family-instruments, and in the latter capacity they are instruments of the action. By concentrating on the family, which is an objective mechanism as well as a subjective relationship, Nichols enables himself to let plot grow seemingly effortlessly out of character, or almost. It matters little whether Nichols himself is a family man or not; here he has simply come across the ideal way of creating a fully structured play without arbitrary externals. The question is: has he succeeded?

Because family life is a constant series of practical actions as well as feelings, it makes ideal television, both in its intimacy and visual minutiae. Something is always going on in the early part of *When the Wind Blows*, because in family life things *must* go on, and so the play can exist on two levels, the verbal and the physical, at all times, which is what makes the lengthy dialogue so tolerable. Indeed, there has never been more monologue in a Nichols TV play: it foreshadows *A Day in the Death of Joe Egg*.

So much new ground was covered here that it would have been almost too much to expect Nichols to have fashioned out a better-made play. It is when the pressures erupt into dialogue in the later part of the play that Nichols fails to produce a proper climax and catharsis for us: *When the Wind Blows* leaves us curiously unpurged. I don't mean that *When the Wind Blows* should have been written like Greek tragedy. But in his highly innovative use of family-as-formal-plot-structure, he doesn't carry the experiment through. Instead, he relinquishes plot and falls back on situation, which by itself is inert and unchangeable. Perhaps he was consciously drawing back from tragedy, which is what this play was beginning to demand.

The Brick Umbrella of 1964 is by comparison a light piece which does not require much extended analysis. Its setting is another wedding. This time we first espy a young man in full morning dress meeting for the first time a young bride coming down the stairs, which seems a little peculiar until we learn that he, Rob, is to give her, Julia, away as a sort of substitute father (her own being dead), since he is married to her sister. The sister couldn't come because of the illness of their child. What follows is – after the ceremony – a reception (at the groom's parents') during which Rob and Julia are briefly smitten and exchange kisses. Mike the bridegroom discovers this, and an ugly situation is narrowly avoided. The play is interspersed with brief flashes of visual fantasy or recall on the part either of Rob or Julia, and at the end, when Rob goes off, Julia looks out the window after him and sees him as a knight riding off on a white charger. So far as I am aware this is the first time Nichols has used fantasy or out-of-sequence visuals by way of a counterpoint with strictly realistic television. Julia, who married Mike it seems on the rebound from an unhappy jilting, is plainly going to have a difficult time with a man who isn't basically her type at all and who surrounds himself with rugger-playing buddies. Meanwhile the knight returns home to a nagging wife and a discussion about his daughter's mouth ulcers.

The play begins ingeniously, the visual situation of a last-minute surrogate father with the bride confusing us momentarily into thinking perhaps that the groom himself is with his bride before the wedding. It is even funnier when we – and Rob – learn that the wedding is in fact a lounge-suit occasion and that he is wildly overdressed for it. Nichols deploys his customary skill and the play is an enjoyable one, but to me dramatically something of a letdown by the time one has finished with it. Again, situation does not quite have the plot to go with it. The family here is not deployed so successfully as an objective mechanism of plot.

The Gorge of 1968 is the first of Nichols's television scripts to be made entirely on film and marks a considerable advance on *The Brick Umbrella* in the integrated use of visual transitions and juxtapositions.

Appropriately enough, the play begins with home movies and continues to be punctuated by Stanley's inept attempt to capture A Day at the Gorge on film. The real day is punctuated by flash forwards to the home movies made of it, as viewed by Stanley, a middle-aged Bristolian, his wife Lily, Ivy and the Canadian Uncle Jack.

[*Home movie*
Exterior. Stanley's house. Day.

The home movie is silent. We hear voices of the people watching but do not see them. Pictures of house from various angles. Milkman delivering]

STANLEY. There we are then . . .

LILY. Home sweet home.

STANLEY. Sixty-seven.

LILY. Lovely colours.

JACK. Sure sure.

IVY. Life-like.

LILY. Very natural.

IVY. You could touch it.

JACK. Sure could. Lilian –

LILY. What, love?

JACK. You want a cigarette?

LILY. No thanks, dear, I got a Mintoe.

JACK. You want a cigarette, Ivy?

IVY. I got a chocolate.[13]

Here is the lower-middle-class Bristolian family, thoroughly at home, looking at its own home.

> [*Picture resumes. Front exterior of a semi-detached house, circa 1900, solid and ugly but in good repair*]

IVY. That's never me.

LILY. Well, it isn't me.

> [*Ivy waves to camera. Gets into car*]

IVY. Well, I was all ready for once.

> [*End of home movie*
> *See them all: Stanley and Lily front seat, Jack, Mike, Ivy back seat.*
> *Car is passing through Sunday morning city streets.*]

STANLEY. I should *think* so. You had twenty extra minutes.

IVY. Not like you to be late, Stan.

STANLEY. D'you think it was *me*?[14]

Nichols says so much in so few words. A transition has been made from a flash-forward (home movie) to a flashback (the main body of the play) yet covering a continuous sequence in time. We have moved forward for the 'film' of the preceding part of the sequence and flash-backed to the subsequent part. This is no mere technical device, for it enables us to compare both the actuality of the feelings of the time with the rather faulty interpretation, appropriately enough from the somewhat scatty Ivy. Nichols does this throughout the play, which is almost a time-unity but discontinuously assembled before us in order to make it one. How like film-making this is!

The family, including Stanley's teenage son Mike, arrive at the Cheddar Gorge – a favourite weekend picnic-spot for Bristolians

– and pitch an elaborate tent, barbecue and all the opulent trim-
mings. Mike makes a secret rendezvous with Chris (she's fifteen), and the two youngsters, the girl ardent, the boy full of
inhibitions, start petting. Chris takes off her jeans 'to sunbathe',
but they are interrupted. Chris runs off without her jeans, and
Mike takes the jeans to avoid their discovery by oncoming
parents in search of the missing offspring. Chris returns to the
hiding-place but can't find the jeans Mike took. She is stranded in
only her pants. She gets to a cave, where an emerging innocent
potholer is punched by her arriving father, mistaking him for a
seducer. Back at the picnic site there are intruders to the peace of
Stanley and Lily on the one hand and the more aloof Norman and
Joyce (Chris's parents) on the other: an itinerant cyclist preacher
doing the Lord's work among the self-indulgent heathen, and
the ton-up gang on their motorcycles. On the return journey
Nichols ends the play with a wholly descriptive passage which is
representative of the visual methods he has employed throughout.

There is no point in pretending that this is other than a pure
entertainment written to amuse and drawn from affectionate
memory. There is even something of *M. Hulot's Holiday* about it.
The reference to Tati indicates that we are indeed into film. The
writing is often purely descriptive rather than dramatic as such
(even when in dialogue), leisurely paced in feeling in accord with
its subject, and spacious. As Siegfried Kracauer points out in his
classic *Theory of Film*, the power of film lies ultimately in its ability
to picture concrete reality, a form of potency which owes nothing
to the canons of dramatic form that must be applied to theatre
and television as such. So thoroughly has Nichols entered into
the spirit of film for this play that he is in danger of forgetting its
televisual context. Funny as they are, Stanley, Lily, Ivy and so on
are not in the M. Hulot mould, and could not be on the small
screen. We would be soon bored with them were it not for their
reactions to continual intrusions from elsewhere: the evangelist,
the motorcyclists and finally the accident. Magnified in cinematic
film, Hulot is funny and continuously interesting even when he
seems merely to be loping along. The characters in *The Gorge*
cannot be this independent of any integral plot; they do not exist
for long without some involvement in incident upon incident.

For all that, it must be said that *The Gorge* is one of Peter
Nichols's best-known and best-loved television plays. It has been

shown all over the world (in consequence of having been made on film and thus being free of the incompatible videotape systems of the time). Nichols seems to possess two basic qualities. One is an English puritanism, which is, to be fair, in the bones of nearly all Englishmen, who instinctively feel that there is something fundamentally wrong about enjoying oneself; the other is a more local characteristic: an easygoing tolerance and ultimate placidity which can only be described as Bristolian. One gets the feeling, which is difficult to pin down in such a craftsman, that in play after play a puritanical element is at war with a more hedonistic, complacent element, and the uneasy juxtaposition of these two brings forth some of the most searching and humane moments in TV drama.

There is an interesting connection to be made between *The Gorge* and Nichols's other TV play of 1968, *Daddy Kiss It Better*, and that is over the visual treatment of time.

The play begins dramatically enough with Ken walking out on his marriage:

> [*Ken opens front door of sixty years old terrace house, slams it behind him, runs down path through garden.*
> *He opens front gate to street.*
> *Front door opened by Mon (for Monica)*]
>
> MON. You'll want your mac!
> KEN. What?
> MON. If you're leaving home you'll want your bloody mac! In case it rains.
> [*Throws mac down steps, goes in, slams door*][15]

But the relationship is far from over, and right from the start Nichols indicates that they will be back together again in the end. They themselves betray their need for one another, as when Ken, inwardly distressed, narrowly misses being run down by a car whose brakes screech. Mon is at the window: 'Mon watches furtively from front window biting lip. A few years younger, fuller face, but as anxious as Ken. She gives way to crying and backs into shadow.'[16] All this, the bust-up and anticipated reconciliation of a marriage, takes place in under a minute before the opening captions of the play. Immediately after them, and mixing from a shot of Ken walking disconsolately down the street, we come across the younger Ken and Monica in bed, before they were married.

MON. . . . Look how fat my legs are.

KEN [*Looking*]. Fat? They're not fat.
MON. And they go straight down like trees . . . not tapering at all . . .
  and they finish in short feet, like pigs' trotters.
KEN. If you're shapeless, what am I?
MON. Your feet are long.
KEN. D'you think feet are ugly?
  [*She shakes her head and smiles.*]
KEN. Feet in general, I mean.[17]

Before the captions, we had a brief scene showing snatches of love, tenderness and concern in the midst of a traumatic separation. Immediately after the captions, we have a scene showing snatches of apprehension over ugliness (with all this implies for eventual disillusion and separation) in the midst of love and tenderness. The two scenes are inversions of each other, the first scene (set in the present) pointing forwards to the actual conclusion of the play, the second scene, its precise inversion, pointing backwards from this conclusion to foreshadow what the play will be about.

Having encapsulated his beginning, middle and end in the first few moments of the play, Nichols frees himself structurally to devote the body of the play to an exploration of loving, courtship, child-rearing, alienation and reconciliation. Through the transparently simple use of flashback (which is most of the play) Nichols recreates the pattern, not as a simple linear movement stretching out to infinity, but as immanent in every moment, its different phases coexistent on the plane of the experienced play on the screen, which is simultaneously the thought and memory process of the runaway husband Ken. At the end of a particularly heavy quarrel, the phone rings:

KEN [*on the phone*]. . . .tell the truth you haven't chosen too good a
  moment . . .
MON [*returning*]. Who is it?
KEN. Your mother. Rang to congratulate us. Apparently it's our
  wedding anniversary. [*Hands phone to Mon*]
  [*Cut to:*
  Day exterior. Ken arrives near some swings in the park. Lights cigarette.
  Watches passing female traffic.
  Couple on bench.
  Youths using slide.
  [. . .]
  Three children at swings. Two girls on swings and boy sitting on the seat of
  his swing, feet on ground.]

BOY. 'Course you won't have a baby.
  [*Girls giggle. One says 'Sssh'.*]
  Tell you why not. Shall I?[18]

The boys and girls tease each other and the boy struggles momentarily with the first girl. She breaks away, and the two leave – 'The boy . . . standing on the swing seat, energetically pushing back and forth, grinning after the girls'.[19]

From the flashback of the bitter quarrel and the untimely call from the mother we return to the present, with Ken witnessing the beginning of life's game all over again in the tentative, juvenile flirtation of the children on the swings. Even the mention of 'mother' brings in the suggestion of the other end of life: the concern of the older mother and grandmother. The whole scheme of life is immanent in these moments of the play: first youthful stirrings, wedding anniversary, moment of ultimate alienation, grandmotherliness, and perhaps – in Ken's passive staring in the park – a hint of the final phase of helpless spectatorship of the pageant. Nichols's true power is demonstrated in this play as a subtly wrought and indeed highly philosophical design, but instead of logical exposition, we have pictorial juxtaposition, the particular rational tool of the television dramatist at his best.

In another flashback Ken is in the pub with an older friend, Vic. Vic is unhappily married and childless, so he opts for the good time with girl friends. Ken envies Vic's good times, but – and here is another of those Nichols poignancies – Vic bitterly regrets what has happened to himself, refuses to believe Ken unhappy in his domesticity, and pours scorn on the cheap thrills of life, the paucities of whose nourishment are all he has to live on. Vic is at odds with the scheme of life and knows it. Ken is not but thinks he is. We too know it, not merely from what Vic says but because everything he is, is at variance with the structure of the play as a whole, which is a recreation of all the phases of natural life. The play's structure reinforces the values that Vic cannot help but be cut off from: a character haplessly at war with the structure, so to speak. And so we have a creative interpenetration on different levels of writing: structure, character and dialogue. The actual ending of the play is typically low-keyed. Ken returns to Mon and promises to revivify their relationship by taking her out more, starting with a 'dirty weekend' in Brighton. Mon takes him back unhesitatingly and then begins fussing and calculating about the babysitting arrangements needed for a resumption of their courtship. The play fades out on her on the telephone, while some of Ken's apprehensions about claustrophobic domesticity begin to return. Yet it is not simply the turning of a wheel, a simple, recurring cycle, for we have definitely moved on to a new phase in the relationship, carrying within itself aspects of its past and its future.

I have not chosen to end this essay with either *The Common* of 1973 or the *Mixed Feelings* series for 1980, written in 1978. The former is an amusing comedy about two couples, the richer of whom are trying to eject a black man and his wife and van from a common immediately outside their fashionable London home and simultaneously seeking to foist an Aftercare centre for ex-offenders on their less-well-heeled borough fellow citizens. The poorer couple consist of a schoolmaster and his wife who become acquainted with the other through the Aftercare public meeting. He is a socialist inculcating his children with left-wing values through his production of a school pageant about Wat Tyler's rebellion. The two men begin affairs with each other's wives, but they have already sown the seeds of their destruction as potential lovers: the rich man trying to make it with the teacher's wife in her flat is interrupted by an irate neighbour round with a petition against the Aftercare centre. With some delightful comedy he abandons his umbrella by sneaking out the back way and has to return to the front to retrieve his belongings, thereby necessarily getting into an argument with the petitioner. Meanwhile the teacher, about to have it off with the richer wife, is interrupted when the fashionable home is broken into by two boys from his class emulating the egalitarianism of Wat Tyler via a bit of burglary. He becomes despised in their eyes (because he got *invited* in) and finds himself arguing with them against his own most hotly held beliefs. It is Nichols at his comedic best, bringing out what incidentally I haven't dealt with at all in this study: his gift for corrosive satire. If I have any complaints about it at all, it is that (i) the cross-swapping of wives ('swapping' is not quite the right term, since neither man is aware of his mate's potential adultery) is almost too mechanically convenient for the plot, and (ii) each man is made of such intellectual straw that he is comparatively easy to knock down; Nichols has set himself a far from difficult task in doing so. And despite the lengthy build-up and splendid classroom dialogue for the Wat Tyler pageant, the sudden inspiration of the boys to go a-burgling would ring a lot truer if it wasn't so convenient for the symmetry of the plot. The mystery of the black man (and the voodoo objects he apparently thrusts through the door of the fashionable house) is lost sight of as he vaporises into a symbolic victim of middle-class hypocrisy.

I prefer to be more reticent about *Mixed Feelings*, partly because I have only been able to read first drafts prior to possible later revisions. It is certainly heavily autobiographical, or so it would seem, because it is about a writer whose career closely resembles Nichols's own and includes portraits of certain persons I know to be taken from life because I share their acquaintance with Nichols. Much of the biography of Nichols Man that I outlined at the outset is included here; if nothing else, *Mixed Feelings* certainly confirms that biography. It seems clear to me that someone, thinking of Nichols as an obviously autobiographical writer, took the logical step of commissioning him for an autobiographical series. I have to say that, after reading the first drafts, I am more than ever confirmed in my view that Nichols lacks the gift of self-projection which is the mark of the true autobiographer. *Mixed Feelings* is certainly neither his *Cider with Rosie* nor his *Glittering Prizes*. The character who is supposed to hold the whole series together is a nonentity. At the end of it all, we do not know what really makes him tick, what the sources of his inspiration are, or what his deepest and innermost experience of life is. And what, indeed, do we know of Nichols the man throughout the entire corpus of his plays? True, I have constructed a biography, but this is of a lay figure only, with a few generalised characteristics: it may provide a key to Nichols's character, but it is not that character itself.

Thus far, we have seen Nichols at his most integrated when dealing with family life: the interpenetration of subjective with objective achieved in plays where characters exist both as themselves and as functions of the ruling organism. I do not think Nichols writes about families simply because he has nothing else to write about; I think the family was necessary to his fully integrated style of drama, his concept of story as an organic development, a fusion of character with function which is both family function and plot function. So we see that he achieves his integration as early as *The Reception* of 1961, for here he explores the family from within, portraying people as Betty, Flora, Lewis and so on but using them as bride, groom's mother, bridegroom and so on. The effect is natural because each of these persons exists simultaneously in both ways. But I think one can go back even earlier to a successfully integrated play, *The Big Boys*, which isn't about family life at all. For here the characters have another simultaneity: a simultaneous existence as individuals and as teachers of children. Instead of the family it is the school which is the ruling organism, and Driver's scene with the little boy is doubly compelling because Driver is both acting out his own subjective needs and functioning as a teacher of boys. His is a compelling portrait because one cannot separate in him the teacher from the man, just as in, say, *Daddy Kiss It Better* one cannot separate Monica the woman from Monica the mother and wife.

The lost souls are judged in these plays as having no part in the organism or as having opted out of it: Larry Argent, Bif Wilder, Vic and – as we shall see – Tony in *Hearts and Flowers*. They are simply not up to the strenuous demands invoked by simultaneity: the protagonists, on the other hand, teeter on the verge of being the same but finally pull through. In doing so, they pull their plays through, because play and organism are the same thing.

The tension between objectivity and subjectivity (a problem one reaches after having successfully surmounted the earlier problem of portraying a living subjectivity) is peculiarly difficult to achieve in television drama. Let us see how Nichols deals with it.

In *Hearts and Flowers* (1970) Bob and Jean, wondering if they are going to have another baby, are rung up in the middle of love-making by Bob's mother Marie. Bob's dad has collapsed and died. Arrangements for the funeral begin almost immediately, and so on to the arrival of all the relatives (including Bob's bachelor brother Tony, a TV personality whose smoothness inclines to unction), the funeral itself and the reception afterwards. During the latter, Tony, who is a lonely bachelor despite his fame, makes a play for Jean who, years before, was his sweetheart before she started going out with his brother Bob. Tony says he 'wants his youth back'. Nor is he repulsed, only interrupted. Later, at the end of the day, Bob and Jean have completed the lovemaking that was interrupted by the death of Bob's father. She is definitely pregnant again. She also has a vague yearning for the romanticism of Tony, symbolised by the rose he gave her which stands in a vase by the bed. Her heart isn't entirely in the loveplay with Bob. Whither the disposition of the heart *vis-à-vis* that particular flower?

Television is a highly subjective medium. In his quartet *Talking to a Stranger* (which is also about a family) John Hopkins manages to convey the tension between the subjective individual and the objective group of four by repeating the story four times in four different plays from four different viewpoints. The aggregate of these is what might have been achieved on stage all at once.

Through his greater experience in portraying the subjective–objective aspects of family life, Peter Nichols is equipped to achieve this in one play. In the first scene, apart from foreshadowing the conclusion of the play, Nichols by now has achieved the ability to portray a television scene wholly objectively by shifting the subjectivities from one character to another:

BOB. I kissed you and you yawned.
JEAN. Did I? Sorry, love, only I'm dead. Bill's been a monkey, tramping chocolate mousse right through the Spanish rope mat . . . and making monster noises during Susan's animal programme . . . Oh dear, it's her school holidays in case you've forgotten.
BOB [*sits up*]. It's not only school holidays.[20]

We see this marriage through both pairs of eyes almost simultaneously. So sure is Nichols in the handling of conflicting family feelings that he easily shifts the subjectivities of the drama from one person to another, thus slowly achieving a wholly objective picture. What the stage can do simultaneously, television – because of its small screen and intimacy – can only do by building up, by criss-crossing (or cross-cutting) from one to another. It is Nichols who teaches us how this is to be written. So masterly is he that he can extend the principle of shifting subjectivity right down to the merest distant relations: each for his moment may have a turn at determining our feelings through allowing us to experience his own.

The function of myth is to help us to come to terms with life and its dangers. In the old days, danger was represented by the occurrence or presentiment of physical death. Now that death is a comparative rarity in our lives, the danger resides in that which advanced civilisation has put in its place: fragmentation of personality, the division of life into self-contained and irreconcilable pieces, monogamy as a bore rather than a form of species-survival, work as the antithesis to life rather than its source,

children as rivals staking claims on one's infantile needs rather
than as guarantors of one's immortality. And Peter Nichols has
created the myths appropriate to all these new dangers,
appropriate also to an age dominated by close-up television.

It is when Nichols also gets to grips with the fact of death in this
modern world that he reaches an ultimate in mythical portrayal,
by bringing together the function of the traditional kind of myth –
which mitigated exposure to the starker realities – with the present kind in its present requirement, to face us with a life made
meaningless by their comparative absence.

His framework is not just any family gathering. It is a funeral,
which is simultaneously a ritualised wish to elevate one human
life – and therefore each of ours – to some significance, a means of
being a little more acquainted with death the unknowable, and a
means of celebrating our own continued survival. Through the
modern funeral the old myth works in with the new, and the
transaction between them is the actual dialogue which comes out
as people reveal their modern attitudes to death, or refuse to, as
the case may be.

The whole play turns on death as an interruption (so many of
Nichols's highest flights are interrupted). It interrupts Bob's and
Jean's lovemaking; it interrupts Marie's comfortable old age. And
there is this poignant moment during the service, involving old
Uncle Will:

ERIC. D'you want a Prayer-Book, Uncle?
VICAR. Psalm Twenty-three.
WILL. I know the words of the Twenty-third Psalm.
    [*They rise.*]
ALL [*reading*]. The Lord is my Shepherd, therefore can I lack nothing –
WILL. Therefore I shall not want – what's this?
ALL. He shall feed me in a green   WILL. He maketh me to lie down
    pasture and lead me forth beside   in green pastures – he leadeth
    the waters of comfort   me beside the still waters
WILL. These aren't the proper words.
ERIC. Ssh.[21]

Will, too, has been interrupted on his normal, placid course;
momentarily he finds that he, too, is no longer with the living. He
is losing the great words of consolation from the Old Testament
which have been with him all his life, because the world has
changed, is no longer using them, is moving on. Within the
context of death, presentiments of death abound. The funeral

procession itself is interrupted – in a beautifully comic moment on the screen – by the intrusion of a white sports-car falling in among the solemn line of black vehicles. That is as much of a presentiment as the exchange amongst the older relations about the fast speed of the hearse in front. Must the world rush Dad, and by implication themselves also, away from itself with such haste?

Nor is it too fanciful to see a presentiment of death in Tony, Bob's TV-personality brother. Tony was once an intelligent, responsive, sensitive and vivacious person with a warm, human concern for life. All these characteristics he has ostensibly retained. Except that something within him has 'died': there is something just a little too unspontaneous in his effusions of sympathy, something a little too glib in what would seem to be his most sincere statements. (As this is seen also from his point of view, he realises this himself.) Having been too long in front of TV cameras, he thirsts for a return to the time when he functioned as a normal human being, unpestered by passers-by, able to love once more the girl he loved before he was famous. Fame has laid a dead hand upon Tony; he has become a eunuch in the land of the fecund, on the verge of becoming a grinning zombie.

Tony's easy adaptability does somersaults of improvisation, as if he were going on 'live', but it is not the same as the real thing, the artlessness of Marie saying, 'I should pop the sausage rolls in the oven about half past eleven Linda',[22] just on her way out the door to her husband's funeral.

This subject fits perfectly with Nichols's other great preoccupation: birth-giving and baby-raising. Fecundity is at the top and tail of this play: pregnancy is suspected before the death and confirmed after the funeral. Life, then, must go on as before. Or rather, it doesn't quite, in the same way. For Bob's and Jean's desire to keep their love-life vibrant has been interrupted by the intrusion of Tony into Jean's consciousness; her lovemaking with Bob at the end of the play sees her vaguely drawn elsewhere, away from him, to thoughts of Tony, perhaps of her youth. Thus the dead hand of Tony is reaching out to touch life here, too. We have a kind of presentiment for Bob and Jean, even if it is represented by nothing more than a flower by the bedside.

Presentiment of what? Death? Death of what? Perhaps of the vibrancy of the sex which creates life. If life is a series of death-presentiments, perhaps the death of full sensual love between two married persons is the first one to appear. And it does appear here – at the end of a play about a funeral.

A play is not simply the sum of its dialogue; a television play is not simply the sum of its pictures. It is made appealing, compulsive and memorable by its structure. If I have concentrated mainly on the internal structure of Peter Nichols's writing to the exclusion of celebrating his uniqueness as a virtuoso stylist, it is because Peter Nichols has not always been given his due as a constructor of plays, an architect of what he writes, in a medium which can glow with such structure but seldom admits to it; for television is the ultimate 'art that conceals art', and Peter Nichols is its artist.

Appendix

Television plays transmitted

26.3.59	*A Walk on the Grass*	BBC
22.5.59	*Promenade*	Granada
23.2.61	*Ben Spray*	Granada
12.5.61	*The Reception*	Granada
28.8.61	*The Big Boys*	BBC
10.3.63	*The Continuity Man*	BBC
22.3.63	*Ben Again*	Granada
2.7.63	*The Heart of the Country*	ATV
25.8.63	*The Hooded Terror*	ATV
31.5.64	*The Brick Umbrella*	ATV
2.8.65	*When the Wind Blows*	ATV
29.7.68	*Daddy Kiss It Better*	Yorkshire
4.9.68	*The Gorge*	BBC-1 *Wednesday Play*
24.9.68	*Majesty* (based on a story by F. Scott Fitzgerald in series *The Jazz Age*)	BBC-2
26.11.68	*Winner Takes All* (based on a story by Evelyn Waugh in series *The Jazz Age*)	BBC-2
3.12.70	*Hearts and Flowers*	BBC-1 *Play for Today*
4.6.72	*Ben Spray* (revival)	London Weekend *Sunday Night Theatre*
21.10.73	*The Common*	BBC-1 *Play of the Month*
5.11.75	*Forget-Me-Not Lane* (TV version)	BBC-1 *Playhouse*

Plays published

(For Nichols's published TV plays, see Appendix 1.)
A Day in the Death of Joe Egg, London: Faber, 1967
The National Health; or Nurse Norton's Affair, London: Faber, 1970
Forget-Me-Not Lane, London: Faber, 1971
Chez Nous, London: Faber, 1974
The Freeway, London: Faber, 1975
Privates on Parade, London: French, 1977

Films scripted

1965 *Catch Us If You Can*
1967 *Georgy Girl*
1972 *A Day in the Death of Joe Egg*
1972 *The National Health*

Interviews with and criticism of Peter Nichols

Ronald Hayman, *Playback 2*, London: Davis-Poynter, 1973, pp. 47–62
Oleg Kerensky, *The New British Drama*, London: Hamish Hamilton, 1977, pp. 59–77
Paul Madden, *Complete Programme Notes for a Season of British Television Drama 1959–1973, Held at the National Film Theatre, 11th–24th October 1976*, London: British Film Institute, 1976 (discussions of *When the Wind Blows* and *The Gorge*)
Gary O'Connor, 'Peter Nichols', in: *Contemporary Dramatists*, ed. James Vinson, London: St James Press, 1977
John Russell Taylor, *The Second Wave: British Drama for the Seventies*, London: Methuen, 1971, pp. 16–35
See also articles in *Plays and Players*, September 1967, pp. 40–1, and March 1978, pp. 14–17

6   **Alan Plater**

ALBERT HUNT

1

In 1973 Alan Plater wrote a film for television called *The Land of Green Ginger*. It's the only one of his TV plays so far to have been made entirely on film – Plater stresses the difference between writing for film and writing studio drama.

'Studio drama works best', he says, 'when the subject of the play is faces.' It's particularly effective, he argues, in 'claustrophobic situations with people locked into a set of relationships. But when you move outside the studio the power of the visual image is much much greater, because there's more to look at. You can go out into the streets of Hull, down to the dockside or some place, you can stand up a character and you point a camera at him, and behind him there'll be a ship and behind him some cranes and behind him the river and behind him the other bank of the river and then some clouds and perhaps an aeroplane flying over, and you've got five, six, ten layers of significance. It's a very basic thing about the job that not many people understand or appreciate. If I'm writing for film I give little drawings. If I'm writing for studio I just write the words.'[1]

Plater wrote *The Land of Green Ginger* in pictures because in one sense the subject of the film is Hull, the city which has been his home since he was three years old. His scripted suggestions for the opening sequence read almost like a poem to the place.

[*The sight and sound of water – the frame filled with the restless and choppy surface of the river while we hear the wind, the cries of the gulls, the distant sound of a ship's siren.*
Panning up to a long shot of the city of Hull dominated by the old town in the centre: the towers of Holy Trinity, the pantiled roofs, the pier and the old paddle steamer alongside.
No need to take in many details at this point: just the flatness of the land and the great width of the river, punctuated maybe by a boat or string of barges going past.

Superimpose main titles.
And if it's a little misty and magical that's all to the good. You don't expect cold
reason in a town that calls a street the Land of Green Ginger.]

The film tells a very simple story. A girl, Sally Brown, who's working in London, goes home to Hull for the weekend. She's a hard-headed, down-to-earth girl: when a journalist she meets on the train says, 'People from Hull, they all have this mysterious Northern mist behind their eyes', she comments, 'Takes a clever feller to talk rubbish like that.' And when he asks her, 'Do you know the Land of Green Ginger?' her off-hand reply is, 'It's a street, isn't it?' – but she's not sure where.

Sally is going home to spend the weekend with her mother: her father's in the Persian Gulf on an oil tanker. Plater shows us the new high-rise Corporation flats where her mother now lives: 'Alcatraz,' says the taxi-driver, but her mother simply says, 'I think they've tried their best.'

The real object of Sally's visit, however, soon becomes clear as she asks for the evening paper. Mrs Brown says, 'If it's shipping movements you're worried about I can tell you. Mike's boat docked this morning.'

On the Saturday morning, Sally goes in search of Mike – Plater uses her trip to show us both the new and the old Hull. The buses, says Mrs Brown, 'don't have conductors any more, like riding around on a weighing machine'. And in Hessle Road – 'The traditional fishing community's High Street on a busy Saturday morning' – there's not only a shop selling fishermen's gear, but there's a Buy-and-Sell Mart ('Telling us all is not prosperous in this little island'), and a Chinese restaurant ('things are changing'). Mike's mother lives in one of the terraced courts that run off one of the side streets – ('and let's find a neat, trim one with well-maintained, handkerchief-sized front gardens').

Mike's not at home, and when she tracks him down in a car he's just bought, he's apparently very casual: he's just off to Wakefield with the boys to see a Rugby League Cup match. Sally wanders the area looking for her old house, but it's been bull-dozed. All she finds is an old trawler skipper she'd once called Uncle. He's drunk and crying.

The next day Mike comes to pick her up in the car he's just bought. They go to Pickering Park and see his kid brother playing football; they go to the Museum of Fisheries. Presently he takes her and shows her the place where the Humber Bridge is going to be built: 'It's going to bring trade and prosperity to Hull. It said so in the paper so it must be true. It's going to be like Klondyke round here, we'll all make our fortunes, ten grand a year, big house near Kirkella golf course, three weeks at Butlins, Hull's going to beat Kingston Rovers in the Final at Wembley by fifty points to nil, City's going to win the European Cup three years running, I'll be the Lord Mayor . . .' He pauses. 'And I'll pack in the fishing.' 'Will you pack it in?' Sally asks.

They go to a show in a Working Men's Club; then they listen to a group of folk-singers, the Watersons, in a pub. The Watersons sing:

> A sailor's life is a merry life,
> They rob young girls of their heart's delight,
> Leaving them behind to sigh and mourn . . .
> They never know when they will return . . .

Afterwards Sally suggests, 'We ought to look for the Land of Green Ginger,' but when Mike asks, 'What the hell for?' she simply says, 'Good question.'

Presently, Sally begins to ask what's happened to 'the old gang'. Tom and Betty 'spend all their time having babies – not much to do in Hull during the winter'; Joan 'married a bloke from Sheffield'; Ken 'got washed overboard. Off Iceland.'

Sally's told Mike she's been offered a job abroad, but now she says she doesn't want it. She wants to come back to Hull, where she can walk down the street and see somebody to talk to. 'Might be drunk or might be crying,' comments Mike – but he's following her drift. And after her pause he says, 'Let's get married.' Before she'll agree, though, she asks him to give up going to sea.

But Mike's just got his skipper's ticket and has wangled to get his own boat. The boat's the one that 'Uncle Jack Adams' had been skipper of: 'He couldn't catch fish' – which is why Sally had seen him crying.

Mike says he's going to make a lot of money, buy his way into a big firm, come ashore: but even if he ends up 'hanging round the fishhouses with half my fingers gone doing odd jobs for a few quid a week' he'll still be a good husband. 'Not to me, you won't,' says Sally – and as she's leaving him she asks, 'Why shouldn't people do decent jobs and have decent lives and live where they want to live?' 'Cause we're all alike,' says Mike. 'We let them all get away with it . . . 'cause we don't know any better.'

On the way back to London, she meets the journalist again. 'Did you find the Land of Green Ginger?' he asks her; and she replies, 'No. We didn't look hard enough.'

I've described *The Land of Green Ginger* in some detail, partly because it introduces us vividly to the city in which Plater has his roots; but also because the somewhat sad story offers a striking contrast to the story of Plater's own career as a television writer.

Why, asks Sally, shouldn't people do 'decent jobs'? But it's a rhetorical question. She and Mike accept what they've got. Over the years Plater has worked at making his own job. And now, talking about his work, he says, 'I leave it to others to decide whether or not I'm an artist. I'd only say I've got the best job in the world.'[2]

Again, Sally and Mike are in the end defeated by the limitations of their own expectations. They allow the limitations to impose on them. Plater sees limitations as something to be overcome. 'If there are no limitations it is necessary to invent them,' he says – and he talks of the architectural triumph of the Parthenon, built at a time when the known maximum span of an arch was three feet. Writing for television, he says, 'You have to make a conscious effort to break the boundaries.'[3] And this is what much of his writing career has been about.

Sally and Mike fail to find the Land of Green Ginger because they don't look hard enough. Plater says, 'I get a bit impatient watching a good deal of TV drama by people who don't seem to be aware of possibilities available that they're not making a grab for.'[4] Plater's not only been aware of and grabbed the possibilities available: he's invented new ones. This chapter is a celebration of his continuing search for the Land of Green Ginger.

2

Alan Plater was born in April 1935 in Jarrow, the town that gave its name to the Hunger Marchers in the Depression. Although his family moved to Hull when he was three, he still had relatives in Jarrow and went back there regularly during his childhood. 'People in Hull would ask me where I was going for my holidays and I would say "Jarrow" and I couldn't understand why they laughed.'[5] In the 1960s, Jarrow gave him the subject matter for one of the few plays he's written out of anger. He was writing a script for a film and was taken out to dinner at the Carlton Grill with the director and the producer. A few days later he went to the funeral of an aunt in Jarrow. 'It occurred to me that the bill for the dinner was roughly the equivalent of an average week's wage in Jarrow at that time.' So he wrote *Rest in Peace, Uncle Fred*, to call attention to 'the bizarre contrast between the meal and the funeral'.

He went to university in Newcastle to read architecture, but spent much of his time in 'iconoclastic' student journalism. When he left Newcastle, after completing only four years of his five-year course, he went back to Hull, where he wrote 'five lousy plays that nobody wanted'. But Alfred Bradley, drama producer for BBC Leeds – 'every Northern writer's Hughie Green' – commissioned him to write a radio play, *The Smokeless Zone* – 'Satire with a capital S'.

It was Joan Littlewood who pointed him in a radically new direction (as she did unknowingly to so many of us). She'd been working in Hull and was quoted as saying, 'You can walk the streets of Hull and hear the people talking poetry.' Plater writes, 'Having walked a great many of the streets without tripping over too many iambic pentameters, this was a puzzling remark.'[6] But, coincidentally, a few days later he started work on the 1961 census in a job which involved talking and listening to householders in Hessle Road. 'It would be romantic and daft to pretend that I found Jerusalem down Hessle Road, but I did listen . . . I discovered what as a native Geordie I should have known all along – that in everyday speech there is a richness and music that makes the voice the most powerful and sensitive instrument for human emotion: and that this exists as a tool for the dramatist at its most useful when the voice speaks with a local accent or dialect. The problem with standard English – and let's accept BBC Radio 4 announcers as a norm to avoid *that* endless debate – is that emotion is inhibited rather than released.'[7]

Eleven years later, in 1972, Alan Plater wrote a television play which illustrated this discovery. In *Seventeen Per Cent Said Push Off*, a post-graduate student, Gavin, whose voice is 'sound, middle-class Guildford but in no way soppy', spends a weekend in the house of a Northern working-class family, the Milners, tape-recording his observations while collecting material for a thesis called 'The Infrastructure of the Working Classes'. His recordings are full of sentences like 'Mrs. Milner appears to be a definitive working-class mother, Mam as they say . . . Her relationship with Mr. Milner appears to be good and friendly.' But what we hear Mrs Milner say affectionately to her husband is 'Come on, get your fat carcase out of the way.'

The confrontation between the two forms of speech reaches its climax when Mrs Milner's married daughter, Betty, whose husband, Sid, is working away, takes him home late on Saturday night after a drink at the Labour Club. After talking grandiosely about picturing 'some sort of world where I don't have a better house than you . . . and where you don't have to sweat and slave' ('We don't slave,' says Betty, 'we're not that stupid'), Gavin tries to reach her in her own language: 'I'm sorry. Give us a kiss luv.' But over the kiss we hear his voice saying, 'The surprising thing about the closely-knit family circles is that there are individual examples of intense loneliness.' And when Betty asks him, 'Will you put this in your book? Is this part of the infra thing?' he, instead of accepting her as a person in her own right by saying, 'No,' can only reply, 'Infrastructure . . . I don't know.' 'That's it then, isn't it?' says Betty – and she breaks away. Gavin is locked in a language which expresses his perception of Betty not as a woman but as a subject for a thesis.

'In plain English', writes Plater of his experience in 1961, 'I was learning that plays spring from talking and not from writing.'[8] It was a lesson that was to affect the future form of all his work.

3

If Joan Littlewood taught Alan Plater to listen to the way people talked, the American writer Paddy Chayefsky taught him to look at the way they behaved.

Chayefsky, as Plater puts it, 'as much as anybody invented the television play'.[9] In the late fifties Chayefsky wrote a series of TV plays about everyday experience, of which *Marty* is a good example. *Marty* is about a butcher who thinks of himself as ugly and who picks up a girl everybody agrees is plain. At first he's persuaded to drop her. But then he suddenly realises he's enjoyed being with her. He defies his friends and goes back to her.

Plater writes of Chayefsky, 'Chayefsky observed that the greatest single asset of television was its simplicity and directness; the ability to watch a face in close-up . . . His consequent philosophy, summarised briefly, was that television drama should be the drama of the ordinary man or woman, revealing the extraordinary core of genius that rests in the heart of each individual.'[10]

Summing up the method he learned from Chayefsky, Plater writes, '. . . you take a small contained situation, and sink a great shaft into the human relationships existing therein. Then you watch what happens at a range of three feet.'[11]

It was a lesson Alan Plater learned to apply during what he regards as his TV apprenticeship, which he served on *Z-Cars* and its successor, *Softly, Softly* (he wrote eighteen episodes of one and thirty of the other). He began writing for *Z-Cars* in 1963 and soon took over from John Hopkins as anchorman for the series – which meant that he was writing an episode every three or four weeks.

He approached the job from the first as a way of learning his craft. 'It was a great opportunity', he says, 'to set yourself tasks.' He would decide to tell a story in which nothing happened, or to tell five stories in the one episode. 'It was like having your own company to work with and you could afford to get things slightly wrong.'[12]

Z-Cars and *Softly, Softly* developed over the years a TV language of their own, based on our familiarity with the regular cast of detectives – Barlow, Watt, Hawkins and the rest. They were the givens of the situation. Plater welcomed their presence – it meant that there were characters he didn't have to create and it left him all the more free to sink that 'great shaft' into the human relationships. The skill with which he became able to do this is demonstrated in the episode of *Softly, Softly* which Alfred Bradley chose to include in a published collection of Alan Plater's plays, *You and Me.* The episode was first televised in 1968 and is called *On Christmas Day in the Morning.*

The story is, once again, simple. Two villains, who have registered at a posh hotel under the name of Wilson, steal several thousand pounds worth of valuables from the rooms of a number of very rich people, including the Lord Lieutenant. They get into the rooms during a Christmas Eve dance by using a pass-key which we've seen being left by a chambermaid called Yvonne. Watt is in charge of the investigation, and from the start we're on his side. He's a likeable and familiar figure, and we sympathise with him because his Christmas is being disturbed. The villains have been presented as smooth professionals, and the interest of the story lies in the way Watt tracks them down.

4 *Z-Cars. James Ellis (Inspector Lynch), Frank Windsor (Detective Chief Superintendent Watt) and Brian Blessed (Fancy Smith) outside Newtown, police station in the final episode of this long-running BBC series.*

Until, that is, Watt confronts the chambermaid, Yvonne. Plater uses the confrontation to set up a complex relationship.

Watt takes it for granted from the start that Yvonne has had nothing to do with the crime. He relaxes by being flippant with her. He's interrupted her while she was serving breakfast and says he wouldn't mind breakfast himself. She tells him he'd better fix it with the management.

The chambermaid is helping out in the kitchen because she needs the money. She needs the money because she has a baby. 'But no feller, see. So I work long hours. People. Breakfast.' Her mother looks after the baby, only she has no feller either: 'My dad was lost at sea.' In a few lines Plater has presented the girl as having had a lot of problems but as having responded with plenty of bounce: when Watt asks her if she ever lets the pass-key out of her possession, she says 'Only when I lend it to anybody that wants to steal things from the rooms.' The line works because we know that she's telling the truth, whereas the detective thinks she's joking. But we're also aware of the implications when she adds, 'You can't take a baby to prison.'

Plater makes us understand precisely why she's acted as an accomplice, and from this point onwards our response to the simple story becomes complicated. Every step forward that Watt takes towards finding the villains means a step towards jail for the girl. Moreover, the relationship between Watt and the girl suddenly becomes friendly. 'Hey,' she says, 'do you fancy a bacon sandwich?' Watt pretends to flirt with her and says 'At least.' Throughout the rest of the story she keeps him supplied with the hotel's food and drink.

Plater uses the relationship to set up a quietly ironic ending. The Wilsons have been caught, but Watt hasn't yet found the accomplice. The Lord Lieutenant has congratulated the Squad – 'He wishes it to be made known,' comments Watt, sardonically.

And then Yvonne brings Watt a cup of coffee. He gives her a pound to buy a present for her baby. And after she's gone, Plater leaves us with Watt sipping the coffee. 'I'll just have my coffee,' he says, 'then I'll go down to Divisional H.Q. . . . Talk to the Wilsons. Find out who gave them the key.'

There are a lot of big questions hovering just off screen. In whose interests are the police working? How far is a girl justified in helping to rob the rich in order to help her baby? And what happens to personal feelings when a policeman is doing his duty?

But the questions *are* off-screen. They're implied in the 'small contained situation' Plater has created on-screen, and which is summed up by a shot of Watt sipping the coffee brought to him by a girl he's about to send to jail.

The episode illustrates two of Plater's most important qualities. The first is his ability to convey 'the passions and frivolities of "ordinary" people in a fresh, unsentimental, yet compassionate manner'.[13] The second is his willingness to bring all his skill and intelligence to what many writers might have seen as the job of writing one more routine episode of a detective series.

The dramatist Edward Bond once commented in *Theatre Quarterly* (after having said, 'A writer does have responsibilities and I accept them'), 'Most of the television I've seen has been a load of old rubbish, and if you're going to write a load of old rubbish you might just as well do it for films.'[14]

Plater would never regard his job as involving the writing of 'a load of old rubbish'. He accepts that much of his work for television is 'honest carpentry, brought about because somebody in an office high up in a glass-fronted building had had an idea'. But he goes on, 'As a result of a phone call or a letter, you are suddenly consumed with curiosity and excitement about, say the suffragettes or Edwardian England or the history of Sadler's Wells Theatre, Grimaldi and all, where, five minutes earlier, such thoughts had never crossed your mind.'[15]

The key words are 'curiosity' and 'excitement'. Bond sees the 'theatre' and the 'writer' as being special: the theatre's job is 'to analyse and explain society', which involves 'forming ideas' – which 'needs the control and scope of a writer'.

Plater sees his job in much more modest terms. 'We're all telling tales in the market place for a living, fundamentally,' he says.[16]

But he sets out to tell the best possible tales he can: and he does this whether he's writing just one more episode of *Softly, Softly* or a new *Play of the Week*. It's this honesty and commitment that make it possible for Plater to create a richly ironic relationship in a simple story – and, in doing so, to extend the possibilities of a popular entertainment series.

4

If Plater had done nothing more than help to make everyday, regional speech familiar and usable on British television, and apply Chayefsky's closeness of observation, not to characters in Brooklyn but to people in Hull and Wakefield, that would have been a considerable achievement. But, having learnt his trade, Plater has consciously and increasingly over the years used his skills to break down what he sees as artificially imposed boundaries and invent new and exhilarating forms of entertainment.

Plater has been aware of constraints since he first began writing for television. 'There are all kinds of boundaries and frontiers,' he says, 'like those between different types of programme and different Departments. It's difficult to span these Departments, and it's very exciting when they are spanned.'[17]

The category of 'drama' has, he says, been limited by a particular concept of theatre: 'We're very constrained by traditions that were inherited from the stage, primarily.' They're traditions connected with the prevailing form of naturalism, where the stage is seen as offering a believable representation of 'real life'; and they've helped to encourage what Plater calls 'identikit' drama. He quotes Tony Hancock as saying if he saw *The Blood Donor* on TV once more, he'd kick the screen in; and Plater adds, 'If I see another play about a middle-aged menopausal business man having an affair with his secretary, *I* shall kick the screen in.'[18]

More important, the naturalistic traditions have inhibited writers from developing new forms. In his early days as a TV playwright, there were formal ideas he had which he didn't offer, because he felt they would be unacceptable.

Paradoxically, some of his first ventures in new forms took place in his television adaptation of his own stage play, *Close the Coalhouse Door*. Because the play had already been accepted as 'theatre', he felt more free to play with ideas. And so he introduced, for example, a scene which looked like the current-affairs programme *Panorama*. 'There was a shouting match between a group of miners and a Government Minister which could have convinced viewers that they were seeing a real *Panorama* programme – but then, immediately, the Minister sang a song. I wouldn't at that time have written such a scene into a new script I was offering as a *Wednesday Play*.'[19]

But as he began to make elbow-room for himself on the

medium, he began to nudge at the conventions. Realising the difficulty of making a major impact on an audience with one play (because television language tends to develop over a series as the audience becomes familiar with the characters and the situation), he wrote a trilogy, in 1968 (*Black, White and Shades of Grey*), which, he says, made him feel he was dealing with 'weighty matters'.

But it was in 1975 that he stumbled on the idea that was to enable him to put on the TV screen a series which communicated what he calls his love for 'the collective joy of people doing daft things' – and to do so in a way which freed him totally from the inherited constraints of naturalist drama.

5

The series was called *Trinity Tales*. Seven people are travelling in a minibus from Wakefield to Wembley to support Wakefield Trinity in the Rugby League Cup Final. In the first episode, Nick the Driver finds himself forced to explain why he's going from Wakefield to London via Lincoln and King's Lynn. He tells the story of adventures which have led to his running away from both a crook, Big George, and the police. Everybody enjoys the story: they all agree that each of them should tell a story on the way to Wembley and that the teller of the best story will be given a free fish-and-chip supper by one of the party, Stan the Fryer, who owns a fish-and-chip shop.

The device of having stories within a story leaves Plater free to demolish the normal conventions of TV drama and to revel in the freedom to draw on a variety of styles.

There's a parody, for example, of Dylan Thomas and of a particularly literal form of television, as Eric the Actor offers an 'evocation of childhood' during a halt in a roadside cafeteria. 'All down the long days of winter, I ran barefoot along steep-sloping, rain-dappled, cobble-stone streets' – and there's a bit of film very like the ad in which a small boy climbs a cobbled street to fetch Hovis. 'And all around me the windows wept in the grey sadness of December' – there's a middle close-up of rain running down a window-pane. 'And all down the long days of autumn . . .' but back in the cafeteria, Dave the Joiner moans, 'Oh, bloody hell,' and they stop Eric the Actor, making him give way to Stan the Fryer. Later Eric the Actor tries again, only this time it's a parody of Raymond Chandler. 'I paused at the corner of East 26th and Main,' he says as we see him in what's obviously an English shopping plaza, pausing. 'The silence was fit to burst your ear-drums and the emptiness crowded in on you. I started walking again . . .' and we see him start walking as Dave's voice-over comments, 'Not a lot going on, is there?'

Plater plays with cinema conventions. As the minibus leaves Wakefield and sets off down the M1, we have a shot of its wheels on the road, like those Hollywood train wheels shots, 'while the show was on tour to Boston and Chicago'. Nick, telling a love story, is embarrassed when the moment comes to show a kiss. Eric tells him to use the 'waves lapping on a seashore'. So Nick repeats the scene, and just as his lips are meeting the woman's we see a shot of gently lapping waves. Later, the woman, in his arms and looking at the camera over his shoulder, says, 'Hey up: here come those waves again,' and the shot is repeated. When they finally climb the stairs to go to bed, there's a shot of the waves *lashing* the shore.

Plater uses Hollywood images again in *The Fryer's Tale*, which is about how a weedy youth called Arthur gets into the British Rugby League team as a way of persuading the wife of a very rich man to go to the pictures with him. When Arthur finally 'has his way' with her, we hear 'As Time Goes By' on the soundtrack and see the faces of Humphrey Bogart and Ingrid Bergman on screen. The camera cuts backwards and forwards between the Holly-wood stars in still shot and Arthur and Dorothy walking. Finally, the camera pulls back from the Hollywood stars to reveal that the still is a publicity photo in a showcase outside the Arcadia cinema – into which we see Arthur and Dorothy walking as the music reaches its climax.

Plater draws on references to the media throughout. After two men in a pub have failed to eat meat pies in a contest, there's a parody of a *Match of the Day* summing-up, with the Brian Clough figure saying, 'It's a good result. It's good for the game. It's good for me and Derek and Mal. It's good for Derby, Brighton and Leeds. It's good for England. It's good for the future of Western European civilisation.' A competition in singing dirty songs becomes the 'Yorkovision Song Contest'. The crooked policeman in all the stories, who calls himself Smith, is played throughout by a well-known TV detective, John Stratton, whom the audience recognises.

But what gives Plater his real freedom to innovate in *Trinity Tales* is the fact that the actors who play the travellers in the minibus are also the actors who play the characters in the story within the story. The concept provides a rich source of comedy.

For example, in *The Driver's Tale*, Big George and Stan the Fryer are both played by Bill Maynard. In one sequence, Bill Maynard, as Big George, is telling Nick how to swindle people by selling them tickets for a non-existent minibus trip to Wembley. If they fall for it, says Big George, it will be their own fault: 'They're the ones who are being greedy.' The scene cuts from Bill Maynard as Big George to Bill Maynard as Stan the Fryer. 'I don't like people calling me greedy,' says Stan.

The Judy's Tale, in which two boys, Sam and Charlie, compete for the favours of a barmaid, Judy (played by the Judy of the minibus), hinges on the fact that Sam and Charlie are played by Nick the Driver and Eric the Actor. The story is told in a pub (Plater calls it the 'present' pub) and takes place in another pub (the 'past' pub). It opens with Sam and Charlie fighting in the Gents of the 'past' pub over which of them is going to take Judy to the Labour Club Dance. The Landlord (Stan the Fryer) stops them from fighting and organises a gentlemanly contest, which includes darts, dominoes, shove 'apenny, the reciting of poems and the singing of dirty songs. At one point, Eric (in the 'present' pub) says to Judy, 'I quite like the way I'm playing the part of Charlie, but the central situation is so chauvinistic. They're treating you like a sex object.' Nick and Eric agree, however, that Judy is behaving with 'dignity' and 'restraint'.

By the end of the contest, both Sam and Charlie are too drunk to claim the prize. Judy's boy friend in the 'present' pub, Dave, has been keeping the score in the 'past' pub and declares himself the winner. But back in the 'present' pub, there's the sound of fighting in the Gents. Nick and Eric are fighting about whether Judy's outstanding characteristic is her dignity or her restraint.

In *The Fryer's Tale* Plater uses the fact that Stan is playing himself in his own story to enable Stan to present himself in a comically heroic light. When the weedy boy, Arthur, falls in love at first sight with the rich wife, Dorothy, she first of all tells Arthur that she can't go to the pictures with him in the afternoon because every afternoon her husband's away she has tea with her sister Jennifer. Then she says she can only love men who achieve something – like playing Rugby League football for Great Britain. Arthur says he'll go and play for Trinity, but Dorothy laughs. The Trinity team is full of internationals. 'Even Stan Fryer, the Coach, he played for Yorkshire, he played for Great Britain . . .' The listeners to the story cut in. 'Is that you she's talking about?' 'Aye: that's me.' 'Crikey, show us your muscles.'

When Arthur finally 'has his way' with Dorothy by taking her to the pictures every afternoon, Stan assures his listeners that the boy never even touched her. Alice the Wife of Batley is determined to find out how Stan knows this. And at last Stan tells her: 'Because Dorothy told all her innermost secrets to her sister Jennifer.' 'And you knew sister Jennifer?' asks Alice. 'No,' says Stan triumphantly. 'I *am* sister Jennifer.'

The invention of having the same performers play two different sets of characters not only makes for comedy. It also completely explodes the style of acting, derived from naturalistic theatre conventions, which dominates television drama.

Naturalistic theatre tries to convince the audience that they are seeing a faithful representation of 'real life'. It's based on the proposition that things are exactly what they seem. In such a theatre, the art of acting is judged by the performers' ability to *become* the characters they're performing, to persuade the audience temporarily to forget that they're seeing a performance. It's a style of acting built up from the inner psychology and feelings of the character portrayed: 'Why am I, as this character, doing and saying this at this point?' Everything is done to avoid calling attention to the conventions.

Trinity Tales reverts to the style of acting which, in Shakespeare, allowed boys playing girls to disguise themselves as boys and to call attention to the fact. ('I shall see some squeaking Cleopatra boy my greatness,' says the boy playing the queen as she's about to die a tragic death.) The style belongs to what the critic S. L. Bethell calls 'the popular dramatic tradition', in which the audience always remains aware of different levels of reality, and playwrights and performers play with that awareness. In *Trinity Tales*, Plater is always reminding us that we're watching television, always calling attention to television conventions.

But the style is directly related to an attitude, a way of looking. It's a sceptical, questioning attitude. 'I've never been able to accept the existence of an objective truth,' says Plater – particularly, he adds, when it's being put forward by politicians who are looking for our votes. And again, 'The camera doesn't lie – but the editor lies all the time.'[20]

Most would-be 'serious' television, from *Play for Today* to the

5 The Man of Law's Tale – Episode 6 in Alan Plater's Trinity Tales, shown on BBC-2 in November–December 1975. John Stratton (Smith, the Man of Law) at the piano watching (left to right) Colin Farrell (Mick), Francis Matthews (Eric) and Paul Copley (Dave).

news and current-affairs programmes, is committed to the principle of persuading us to believe in the truth of what we see on the
screen: it was on telly, so it must be right. *Trinity Tales* invites us
to view these claims less than reverently. In *The Fryer's Tale*,
Arthur, who's just been interviewed in a mock sports programme on telly, suddenly turns up at Dorothy's door. 'How did
you get here so quickly?' asks Dorothy. 'You were on television
four minutes ago.' 'That was recorded,' says Arthur, and he
points to an image on the screen within the screen. 'That's recorded, what you're seeing now . . . Nothing's ever what it
seems, including me.'

Naturalistic drama asserts that things are what they seem.
Trinity Tales warns us that nothing is ever what it seems. The
form and style of the series leave us in a state of (to paraphrase
Brecht) 'cheerful and militant' questioning. A song at the end of
The Judy's Tale sums up the series' attitude. It's sung in a pub
that's been tarted up by the brewers and is accompanied on a
piano that's been forced open after having been locked up by
order of the magistrates.

> As you limp along Life's Highway
> You meet strangers every day,
> Offering you the fruits of Heaven,
> This is what you have to say . . .
>
> Knock it off
> Knock it off
> Don't say yes say
> Knock it off.

I'd be tempted to describe the style of *Trinity Tales* as Brechtian
– but Plater's beaten me to it. In *The Joiner's Tale*, after a song ('I
love my work, and I love my wages,/Love my boss and he loves
me'), Smith the Policeman says, 'I find this extremely far-
fetched'; but Eric comments, 'It all has a kind of Brechtian quality,
it seems to me.'

Not even Plater's own style is spared his mockery. He doesn't
want people to believe *him* unquestioningly, either. But then,
neither did Brecht.

6

In *Trinity Tales*, Plater fused a celebration of the 'collective joy of
people doing daft things' with a gleeful and irreverent question-

ing of what he calls 'generally acknowledged truth, generally acknowledged reality'. This spirit of celebration and questioning has continued to flow through his later work. The celebration is at the heart of the comedy series which took Plater to the top of the charts – *Oh No! It's Selwyn Froggitt*. The questioning is pushed further than before in a play still (at the time of writing) to appear on the screen, *The Blacktoft Diaries – True or False?*

The *Selwyn Froggitt* series developed directly out of *Trinity Tales*. Bill Maynard, who played Stan the Fryer in *Trinity Tales*, had this idea for a character, based on a man he'd known for a long time. Plater recalls how Bill Maynard had described the man. 'Our real-life Selwyn has the habit of walking into a bar and tickling people under the arms. This fellow knew that this guy was going to do this. So he had his pint in his hand, and as he was tickled he pretended that the tickling had caused him to throw the pint backwards all over the real-life Selwyn, who said, "I'm sorry – let me get you another drink."' Plater adds, 'Selwyn is the kind of man who, if you hit him, he'd be grateful that you weren't hitting him harder.'[21]

Selwyn Froggitt, in the series, works as a labourer for the Council of a small industrial town, presumably in Yorkshire (the filmed sequences were shot in Skelmanthorpe, a West Yorkshire village at the foot of the Pennines between Huddersfield and Barnsley). But although he's only a labourer, he sees himself as a very important person – he goes to work on a bike which he leaves in the Council car park and he constantly refers to *The Times*.

His life is centred on the house which he shares with 'me mam', 'our Maurice' and, in the later series, 'our Maurice's wife', Vera; on the bar of the Working Men's Club, which he shares with three cronies; and on the Club's Committee Room upstairs. (Plater's delighted at the number of people who have told him that it's the first time they've seen the workings of a Club Committee accurately portrayed on television – 'accurately,' Plater stresses. 'Not realistically.')

Selwyn blows through these environments with hurricane energy and enthusiasm, leaving a trail of well-meant disaster in his wake. He's a huge man, but, as Alan Plater sees it, 'rather different from most fat men in comedy'. Characters like Oliver Hardy and W. C. Fields are, says Plater, 'slow-moving, dignified'. Thanks to Bill Maynard, Selwyn Froggitt is 'a very large piece of muscular quicksilver'.[22]

In a typical episode, Selwyn has to sleep downstairs on the couch because 'our Maurice' and Vera have taken his bed. He finds it hard to sleep on the couch – 'I wake up every time I drop off.' But he finds a reason to be grateful for the inconvenience. 'I told me mam,' he says to Maurice. 'Actually I prefer sleeping downstairs. You don't have to get up in the morning. You're here already, aren't you?'

His cronies in the Club offer him a hammock in the Committee Room. But they tie a rope to the hammock, using 'a single, blackwall slippery hitch knot' which will slip if the rope's pulled. They know Selwyn always sleeps with the door open – 'Otherwise I start imagining things' – so they take the other end of the rope downstairs, planning to pull it just as Selwyn is falling asleep.

Only before they can pull it, Selwyn appears, carrying his end of the rope in his hand. 'I cut it off with my penknife,' he explains. 'I don't know who tied that knot, but they don't know much about tying knots. That was a single, blackwall slippery hitch. You give a little tug at that and I would have come crashing down. I'd better make it secure, you see. I mean, I know all about knots – there was an article about it in *The Times*.'

As he turns to go back to bed, he says, 'Thanks ever so much for that hammock. It's swinging.' Next morning the phone rings to wake him. When he tries to reach the phone, he falls out of the hammock.

He falls, but, as always, he's not hurt. Selwyn couldn't be hurt, just as he couldn't swear or talk about sex or tell dirty jokes. Selwyn, says Plater, is 'so earthy, so basic. Sort of a child in man's clothing. He's got the vision of a child, the imagination of a child. You can't give him sophisticated jokes.'[23]

Selwyn Froggitt is essentially an innocent; which is why, in one sense, it was surprising, in the decade of *Are You Being Served?* and *The Sweeney*, to find that he'd suddenly become a folk-hero. It happened midway through the second series, in February 1977 (Selwyn had first appeared on Yorkshire TV in 1976). 'This newspaper rang me', says Plater, 'and said, "What does it feel like to be number one in the charts?" I didn't even know we were number one.'[24] Watching the programme became like being a member of a club. People would greet each other on the streets with Selwyn's thumbs-up gesture and his catchword, 'Magic! Magic!' When Bill Maynard took his seat at the Rugby League Cup Final, people all around put their thumbs up: 'Magic! Magic!' 'Hooligans' on the terraces at soccer matches sang, 'Ma-gic, Ma-gic', to the tune of *Amazing Grace*. On walls people wrote, 'Selwyn Froggitt Rules – O.K.?' Car-stickers appeared reading 'Selwyn Froggitt for King'.

The key to Selwyn's popularity seems to lie in Alan Plater's remark that strangers would often say to him, of Selwyn, 'We've got one at work.' Selwyn is immediately recognisable as one of *us*. He sums up Plater's commitment to the extraordinariness of the 'ordinary' man.

For Plater himself, *Oh No! It's Selwyn Froggitt* meant an extension in two directions. First, it involved him, more than any of his previous work in television had done, in working with a team. In *Theatre Quarterly* he'd written, 'Art *can* emerge from lonely pondering in a white tower, but I'm fairly certain that lads and lasses getting together on the shop floor is as effective, and definitely more fun.'[25] In the theatre he'd worked with groups to make plays like *The Fosdyke Saga*. But he'd experienced that kind of collectivity much less frequently in television; and *Selwyn Froggitt* was essentially a team show. Each episode was worked on with the team for a week. The script Plater took in on the Sunday was, he says, no more than a basis for negotiation. They'd play with it together until the Wednesday, when the producer, Ronnie Baxter, would decide on the final version. Then they'd rehearse for two days and record the episode live in front of an audience on the Friday night. The recording of each half-hour episode seldom took longer than an hour and a half, and the teamwork was strong enough for Plater to drop out midway through the third series without the quality being affected.

Secondly, it meant that Plater, the 'dramatist', had totally crossed the boundaries between drama and light entertainment and had done so, not by 'writing down' to the masses but by using his 'curiosity and excitement' to give life to an archetypal figure who became part of the communal imagination.

Plater handed over Selwyn Froggitt to other writers in the course of the third series. He'd decided to do so because he'd come to the conclusion that television rests too easily on its safe successes. He was, as always, looking for yet more extensions.

One extension involved him in writing a rock musical, *Curriculi Curricula*, about 'a boy who loses a girl, finds her again, and rides off with her on his motorbike into the sunset'. Another, *The Blacktoft Diaries – True or False?* involved directly confronting another traditional boundary – that between drama and documentary.

7

The distinction between drama and documentary has, of course, been frequently challenged before. The school of TV drama which virtually began with *Cathy Come Home* is one which presents social issues, such as housing or Borstals, in such a style that it's difficult to know where the documentary ends and the acting begins. When the BBC controllers refused to screen Roy Minton's *Scum* (about life in Borstals), they argued that the presentation was so 'brilliant' that viewers would believe they were seeing a picture of a real Borstal. (Minton argued that all the incidents he showed were true, but claimed the dramatist's right to concentrate time and space.) But this school of playwriting works on the assumption that viewers accept documentaries as 'true', and that therefore plays should try to persuade the viewer that they're as 'real' and, therefore, as 'true' as the documentaries.

Plater's aim in *The Blacktoft Diaries* is precisely the opposite. He's not trying to make a play that looks as 'true' as a documentary. He's asking us how we can be so gullible as to believe that because something is documentary it must be true.

The Blacktoft Diaries tells the story of events in the small Humberside community of Blacktoft between 3 and 7 November 1955. The events are recorded in a diary kept by Mrs Brown, who runs a Literary Society in the front room of her house. On 3 November, the meeting of the Literary Society seems very ordinary: George the Postman reads new pages from his verse play, *Flight Into Madness*, Mrs Garton displays her embroidery of Wordsworth's 'I wandered lonely as a cloud' (she's spelt 'daffodil' with only one 'f'). But the meeting is joined by a stranger, Mr Dvorak, whose trousers are wet and wrinkled as if he's just waded ashore from a small boat. Afterwards Mrs Brown invites him to stay for cocoa, and he surprises her and her husband, Harvey, by offering them £100 for the use, for a few days, of their back bedroom, which commands 'a good view of the surrounding plains'.

Over the next few days Mrs Brown's diary reports on the stranger's comings and goings. He makes long telephone calls in a foreign language from a nearby telephone box. He's very moved by Russian music on the radio and talks of 'the struggle'. When he hears bangs and sees flashes on Guy Fawkes night, he flings himself to the ground. 'If he wasn't a cash customer,' says Harvey, 'I'd say he was round the bend.'

The Browns see a piece of wire poking out of his bedroom window, but when they ask him what it is, he simply confirms that it's a piece of wire. The climax of the story is reached on Remembrance Sunday, when he leaves the house wearing sinister-looking wellington boots. Before he leaves he orders them not to go into his room, but Harvey, arguing that an Englishman's home is his castle ('that's in Magna Carta or Domesday Book or Habeas Corpus'), disobeys the order.

As the Browns open the door of Mr Dvorak's room, a loud alarm bell rings. They shut the door quickly, but not before they've seen what they recognise as a radio transmitter – they recognise it because they've seen one before in either *Target for Tonight* or *In Which We Serve*.

Mr Dvorak stays out until one o'clock the next morning – 7 November. He's angry that they've opened the door and seen the transmitter but gives them another £100 to agree that what they've seen is a knitting machine and to forget everything. Then he makes what is to them a puzzling speech about smuggling Trojan horses into the citadels of evil and reaction and helping to protect the soldiers in the horses when they're in danger. 'I believe that because of the work I have done here, our soldiers are no longer in danger.'

Just before they all go to bed, Mrs Brown happens to mention her diary. Mr Dvorak shows a sudden interest and asks if he can read it before he leaves the next day. In the last entry in the play, Mrs Brown records the day's events and concludes, 'Perhaps I shouldn't write all this if he's going to read it in the morning. But he'll probably forget.'

That night, we're told, there was a debate in the House of Commons during which Mr Macmillan denied that Mr Philby had anything to do with the disappearance to Russia of the diplomats Burgess and Maclean.

But the Browns, too, have disappeared. After a few days George the Postman climbs over the fence, has a look round the garden and finds Mrs Brown's diary, wet with the rain, on the remains of Harvey's bonfire. The diary, says George, 'kicked about my shed for years. Then one of my mates picked it up and said he knew some feller that collected old diaries and that feller showed it to some other feller that does things for the telly . . .'

The play is full of ingenuity and fun. When the Browns, for example, are arguing about whether or not Harvey should follow Mr Dvorak to find out what he's doing, Mrs Brown suddenly remembers that it's time for the two-minute Remembrance Day silence. They pause in their positions on the screen and remain silent until Mrs Brown gives a nod and the argument continues. Much of the comedy springs from the contrast between the total innocence of the Browns and the pretensions of Mr Dvorak. When he's deeply moved by Russian music on the radio, Mrs Brown says she doesn't know what it was because it certainly wasn't in the *Radio Times*.

But what carries the play's statement is its form. It opens in what Plater describes as 'True News/Documentary style', with helicopter shots showing the Humber estuary where it opens out to the North Sea. A familiar voice describes what we're seeing, as if we were looking at a travelogue: 'The estuary of the River Humber lies on the East Coast of Great Britain, opening out into the North Sea. If you sail up the river, past the port of Hull, beneath the new Humber Bridge' – the camera moves with the commentary – 'you arrive at a stretch of water known as the Blacktoft Channel' – and the camera picks up a stretch of sluggish, muddy water.

The camera shifts to show the Narrator in conventional documentary style, standing at a vantage point overlooking the channel. The Narrator turns out to be a familiar figure – Plater superimposes his name over the picture. The name is that of James Cameron, the 'feller that does things for telly' – in recent years, of course he's been particularly associated with a series showing old home movies. Cameron turns and talks, reporter-style, straight at the camera.

'This is a quiet rural area, with a scattering of small communities . . . Gilberdyke, Saltmarshe, Yokefleet, Staddlethorpe, Blacktoft itself. To the people who live here, it is an area of vital importance. To the rest of the world, and in the nicest possible way, it probably doesn't matter a damn. Yet, for a few days in 1955, it was at the heart of a major international crisis, later to become a landmark in the history of espionage, Whitehall scandal and embarrassment at Westminster. It may seem unlikely, but *if* we are to believe the evidence of the Blacktoft Diaries – and we shall examine the if in due course – this quiet backwater was witness to many strange events and bizarre secrets.' He walks out of shot as the main titles are superimposed over film of the waters and the muddy bank.

This introduction sets the tone of the whole play. There's no easy parody: the sequence *is* documentary, and the presence of James Cameron, a reporter we've been taught over the years to believe and respect, reinforces the documentary quality. But Cameron's key phrase is '*if* we are to believe', which is what the whole play is going to be about.

Plater continues in the documentary style. We follow James Cameron as he walks along a country road. 'Before we consider the events that might – or might not – have taken place along this road, in and around this telephone kiosk' – we see a shot of the kiosk – 'and especially in and around this house' – a deserted house is carefully picked out – 'let us first think a little about November 1955, refresh our memories about what is laughingly called the Spirit of the Times.'

Plater takes us into a montage sequence, made up of stills and archive material, with Cameron's voice over. The sequence uses a television language that's as familiar as the detectives in Z-Cars, that of such pop history series as *All Our Yesterdays*.

'Great Britain had a nearly-new Prime Minister called Anthony Eden, leading a newly-elected Conservative Government aged five months with a majority of 59' – we see pictures of Butler, Macmillan, Lloyd, Thorneycroft. 'This Government was intensely preoccupied with strikes, inflation and the state of the economy. Preparations were being made for urgent talks with both sides of industry. Not for the first time, nor, as we know, the last.

'The people, as they are generally known, had somewhat different preoccupations. To judge from the Hit Parade, one of their favourite heroes was Mr. Johnny Ray' – there's a still of Ray and a fragment of 'The Little White Cloud That Cried' – 'more of that anon, but not perhaps for some time. The leading lady of song was Miss Ruby Murray' – there's a still of Ruby Murray and a snatch of one of her songs – 'while the principal rival to Mr. Ray and Miss Murray was a transatlantic group of indiscriminate sex known as The Singing Dogs' – there's a shot of a group of dogs and a fragment of 'How Much Is That Doggy in the Window?' 'Innocent days, then, of canine absurdities in the Top Twenty, and, you will not be surprised to hear, clashes between Egyptian and Israeli troops in the Gaza strip. While in this house, in November 1955, a woman was keeping a diary . . .'

'The camera doesn't lie – but the editor lies all the time,' says Plater; and 'News doesn't exist until it's reported.'[26]

In this sequence Plater has offered a demonstration of the way television presents the world. It presents the world through the eyes of experts, and experts who take up a particular point of view. The point of view is reflected in the language they use, just as Gavin's point of view, in *Seventeen Per Cent Said Push Off*, is reflected by his language.

The language of television news is that of the well-educated, highly articulate, middle-class Britisher, who's smoothly confident that his world picture is not only the right one but the only possible one. Cameron is playing the expert – his language takes on the slightly superior tone of a man who's mildly amused by the frivolities of 'the people, as they are generally known'; he refers condescendingly to '*Mr.*' Ray and '*Miss*' Murray.

Cameron's version of 1955 is highly selective. But once it's been presented, it becomes the definitive version. The year 1955 *is* a new Tory Government, the Hit Parade, the Gaza strip, history frozen forever in film.

But the key word is 'playing'. Cameron himself is consciously playing a modified version of himself, and in doing so is implicitly commenting on television's right to set up its version of reality, as if that version were the only possible truth. And *The Blacktoft Diaries* works precisely through this kind of 'play'.

We've seen the river, the country road, the telephone box, the house. But what about the woman in the house? Are we to believe she really existed? She's clearly not 'real' in the sense that the telephone box is real – she's obviously played by an actress. But then, Cameron tells us that she's played by an actress: 'What you will see is, in modern jargon, a simulation, with actors and actresses playing the parts of the people described in the diaries.' And the scenes, he warns us elsewhere, only show the recorded highlights. So perhaps the actress is simulating a 'real' woman, as real as Johnny Ray. But what does that do to the history of 1955? Is her disappearance at the end of the story any less 'historical' and any less believable than that of Burgess and Maclean? (What, in any case, could be less believable than that the head of anti-Soviet espionage in Britain should be a Soviet spy?)

At the end of the play, Plater confronts the questions. Cameron interviews George the Postman, who allows himself to be shown only with his back to the camera. The story of his finding of the diaries is very convincing. But when he's asked if he ever wrote a verse play called *Flight Into Madness*, which the diaries say he has, he's genuinely angry: 'Don't be bloody daft. Whoever heard of a postman writing plays?' Cameron sums up the contradictions. 'It is a tantalising story, leaving us with more questions than answers. Was Mr. Dvorak really organising the Philby cover-up from this quiet backwater? Did he dispose of his hosts when it became clear they knew too much? Did he throw away the incriminating diary on the still smouldering bonfire where it was preserved by a sudden shower of rain? Or was the whole thing an invention? Was the diary written as an imaginary piece of creative fiction for the literary club? If it comes to that, is it any business of television to be concerning itself with truth in the first place? And is there such a thing as truth?'

Cameron ends by affirming official history. 'There are matters of public record that we can be certain about. We know that on the evening of November 7th 1955, the Home Secretary denied that Philby was the third man. We know that on the same evening Miss Ruby Murray appeared on the Royal Command Performance. As did Mr. Johnny Ray. But not, mercifully and understandably, The Singing Dogs.'

By this time, though, Plater has completely dislocated our sense of what is normal. He's destroyed the conventional boundaries between fact and fiction, documentary and drama, the serious and the trivial, the public and the personal. And he's done so, not to mystify and confuse, or fool us into thinking that we're seeing something that's 'true', but to put us in a position where we can look more clearly, more questioningly, more critically – and feel confident in our own irreverence.

In the last scene of the play, Cameron shows us a photograph of a headstone in a graveyard. On it is the name of Emily Garton, the woman who, according to the diaries, had embroidered Wordsworth. And beneath the name is an inscription: 'She wandered lonely as a cloud . . .' 'Well – don't we all?' asks Cameron – and the camera zooms out over the river and towards the estuary as we hear Johnny Ray singing 'The Little White Cloud That Cried'.

'There are all kinds of boundaries and frontiers . . . between different types of programme,' says Plater. 'It's very difficult to span them . . . and it's very exciting when they're spanned.'[27]

They're spanned in *The Blacktoft Diaries*: which is why, to me, it's one of Plater's most exciting plays.

8

Towards the end of *Seventeen Per Cent Said Push Off*, Mr Milner, the father of the working-class family, surprises the post-graduate student, Gavin, by referring to 'working-class solidarity against the bourgeoisie'. 'I didn't know you were a political man,' says Gavin, and Mr Milner says, no, he's not any more, although they used to talk a lot in the army about 'what sort of world we'd make' after the war.

They got very near to it, he says, but there were all the city gents in their big boots waiting to kick it all to bits. After a time you get tired – too many night shifts.

'And don't you think it'll ever change?' asks Gavin; and Mr Milner replies, 'Maybe change round the edges a bit, but your people won't relinquish their power, our people won't take it, your people'll go on saying we can have six per cent rises and we'll ask for fifteen and we'll settle for . . . Well,' he adds, 'I've got my telly. Got my football match and my pint of beer . . . best bitter . . . the opium of the masses. That's not bad, is it?' He thinks for a moment. 'We know the terms,' he says. 'We know the rules. But we've never fought the war.' 'Why?' asks Gavin, and Mr Milner replies, 'Scared of losing. Or scared of winning. Not sure which.'

Alan Plater's attitude to Mr Milner is complex. He's not in any way patronising, doesn't take up the conventional intellectual position that the working classes are living narrow, deprived lives and have sold out by settling for telly, football and beer. He shows Mr Milner as intelligent, aware – 'We know the rules.' Mr Milner's wry reference to 'the opium of the masses' is full of consciousness. Milner knows that in one sense it's true, that he *has* settled for less; but he also knows that that's how people like Gavin see him and that the way they see him isn't true. And when Plater puts into his mouth the sentence 'That's not bad, is it?' Plater knows that's true as well. Television, the football match, best bitter – they're all enjoyments that Alan Plater shares with Mr Milner. He doesn't regard himself as living a more richly cultured life because he's involved with 'drama'. 'The experience we define as "high drama" may take place on a football field, in a boxing ring, in a concert-hall, in a pub on singalong night, or between the couple at the next table in a restaurant when we all pretend not to listen though we're listening like hell to every hostile syllable.'[28] Drama's part of the 'life of the streets' – part of an experience that both he and Mr Milner share.

Plater, like Mr Milner, enjoys the telly. But it's this very enjoyment – his commitment to making enjoyment – that's led him, as a writer, not to be scared of 'winning the war'. Working in an industry which tends to impose its own limitations, Plater has seen the limitations as boundaries that can be extended. He's extended them by working at his job, mastering it, and then using his mastery to create new possibilities.

But the new possibilities haven't been created out of any spirit of self-indulgence. Alan Plater has always remained aware of Mr Milner. It's for the millions of Mr and Mrs Milners that he's making entertainment – for them and about them. And precisely because he knows that the Milners aren't the stupefied masses that exist in the minds of the makers of packaged telly, he can write using all his own intelligence, wit and ingenuity, dare to create new forms, not be afraid to ask hard questions.

In his *Theatre Quarterly* essay he writes, 'I don't want to sound too evangelical about it, but if I have a theatrical mission, it is to synthesize the best of our two theatrical traditions: to write plays of serious central intent, but to achieve the intention using as much as possible of the energy, the emotional charge, the earthy reality, the vulgarity and grace of the music-hall.'[29]

Alan Plater's work for television has demonstrated that it's possible to write programmes of 'serious central intent' while using and extending the language of popular TV entertainment.

He's used that language both to call attention to the enforced poverty and to celebrate the richness of the lives of the people he's writing for. And in doing so he's moved far beyond the bounds of 'Television Drama'.

'Increasingly', he writes, 'I lean to the concept that comedy is king, because the hero has to go on living with the reality of tomorrow.'[30] To go on living with it – but also, like Alan Plater himself, to set about changing it.

Alan Plater recognises the reality – he looks at it from a distance of three feet. And demonstrates the possibility of change.

Appendix

Selected television plays transmitted

SS = Softly, Softly (followed by series and episode)

1963–5	*Z-Cars* (18 episodes)	BBC
8.3.64	*Ted's Cathedral*	BBC
11.5.66	*The Short Cut* (*SS*/1/19)	BBC-1
8.6.66	*Best Out of Three* (*SS*/1/23)	BBC-1
30.11.66	*Sleeping Dogs* (*SS*/1/31)	BBC-1
18.1.67	*James McNeil, Aged 23* (*SS*/2/38)	BBC-1
8.3.67	*The Same the Whole World Over* (*SS*/2/45)	BBC-1
5.4.67	*A Piece of Waste Ground* (*SS*/2/49)	BBC-1
18.10.67	*Material Evidence* (*SS*/3/3)	BBC-1
29.11.67	*The Mind of the Beholder* (*SS*/3/8)	BBC-1
20.12.67	*Who's Mr. Smith?* (*SS*/3/11)	BBC-1
1.1.68	*Murphy's Law* (episode 1 of trilogy *To See How Far It Is*)	BBC-2 *Theatre 625*
8.1.68	*The Curse of the Donkins* (episode 2)	BBC-2 *Theatre 625*
15.1.68	*To See How Far It Is* (episode 3)	BBC-2 *Theatre 625*
14.3.68	*If I Can Help Somebody* (*SS*/3/23)	BBC-1
17.7.69	*The Whips Are Out* (episode 17 of *The First Lady*, 2nd series)	BBC-1
22.10.69	*Close the Coalhouse Door* (based on a story by Sid Chaplin)	BBC-1 *Wednesday Play*
13.11.69	*Write Off* (*SS*/5/10)	BBC-1
15.1.70	*Standing Orders* (*SS* Task Force)	BBC-1
28.1.70	*Rest in Peace, Uncle Fred*	BBC-1 *Wednesday Play*
22.5.72	*Seventeen Per Cent Said Push Off*	ATV *Playhouse*
19.10.72	*Tonight We Meet Arthur Pendlebury*	BBC-2 *Thirty-Minute Theatre*

26.12.72	*The Reluctant Juggler* (episode 6 of *The Edwardians*)	BBC-2
10.10.73	*No Life for a Woman* (*SS Task Force/5/5*)	BBC-1
18.11.73	*Oranges and Lemons/Brotherly Love*	London Weekend
2.1.74	*Trouble Maker* (*SS Task Force/5/16*)	BBC-1
6.1.74	*The Needle Match* (episode 3 of *Sporting Scenes*)	BBC-2
24.1.74	*The Land of Green Ginger*	BBC-1 *Play for Today*
10.9.75	*Protection* (*SS Task Force/7/3*)	BBC-1
21.11.75	*The Driver's Tale* (episode 1 of *Trinity Tales*)	BBC–2
28.11.75	*The Fryer's Tale* (*Trinity Tales* 2)	BBC-2
1.12.75	*Willow Cabins*	Yorkshire
5.12.75	*The Judy's Tale* (*Trinity Tales* 3)	BBC-2
12.12.75	*The Joiner's Tale* (*Trinity Tales* 4)	BBC-2
19.12.75	*The Wife of Batley's Tale* (*Trinity Tales* 5)	BBC-2
26.12.75	*The Man of Law's Tale* (*Trinity Tales* 6)	BBC-2
10.11.76	*At Risk* (*SS Task Force/8/10*)	BBC-1
1.5.77	*Short Back and Sides*	Yorkshire
15.6.77	*Rich Is Best* (episode 1 of *Middlemen*)	BBC-1
22.6.77	*A Little Bit of Heaven* (*Middlemen* 2)	BBC-1
29.6.77	*A Young Lady from Gloucester* (*Middlemen* 3)	BBC-1
6.7.77	*A Bag of Mixed Nuts* (*Middlemen* 4)	BBC-1
13.7.77	*Read Any Good Books Lately?* (*Middlemen* 5)	BBC-1
20.7.77	*Fresh Fields and Slightly Soiled Pastures* (*Middlemen* 6)	BBC-1

Plays published

(For Plater's published TV plays, see Appendix 1.)
The Mating Season, in: *Worth a Hearing: A Collection of Radio Plays*, ed. Alfred Bradley, London: Blackie, 1967
Close the Coalhouse Door, London: Methuen, 1968
Excursions; And a Little Love Besides, in: *You and Me: Four Plays*, ed. Alfred Bradley, London: Blackie, 1973

Films scripted

1970   *The Virgin and the Gypsy*
1975   *Juggernaut* (additional dialogue)
1976   *All Things Bright and Beautiful*
        It Shouldn't Happen to a Vet

Selected radio plays transmitted

1961   *The Smokeless Zone*
        Counting the Legs
1962   *The Mating Season*
        The Rainbow Machine
1963   *The Seventh Day of Arthur*
1966   *Excursions*
1967   *The What on the Landing?*
1970   *Fred*
1973   *The Slow Stain*
1976   *5 Days in '55* (*The Gilberdyke Diaries*)

Criticism by and about Alan Plater

(For some of Plater's articles, see Select Bibliography. Note particularly *TQ*, 7, 25 for a listing of work in various media.)
Yorick Blumenfeld, 'The London Show', *Atlantic*, Boston, August 1969
Peter Fiddick, 'Trinity Collage', *Guardian*, December 1975
Alan Plater, 'What's Going On Behind the Coalhouse Door', *The Sunday Times*, 9 February 1969
    'One Step Forward, Two Steps Back', *New Statesman*, 3 November 1972
    'Views', *The Listener*, 29 November 1973
John Russell Taylor, 'British Dramatists: The New Arrivals', *Plays and Players*, January 1971
    The Second Wave: British Drama for the Seventies, London: Methuen, 1971, pp. 181–6

7   Dennis Potter

PHILIP PURSER

DENNIS POTTER'S TITLES are meticulously chosen even when they're filched from popular songs, but none gives such a clue to the ruling passion of his work as the one he picked for a now forgotten – indeed, lost – little play of 1966, *Emergency Ward 9*. It was, obviously, set in hospital, which was a recent experience of Potter's, and one unfortunately to be repeated many times, but the theme is not noticeably derived from personal suffering, nor in fact much concerned with suffering at all. It's a slight comedy of attitudes between patients in the ward, one unruly and working class, one prim and middle class, one black. The point is that Potter seemed deliberately to be adapting the formula of the popular hospital soap operas of the day, and was quite certainly echoing – down to the way it was universally misread – the name of the most popular of all. *Emergency – Ward 10* was the first twice-weekly serial on British television, running from 1957 to 1967.[1] Though it was supposed to roam over all the departments of a big general hospital, with Ward 10 a purely representative location for the drama and urgency invoiced in the title, its devotees steadfastly ignored the dash whenever they talked about their favourite programme, thereby transforming it into the annals of a mythical 'emergency ward' where all the hopes, disasters, sunshine and tears of hospital life could be handily concentrated. In this respect they displayed a better understanding of the nature of soap opera than the programme-makers, and Potter followed suit. The play affirmed his allegiance to television as the true national theatre and common culture of the people. That was the audience *he* wanted to reach, though it was to be many years before he achieved anything like mass popularity in terms of ratings. He is, or at least was until 1979, extraordinarily indifferent to the stage adaptations he occasionally made from his television originals, or to the two or three screen plays he has written to commission;[2] while frequently and publicly despairing

of the use made of television both at the sending and the receiving ends, he remains its ardent champion.

Dennis Christopher George Potter was born in 1935 in the
village of Berry Hill in the Forest of Dean, the son of a coalminer.
Every writer is the product of his upbringing, but here time and
place and community conspired together with unusual attention
to detail. A working-class background (or working-class pass-
port, as Alan Brien has termed it) was almost a literary requisite in
the early sixties, in the wake of Alan Sillitoe and Shelagh Delaney
and *Billy Liar*, and the best qualification of all was a dad out of the
pits. So many gnarled specimens were depicted in films and
plays, failing to understand their soft, déclassé sons, that by the
end of the decade the funny television show *Monty Python's
Flying Circus* could mount an inversion of the formula in which
the father, now a scarred old author, berated the son for opting
for the security of a well-paid job at the coalface. 'Civic luncheons, lad? Ah've eaten more civic luncheons than tha've had
hot dinners.' It is a small but impressive indication of the vigour of
Potter's dialogue and characterisation that *Lay Down Your Arms*
(1970) went out only a few weeks later containing the straightforward version (coalminer father, scholarship boy) and still
managed to give the scene freshness and love. Potter's
relationship with his father, whom he had also 'put' into
Stand Up, Nigel Barton, as finely played by Jack Woolgar, was
exceptionally close, and the strains of finding himself drawn
into a world far removed from his home and family were very
real.

The Forest of Dean is, or was in Dennis Potter's formative
years, a peculiarly remote, inward-turned corner of England.
'Enclosed, tight, backward' were his own adjectives I quoted in a
magazine profile.[3] Until he left home he had never seen a flush
toilet or a washbasin with running water. The slops were thrown
on to the vegetable patch as fertiliser. There were neighbours
who had never been out of the Forest in their lives. And although
the working population was an industrial one, the scenery was as
rural as that of Hardy's Wessex. Directly or indirectly it is the
setting for a great deal of his invention. When Potter was fourteen the family moved to London, staying with relatives in Hammersmith. After two and a half years Potter's father tired of odd
jobs in the building trade and went back to the Forest and the
mines; but Dennis, doing well at St Clement Dane's Grammar

School, stayed on. Hammersmith, especially Hammersmith Bridge, is another favourite location.

He won a place at New College, Oxford and after two years' national service which we will consider when they surface in dramatic form went up to read Philosophy, Politics and Economics. Brought up in a solidly Labour, chapel-going community he threw himself into left-wing politics but also acted, debated and edited *Isis*. In his third year he wrote his first book, *The Glittering Coffin*, a swipe at Oxford, the class system and metropolitan culture in the mood of the 'angry young men' of the day. Like many an undergraduate shocker, it was written with one eye on Fleet Street and the hope of attracting an offer, as a notorious young writer, from one of the papers. This came to pass for Potter but not immediately, for *The Glittering Coffin* was not published until 1962 and in the meantime he had been accepted as a BBC general trainee, the one lucky spermatozoon from the hundreds of arts graduates who used to apply every year at this time. Potter worked on *Panorama* and according to popular legend wrote his first-ever lines of dialogue when for an early book programme he furnished the little dramatised excerpts from novels which were then thought to be the only way of making literature visual.

His most important assignment, though, was to work with the film-maker Denis Mitchell,[4] under whose supervision Potter wrote and directed a documentary called *Between Two Rivers* (1960) about his beloved Forest of Dean and the threat to its particularity posed by television and the Light Programme and advertising and all the other manifestations of a popular, generalised culture. The angry tone of the commentary caused most comment, anger still being a quality eagerly sought in young men. I quote from my review in the old *News Chronicle*,[5] not with any great satisfaction but because it is to hand and because I spotted the fact that Potter was to some extent putting it on.

He hates the idea of this once-proud, distinctive mining area becoming submerged in a colourless, supermarket England. He hates status-seeking, hidden persuasion, the acquisitive urge, publicists, pop music and pop TV. He likes brass bands, pubs, working men's clubs, methodist chapels, independence and that most comforting of concepts, 'community'.

Most young men of sensibility could produce a similar reaction, and in his vehemence Mr. Potter came close to over-stating his case. People and places that on his own admission had oppressed and confined him only three or four years earlier were now bathed in golden approval. Though it was a shame the old pub was to be modernised, I must say it was pretty bleak as it stood.

Potter's relationship to at least two of the bogeys on that list (television and popular music) must have been ambivalent even then. Certainly he went over the same ground in a much less strident and more tolerant – indeed, often gentle – voice in a monograph called *The Changing Forest* (1962) for a Secker & Warburg series to the brief of 'Britain Alive'. Meanwhile *Between Two Rivers* had failed to please his superiors at the BBC. Denis Mitchell took no more pupils. Dennis Potter, disillusioned with broadcasting and impatient of the political neutrality expected of broadcasters, went off to the *Daily Herald* as a leader-writer. The episode was an early demonstration of the Potter knack of generating controversy, but it may have left scars of a different – and graver – sort. He already felt guilty about the elitist education (as he called it) which separated him from his working-class compeers. The reactions of family and friends and neighbours to his film made him secretly afraid that he had patronised them, made use of them and, worst of all, pronounced upon them. In later years he would sometimes date his illness from this moment.

In November 1962 the BBC launched its satirical Saturday night *That Was The Week That Was*, which became first a national sensation, then a national institution. Potter and a *Herald* colleague, David Nathan, formed one of the writing partnerships that flocked to exercise their wits on the lovely new audience that was suddenly available, a bourgeoisie waiting to be affronted. By definition most of the material was pretty ephemeral, but a reminder of four or five Nathan–Potter contributions is preserved in print in a *TWTWTW* compilation.[6] Two of them are openly political: the Conservative Party had just issued a pamphlet tearing some Labour proposals out of context, so Nathan and Potter applied the same technique and same rhetoric to the Tory record; neater and more enduring, really, because it draws on a recurring human foible, is a sequence of remarks made about Clement Attlee by his political adversaries over the years, gradually warming from hostility to benign approval as Attlee passes out of power and into history. The item likeliest to be remembered, however, was called 'Mother's Day'.

What is a Mum?

A Mum lives with a Dad and 2.4 children in a rented house where the neighbours notice her washing on the line. A Mum relies upon secret ingredients and instant cake-mixes. She has kids with dirty teeth who regularly shout 'Don't forget the Fruit Gums, Mum.' A Mum is full of faith. She thinks every wash-day is a miracle. And since she adds the extra egg to everything except the bacon, she is probably constipated as well.

And so on. If wit was shit, as they say in Suffolk, tha'd be constipated, too, Dennis and David. But it was a neat enough concatenation of all the most grating assumptions aired in the TV commercials of the day, and with Mum impersonated by Rose Hill it seemed at the time to be a funny and scathing *aperçu*, as well as an early example of the obsession with the ruses of advertising which was to colour several of Dennis Potter's plays.

While covering a political progress by Hugh Gaitskell for the *Daily Herald*, Potter suddenly felt his knee lock as he was trailing along the street in the wake of the party. It was the first serious intimation of the mysterious illness, eventually diagnosed as psoriatic arthropathy, which was to beset him on and off – but increasingly on – for the next fifteen years. He would suffer intense skin irritation coupled with painful stiffening of the joints; his hands in particular were affected, in the end permanently. Treatment by various drugs brought some relief but distressing side-effects. Only the intervention of doctors who read of his plight and suggested, in 1977, a trial with a new drug, Razoxin, finally brought about a substantial and sustained improvement in his health.

One immediate consequence of his illness was that Potter had to be taken off his existing duties at the *Daily Herald*. The paper gave him the job which he wryly defined as the refuge of the sick and the crippled, that of television critic. Actually, morning-paper reviewing was quite a nervy task when a good deal of television was still live and there were few previews for the press. Some hundreds of words of judgement might have to be telephoned in by a deadline only five minutes after the show finished. Potter evidently enjoyed both the subject and the spontaneity demanded of him. Television could be 'dreary, repetitive, sordid, commercial and second-rate', he had written in *The Changing Forest*, and it was regrettable that this was so often what the folks chose to watch; but television was also the only unstuffy

medium capable of reaching everyone and independent of the
snobberies and superiorities of an educationally privileged
minority. To yell for the best in television and deride the worst
was an honourable calling; and what truer, less stuffy way of
doing it than by spilling out the hot reaction, without the opportunity to sit down and compose mandarin second thoughts?
Though after two years Potter took advantage of a period of
remission in his illness to pursue an old ambition to enter politics,
and never returned to a staff job on a newspaper, the instant
satisfactions of journalism would always attract him. He wrote a
personal column for his old paper – by now the *Sun* – in the
mid-sixties; he contributed book reviews to *The Times*, and
throughout most of the seventies acted as television critic first for
the *New Statesman*, then *The Sunday Times*.[7] Whether he applied to
these last tasks the whoopee-doo of extemporisation I don't
know, but he told me once that his measured book pieces for *The
Times* were sketched out only in note form and then ad-libbed
over the telephone to a patient Printing House Square copytaker.
By this time, it has to be added, his hands were irretrievably
injured by the illness; typing was out of the question, and dictation to a typist, judging by the fury it induced in the temporarily
crippled writer–hero of *Only Make Believe* (1973), did not suit him.
He had to master a new longhand with pen wedged in his fist,
and while it is unlikely that this necessity will have much
affected his dramatic works, his only published novel *Hide and
Seek* is written in such an obsessive prose that you can almost
see, through the print, the lined paper and crabbed racing
hand.

Potter stood as a Labour candidate in the 1964 General Election
that brought Labour back into power after thirteen years, but
against Derek Walker-Smith in the safe Tory seat of Hertfordshire
East a young and emotional tyro stood little chance. Potter found
the campaign exhausting and the baby-kissing and glad-handing
sickening. Politics were not for him. He now knew for certain that
what he wanted was to be a writer. Like most young journalists,
he had started a novel in his spare time. A friend, Roger Smith,
had become a story editor in BBC television drama. Why didn't
Dennis turn his plot into a television play instead? If accepted, it
would bring a much quicker return than slogging on to complete
the statutory seventy thousand words and then waiting the best
part of a year for publication. And, of course, it was in accord

with all his cultural ideals. Potter accepted the suggestion and with it a challenge that might have been framed for him.

The Confidence Course went out as a *Wednesday Play* in February 1965. The plot concerns a trio of smooth operators endeavouring to enrol a group of potential pupils into a personality class supposed to make the recipient happier, more successful and, obviously, more confident. They are defeated by a kind of Holy Fool among the aspirants who keeps breaking in with dissertations on such Potterish preoccupations as the advertisements in the London Underground and finally, by casting doubts on the list of attributes the Confidence Course claims to bring out, converts everyone back to the comfort of being unconfident. It seemed to me at the time to be a consummation rather too easily obtained, but, alas, nothing of the production survives. In the expressive and understandably aggrieved jargon of the National Film Archive, the recording has long since been 'junked'. Nor is it the only one. The tapes of *Message for Posterity* (1967) and *Angels Are So Few* have also been wiped. *Emergency Ward 9* belonged to a fad for half-hour studio plays on both BBC-2 and ITV (Rediffusion) around 1966–7 prompted partly by stinginess, partly by a kind of Pre-Raphaelite urge to get back to the roots of television drama as a live, compact, enclosed performance, and by definition has vanished into the great blue yonder. *Cinderella* was rejected at the script stage, though not without earning the author some of his customary publicity in the process.[8] *Shaggy Dog* (1968) I saw but have quite forgotten. Scripts, of course, exist, and in one or two cases I have consulted them to check points of detail; but Potter has written somewhere of the 'soup' of television, the non-stop swirl of sport and news and second-hand movies and idiot panel games from which every programme has to sing out or go under. In braver moments he has intimated that he likes his own work to be experienced in this context rather than in the isolation of the Steenbeck Room, so I propose to pay him the compliment of relying chiefly on what the good critic Maurice Richardson used to call the cauliflower-shaped taperecorder.

In his first fifteen years as a television dramatist Potter completed twenty-five single plays, of which all but *Cinderella* were produced, though another was famously never transmitted; two original six-part serials; and two serials and one single episode adapted from literature. Though many of them reveal recurring obsessions, and some of them even share a circumstance in the plot, to try and classify the single plays alone would require one of those complicated patterns of eccentric and partially overlapping circles – however recognisable the tone of voice may be. The nearest thing to a common factor is that most of the time Potter is dealing in what he has himself defined as 'interior drama'.

I'm much more concerned with interior drama than with external realities. Television is equipped to have an interior language. Certainly one of the strands in TV drama is that of the interiorising process, the concern with people's fantasies and feelings about the shape of their lives, and about themselves. It seems very important to me that television should be concerned with that, because the people watching it are watching it in a very peculiar way, with all their barriers down. You've got a huge audience on the one hand, and yet it's also a series of very informal, very tiny audiences, multiplied X times, and the interior drama, if you like to call it such, can work in those conditions almost better than anything.

This pronouncement comes from Paul Madden's useful interview with Dennis Potter in the duplicated programme to the season of British Television Drama held at the National Film Theatre in October 1976. Potter was represented by his two Nigel Barton plays from late 1965 and, pausing only to forgive him for 'interiorising', we might as well deal with them at this point. Both are autobiographical, though Potter was at pains in the same Madden interview to stress that he likes using only the external circumstances of his own life. The hero's hopes, fears, fantasies and revulsions are not necessarily his own. The autobiographical element is a framework for the play rather than the play itself. *Vote, Vote, Vote for Nigel Barton* was written first, as an angry lampoon on politics inspired by his Hertfordshire candidature but owing something to *TWTWTW* and his two years as a critic. Having been on the receiving end of so much television drama, he told Madden, he was anxious not to furnish merely more of the same when he changed roles. He wanted to use a brisker narrative style and, in particular, experiment with direct address to the audience. A political subject with everyone making speeches was obviously suitable. It is interesting to note how in *Pennies from Heaven* thirteen years later Potter – or his director then, Piers Haggard – used the same, if by now familiar, device of opening on the politician as if he is making a speech direct to camera and only pulling back after a moment to relocate him within the geography of the play.

Stand Up, Nigel Barton, which fortuitously went out first, is the better play in Potter's own opinion. Certainly his command of what is soon to become the identifiable Potter style is surer, though there is also an early warning, in an Oxford party scene populated by vapid upper-class undergraduates, of the rather silly and curiously anachronistic caricatures Potter sometimes draws instead of characters. The action flicks to and fro between present and remembered time to follow Nigel through the same convulsive process that heaved his creator from miner's cottage to dreaming spires, only instead of making a television film Nigel takes part in one. He watches it with his family at home. His father sweeps out in disgust. Nigel catches him up and they head for the pub together, but the last scene direction in the published script has father and son walking away from the camera 'separated by a mutual anxiety'.[9]

The most original device in *Stand Up* is to have all the children in the remembered classroom scenes, including Nigel himself, played by adult actors 'imitating childish manners and movements in a horribly precise style'. It is possible that Potter had seen an item in the current-affairs programme *Tonight* in which a number of adult contributors to a collection of memoirs called *John Bull's Schooldays* were sat at little school desks to discuss the book.[10] It was still a brilliant extension of the conceit to apply it to drama; Nigel is one minute able to address the viewers directly with the hindsight of the man and lapse the next into the boy taking the first steps along the road to the scholarship that is to distance him from his fellows. And a sharp, unexpected reminder of the nature of childhood comes from seeing actors slipping into the giggles, snivels, innocences, treacheries and capricious alliances of infancy. Fourteen years later Potter expanded the novelty into the whole device of his little masterpiece *Blue Remembered Hills*.

The remaining play written to the autobiographical convention is *Lay Down Your Arms* (1970), which drew on Potter's two years' national service between school and Oxford. In company with Michael Frayn and other misfits he was sent on one of the army's celebrated crash language courses which had been instituted to provide an ample supply of interpreters should the Cold War produce some warmer skirmishes, and ended up as a Russian-language clerk in the War Office. What the play makes of this employment is a good illustration of the liberties Potter feels free to take with his own – or anyone else's – history. He deferred the action a year or two in order to have it taking place during the Suez crisis, a time of righteous indignation for all left-wing writers, added a visit by the Moscow Dynamo football team for good measure and converted the bunch of officers with whom his hero had to work into a collection of upper-class numskulls as caricatured as anyone in *Nigel Barton*.

One tiny bit of business remains sharply in my mind after more than ten years: the ritual of the morning coffee or afternoon tea, with the clerk carrying a tray of mugs to each officer in turn for the drill of being offered first the sugar and then the use of the communal stirrer. Obviously it was an even more vivid memory to Potter, perhaps because it encapsulated a distinction between officers and other ranks which seemed especially fatuous and especially humiliating when everyone was in civilian clothes. Potter uses it in drawn-out detail, twice if not three times, as a piece of the apparatus of life he reproduces very carefully while whizzing off in all directions for the imaginative content of his plays. Here, he never quite settles whether to go for a serious diatribe (Suez), a farcical climax (his hero trapped by his fantasies into impersonating the Dynamo goalkeeper) or a happy ending (anxious quest for a girl friend succeeding at last). The production was nevertheless an entertaining instance of what might be called the virtues of transience in television drama, which is something I want to expand on later but brutally simplify just now to mean that at the particular season it went out, the play's evocation of another particular season seemed very apt. Though it wasn't the first time Potter had taken his title from a popular song and used the same song on the sound-track, it was, until *Pennies from Heaven*, the only occasion on which the song was at all contemporaneous with the events of the play, and belted out by Anne Shelton in the authentic mid-fifties version it carried all sorts of resonances – not quite nostalgia, more than simple re-membrance – besides furnishing an ironic chorus to the martial and amatory strands of the story. Potter and the director, Christopher Morahan, also demonstrated a casual mastery of the narrative devices which Potter now commanded: newsreel clips, overlapping voices, flashbacks, a little play within the play and that familiar scene between coalminer father and grammar-school son which even Monty Python hadn't been able to blight.

A natural companion piece to *Lay Down Your Arms*, if more

sombre in tone, is *Traitor* (1971). Potter's renegade British agent self-exiled in Moscow has some antecedents in common with Kim Philby, including a responsibility for the betrayal and death of former allies, but biography is no more Potter's concern here than self-revelation is in his autobiographical pieces or Christology in *Son of Man*. It is an attempt to bring alive as 'Adrian Harris' one kind of person who might have behaved as Philby did and offer an explanation of why he did so. The proposition of the play is beautifully explicit, with a party of English correspondents climbing flight after flight of stairs to their quarry's bleak Moscow flat, speculating the while as to why he has invited them and what they will hear. And notice again this curious whiff of impermanence about the production (director, Alan Bridges), as if it were deliberately geared to transmission at this very conjunction of the planets on 14 October 1971. Instead of one of the heavyweight actors who might have been expected, Bridges cast as Harris John le Mesurier, an actor identified not merely with comedy but with the immensely popular *Dad's Army*, then in the third year of a run which lasted from 1969 to 1978. By being such a familiar of the screen, I noted at the time, he lent proceedings 'a curious and rather valuable quality of being about someone whose picture really was on the front pages day after day, a while ago now'.[11]

Potter's explanation of Harris's behaviour is revealed by the characteristic injection of flashbacks and lightning interior images as he answered his visitors: childhood under the shadow of an eminent archaeologist father, the one direct borrowing from Philby's background; schooldays transposed from the village primary of Potter's experience to a posh prep school but with Authority stamping down even more harshly on childish individuality and infirmity, e.g. the young Adrian viciously persecuted for stuttering over a line from Blake; the upper-class mill grinding on through public school and Oxbridge to the Foreign Office, while in newsreel clips the poor languished in slums and the unemployed marched.

'Traitor?' muses the exile in his Moscow flat, ' – to my class, yes. Not to my country, not to England.' For his England is the England of Constable landscapes and, ironically, the romantic socialist visions of the very poet for whom he had been made to suffer in the classroom. His hatred is of his upbringing, not his fellow countrymen, but by a further irony it is his upbringing which had prevented him from ever knowing his fellow country-men. Only to an ex-public schoolboy in the party of journalists, significantly, can he really make himself understood. If less glib and more sophisticated an explanation than I have perhaps made it sound, in retrospect it is still not strong enough to support the disconcerting durability of a Philby's or an Adrian Harris's convictions. Not for the first time, the play itself seemed less persuasive than the glittering extemporisation on patriotism and treason which Potter delivered on *Late Night Line-Up* afterwards. Who was it that, in praising Shaw's prefaces, wondered why he bothered to append those silly little plays?

Potter's own patriotism is intense and localised. He did not go abroad for the first time until well past forty. Even to venture out of England for the 1977 Edinburgh TV Festival was an ordeal, he told the delegates. His England is the Forest of Dean, Hammersmith Bridge and a fervent old-fashioned socialism rooted in chapel and pit. His scorn for the superficial, flag-waving, who-won-the-war-then patriotism is correspondingly fierce. But so is a distrust of foreigners and foreign influence which can only be described as xenophobic. When these two impulses coincide, as they did in the thoroughly bad and best forgotten *The Bonegrinder* (1968), it is difficult not to suspect that it is Dennis Potter himself, like one of his Puritans who protest too vehemently at filth and unchastity, who is secretly and ashamedly the Little Englander.

Traitor slides us towards the plots which Potter has acquired from legend or observation rather than from his own depths, and which therefore tend to take place a little less inside the head. In this early-to-middle period, *Alice* (1965) is a sympathetic study of Lewis Carroll, *Where the Buffalo Roam* (1966) a lurid parable about a youth with a Wild West fixation, *Message for Posterity* (1967) the clash of an indubitably Churchillian elder statesman with the doughty old painter who has come to do his portrait. The most interesting, on several counts, is *A Beast with Two Backs* (1968), which Potter took from a Forest of Dean story he had perhaps heard as a boy, of how the locals once attacked and killed a dancing bear which came wandering into the area. Potter gives the episode an authentic folk-tale atmosphere while rooting it firmly in period (the 1890s) and place. It is the only play of his set solely and specifically in the Forest and the first to be shot (by the veteran director Lionel Harris) wholly on film. But I suppose the piece which still dominates this particular batch is *Son of Man*

(1969). Potter wrote it at a bad time in his illness and a time of change in his political convictions. He was still a socialist, as he is today, but during the revolutionary fever of 1968 he happened to come into contact with some of the leading zealots and was suddenly disenchanted with the materialism of their aspirations. From childhood he had been susceptible to the intimidating face of religion – in an oft-quoted reminiscence, the Valley of the Shadow of Death was, for little Dennis, a sunken lane near his home down which he scuttled with his heart in his mouth. Now in his pain and his disillusionment, he saw the reverse side. He was overcome by – and wished to communicate – the enormity, as he put it, of Jesus's simple message of love.

It is difficult now to evaluate either that 1969 production or the script underlying it. The common reaction was respect rather than enthusiasm among those disposed to accept the play, resentment rather than indignation among those who disliked Potter's indifference to the divinity of Christ and concentration on the humanity of Jesus. The scene everyone remembers is Colin Blakeley, as a muscular, earthy, journeyman carpenter of a Messiah slapping the cross (in an early confrontation with the machinery of crucifixion) and lamenting the abuse of good timber which might have been turned into tables or chairs. Otherwise it seems to be one of the few Potter plays which somehow missed the tide when they were first done, and it will be seen clearly to be a HIT or a MISS only if it is one day re-produced, with different actors, a different attack and a different set of expectations.

Seven plays written between 1970 and 1976 are linked by filaments sometimes so fine that they seem only to be coincidences, the author nodding over his typewriter and inadvertently punching up the exact sentiment he gave another character in another world, sometimes so specific – in the production and casting if not in the text – that the connection is proclaimed. In *Only Make Believe* (1973), a play about the writing of a television play, and more particularly the use an author makes of his own experiences, the play in question is *Angels Are So Few* (1970), and clips from it are sewn into the action. As an extra nudge in the BBC production, the actor playing the author was Keith Barron, previously Nigel Barton in the Nigel Barton plays. The relationship between an author and his character is also the device of the novel *Hide and Seek*, which, published in 1976, is clearly an honorary member of this group. The relationship between an author and the actor – or in this case, actress – inspiring his play is one of the concerns of *Double Dare* (1976). The relationship between an actor and the parts he plays is the sour joke of *Follow the Yellow Brick Road* (1972).

Another regular obsession is voiced by Jack Black, the paranoid hero of that play and star of the dreadful TV commercials which punctuate its narrative. Despite the ignominy of being pushed into a pond by a Great Dane avid for Waggytail Din-Din or creeping downstairs in the dead of night to catch his wife at the Krispy Krunch biscuits, he professes to prefer the sunny world of the commercials, where families are happy and husbands and wives love each other, to the sordid home truths of the television drama of the day.

JACK. Filth – that's what *oozes* out of these plays. Filth of all kinds to mock virtue and to encourage doubts. They turn gold into hay, these people. Angels into whores. Love into a s-s-sticky slime – and Jesus Christ into an imbecile bleeding and screaming on a cross. God! I hate them. I bloody hate them, and their rotten, festering, suppurating scabs of ideas![12]

Potter is, of course, settling a few old scores. The language is the language of the most ignorant and least temperate among those who sought to 'clean up' television at this time. 'Filth' was almost an obligatory word. In just such terms had Potter's own plays been described: the angels turned into whores may be a sly reference to *Angels Are So Few*; the line about Jesus Christ is certainly an allusion to *Son of Man*. But Black is no yahoo. He is the hero of this play, the character with whom the audience is invited to identify. In common with other Potter characters, and for that matter with a substantial section of humanity, he is both attracted and repelled by sex; the panting excitement of the moment is instantly followed by a Swiftean disgust with the bodily plumbing involved; ideals of love and ethereal sensation wither before the readiness of others to feign, sell or otherwise betray their intimacies. In Jack Black's case the revulsion dates from the discovery, glimpsed in flashback, of his wife not at the Krispy Krunches but satisfying a rather different appetite, with a naked man. In *Double Dare*, by a complete reversal, the playwright's disgust is focussed on a commercial made by the actress he wants, in both senses, in which she was evidently willing to fake the most intimate caress available to a woman in order to sell a chocolate bar.

Illusion and reality, performance as against genuine behaviour, the transmutation of life into fiction, the consolations of
fantasy, the eternal struggle between the id and the ego – the
permutations are always ingenious, often funny and made absolutely plain by Potter's technique, now fully developed, of cutting instantaneously between present and past, between objective and subjective versions of events. But it has to be said that the
interplay of author and character or actor and role cannot help
seeming too easy, too private a metaphysical concern. It's one
that any writer is going to have his nose rubbed in; it is not one
that necessarily fascinates everyone else. Certainly the most exciting – if ultimately disappointing – of the seven plays, *Double
Dare*, toys with an altogether more heady set of speculations. The
actress playing the actress who is helping the dramatist overcome
a nasty case of Writer's Block also plays a call-girl visiting a
boorish, red-faced client in the same hotel. Cross-cutting between the room dominated by the typewriter and the room
dominated by a bed makes a familiar Potter connection between
sex and creativity. But what is this trick of the dramatist's of
anticipating what the girl is going to say? Why does he keep
quoting from Dante Gabriel Rossetti's *Sudden Light*?

> I have been here before,
>   But when or how I cannot tell:
> I know the grass beyond the door,
>   The sweet keen smell,
> The sighing sound, the lights around the shore.

It looks as if Potter is going to explore something he hasn't
explored before, the possibility much loved by J. B. Priestley and
of appeal to anyone who has experienced one of those sensations
of *déjà vu*, that time unfolds in loops and there may be a Second
Chance or at least some precognition of things to come. But he
settles for a variant on the solipsist dénouement he has already
used in *Schmoedipus* (1974): actress and whore are the same person and the red-faced client is the writer's *alter ego*; it's all in the
mind.

Schmoedipus is one of three or four plays in the group sharing
the same little circumstance of a young man who turns up on the
doorstep of a private house and claims acquaintance with someone within. In *Schmoedipus* it is the housewife, and he says he is
her long-lost son, which she is delighted to accept; but in the end

– if much more skilfully and compassionately than this bald summary can indicate – he is revealed to be a figment of her guilt and yearnings. In *Joe's Ark* (also 1974) the visitor is real and legitimate and means well, a friend from student days of the young girl in the house who is dying of cancer. In *Brimstone and Treacle*, recorded in 1976 but never transmitted, he is still real, if hardly human and certainly not legitimate. He is a genuine devil complete with cloven feet;[13] his pretence of having known the now brain-damaged, inanimate daughter of the house is a whopping lie; and he means very badly indeed. His sexual possession of her body – twice – is truly shocking. But it achieves what all her parents' wan efforts have failed to bring about: it jolts her back into sapient life. Potter is deliberately inverting the proposition of *Angels Are So Few* (which had a real angel) and the pieties of *Joe's Ark* to see if the other side has anything to offer. 'Why don't people accept evil when they are offered it?' the little demon wonders, genuinely puzzled.

Denied transmission by Alasdair Milne, then BBC Director of Programmes, *Brimstone and Treacle* became the focus of much agitation about censorship. The text was published first in the *New Review*, then as a paperback. The tape was shown on closed circuit at the 1977 Edinburgh Television Festival at which Potter was due to speak, and delegates were moved to send a telegram of protest to Milne. A stage version was produced shortly afterwards (October 1977) at the Studio Theatre, Sheffield; a further production was mounted at the Open Space, London, in February 1979. Alasdair Milne's grounds for his decision[14] were that the rape scenes would provoke such outrage that Potter's 'point of serious importance' would be prevented from getting across, and certainly it is not easy to watch an inanimate girl being unbuttoned – or in the Sheffield stage version, even more explicitly, having her plastic pants lowered – preparatory to being violated. But rationally it is the outcome of the assault which demands the bigger swallow of acceptance. Is Pattie's (the girl's) reclamation any less fortuitous a turn-up than one I still remember from a boy's magazine story and rejected as unlikely even at the age of ten, whereby the hero took his crippled friend for a ride on his motor-bike, they crashed, the friend's leg was injured, but at the hospital, gosh, they found that the new injury had corrected the old infirmity? After all, brain damage is usually held to be irreversible. I believe that Potter does make the miracle work, if only because a miracle is obviously admissible in any play that contains a paid-up supernatural being. Where, on reflection, he forfeits the more extravagant claims made for *Brimstone* after its banning is in what look suspiciously like stand-by elements in the plot. One is a set of National Front attitudes on the part of the girl's father, which he is made to re-examine by the visitor's acting, appropriately, as Devil's Advocate as he leads the conversation to the logical conclusion of concentration camp and gas chamber. The other is a tatty little injection of secret guilt into the father's concern for Pattie. The accident which turned her into a cabbage, it transpires, happened as she ran headlong from discovering Daddy in the arms of her best friend.

The poor bastard has enough sadness to bear, you might think, without this added burden. An interpretation, I suppose, is that the demon doesn't really exist – he is the phantom representation of Daddy's secret self just as the client is the playwright's secret evil self in *Double Dare* or the visitor in *Schmoedipus* is the heroine's phantom son – but to support this logically the paternal lusts should have been directed at Pattie herself, not at her friend. Potter has written of the fierce religious beliefs he absorbed in the revivalist chapels of his boyhood, the certainty that there was an eagle-eyed God noting every sin and programming due retribution. It looks here, as it looks in many of his works, as if he is still reluctant to accept that ill fortune can descend at random and needs at all costs to trace it back to one fatal lapse. In this respect he follows the author he presumably much admires and has twice adapted for television, Thomas Hardy. The trouble is that the visual shorthand he employs is always in danger of seeming too glib, too mechanical. These recurring scenes, flashes of memory, fleeting visions, are removed only in style from the ponderous flashbacks, invoiced by a rippling screen or echoing music, at which we smile in old Hollywood epics.

All television drama is collaborative, and Dennis Potter's connection with a comparatively small number of producers and directors has been vital to his developing confidence as a writer. No fewer than nine of his early plays were directed by Gareth Davies. Barry Davis, Alan Bridges and, more recently, Brian Gibson have each directed at least two plays. But the relationship with the producer, who in television acts as impresario, moving spirit and buffer between the author and everyone else, has evidently been even more important to Potter. Kenith Trodd, a friend from early political days, is a former story editor at the BBC (he worked on *Emergency Ward 9*). In 1968 with Tony Garnett, David Mercer and the late James MacTaggart he set up an independent production company, Kestrel Productions, for whom Potter wrote *Moonlight on the Highway* (1969). When Kestrel folded after a few years in the face of the programme companies' reluctance to share whatever credit was available with a subcontractor, Trodd became a straightforward freelance producer and the man who has nursed most of Potter's later works on to the air. Their maiden collaboration, *Moonlight on the Highway*, is not only an adroit and intriguing comedy but also Potter's first real raid on the mythology of popular music. His hero runs a society dedicated to the memory of Al Bowlly, the crooner killed in the London Blitz; Bowlly's songs swirl in and out of the action, his photographs are everywhere; and when the hero tries to charm a girl he's met, they are Bowlly's words he reaches for.

It was when, years later, he was brooding over an idea for a further play about Bowlly and found he was really more interested in the songs than in the singer, Potter has said in an interview,[15] that he began to hatch the work which has brought him a wider audience than anything else. *Pennies from Heaven* (1978), described as a play in 'Six Parts with Music', is in fact a serial *to* music, in a particular and quite novel sense of the words. Some sixty original recordings from the Bowlly era, including some by Bowlly himself, are woven into the story. Since Potter's hero, Arthur, is a sheet-music salesman of the period, this may seem perfectly natural, but the use to which Potter applies the songs is far from naturalistic. Without any hesitation or change of expression, characters step out of the play and into a rendition – I choose the word with care – of the number, miming to the original voice or voices and frequently adding a snappy little dance routine for good measure. Sometimes it is in enhancement of the mood of the scene, as in a Hollywood musical of the era, more often in ironic contrast to it. When, at the outset, Arthur's amorous advances are rebuffed by his pretty but cold and socially ambitious wife, he slips into 'The Clouds Will Soon Roll By'. Driving to Gloucester next morning, 'Prairie Moon' sets the optimistic mood of the journey and is also the song which he is carrying in his attaché case to push in the music shops along the way. Tracking down the pretty schoolteacher from the Forest of Dean (of course) who has taken his fancy, he croons 'Love Is the

6 *Bob Hoskins as Arthur and Cheryl Campbell as Eileen in Dennis Potter's six-part serial* Pennies from Heaven, *shown on BBC-1 in March–April 1978.*

Sweetest Thing'. Sometimes a song is used more than once or used in opposite contexts by different parties. In one really surrealist instance the mysterious 'Accordian Man' whom Arthur also meets on the road leads a workhouse ensemble of sleeping tramps through 'Serenade in the Night'. The overall proposition is that, however false, rose-hued and saccharine the songs may be, the dreams they peddle are as necessary to human survival as the promises of religion used to be; indeed, they represent what heaven once represented to the devout, a truer and more enduring reality than the mundane ups and downs of the day. 'Songs', someone says, 'are the same as pictures. They drop into your head and 'elp you to understand things.'

This gives Potter his ending, widely but gratuitously thought to be Brechtian, whereby Arthur – sentenced to death for a murder he did not commit – is dematerialised from the execution shed to turn up 'like a bad penny' by his loved one's side on Hammersmith Bridge. 'The song is ended but the melody lingers on,' he says as the title song plays and the credits roll. It is, of course, an old-established dramatic get-out, used by John Gay in the original *Beggar's Opera* long before Brecht's version, by Jean Anouilh in *L'Alouette* and by Elliot Silverstein in the movie *Cat Ballou*. The author shifts into the Great Key and the players step away from the scaffold. Why not? My difficulties with the 1978 production, blurred at the time, sharper in retrospect, in fact had little to do with any of the conventions, though I must say the injection of the songs did lose its novelty over six weeks and an increasing proportion of them seemed to be there because it was time for another break or they were favourites of Potter's which he hadn't otherwise been able to place, and in either case were cued in a rather literal and certainly non-contrapuntal way – 'Radio Times' for instance, by the happy accident of a railway traveller immersed in the *Radio Times*. But the real stumbling-block is that Potter's objective England of 1935 is not really any more substantial than the dream world of the songs. It is drawn not from life but from superficial associations with which the thirties are lumbered. It was a good decade for murder, so there are a couple of murders. Prostitution flourished. Tory M.P.s were corrupt hypocrites clinging to their military rank. Head waiters put jumped-up diners in their place. Buskers entertained the cinema queues. You get the feeling of time and place assembled from Great Western Railway posters, old Sunday papers and the novels of Patrick Hamilton.

The detective on Arthur's trail speaks in the accents of a floor-walker and coughs genteelly, *ahem*, behind his hand. His idea of justice is summed up in an exchange with Arthur's wife Joan, characteristic of Potter's humour but indicative, again, of this rather tuppence-coloured, derivative picture of a harsh bourgeois society. Arthur's best chance, the detective tells Joan, is to give himself up. 'What? And hang?' – 'He'll have a fair trial first.' As for Arthur himself, he is – or was in Bob Hoskins's performance on television – an extraordinary mixture of a few period cockney features with the truculent whine and interrogative interjections ('Innit?', 'Aren't I?') of the Greater Londoners heard complaining on the radio any morning today.

The most prominent consequence of the original production was a revival of interest in the songs it pressed into service, with Dennis Potter's name written large in the advertisements for two *Pennies from Heaven* albums of 'Original recordings of 40 years ago by the most famous Bands and Vocalists of those Dizzy Dancing Years!' Though the show was subsequently bought for the cinema, with a screenplay by Potter transposing the action to Chicago, it seemed to me to belong absolutely to the whizzing traffic of television which Potter half enjoys and half regrets: something to hop on to and enjoy at the time, without too much brooding.

An apparent anomaly of the close Potter–Trodd partnership is that while Potter has, as recently as 1976, gone on record as preferring electronic drama to film,[16] Kenith Trodd is a leading advocate of putting it all on to film and the compiler of the famous 'Trodd List' of the first three hundred British television dramas so to be made. His third production of a Potter script, the wry newspaper comedy *Paper Roses* (1971) for Granada, was filmed; so were *Double Dare*, at Ealing Studios, and the piece which followed it on the air a week or two later in 1976, *Where Adam Stood*. Potter took this from an episode in Edmund Gosse's *Father and Son* in which Gosse recalls the impact of Darwin's theory of evolution on his stern Victorian papa, a leading natural scientist but also – as a member of the Plymouth Brethren – a fundamentalist Christian committed to the literal truth of the Bible. His struggle to reconcile his beliefs with what he recognises to be irresistible scientific argument is played out against a small clash of wills with the boy Edmund as the two of them (the mother is dead) spend a holiday together in the West Country. It is on any estimation one of the half dozen best things Potter has done, and I would rate it as one of the two indisputable masterpieces: intellectually faultless, warm, tender and sly, with the boy unwittingly turning a prayer session intended to disabuse him of his desire for a model boat into a demonstration of the Darwinian principle of learning to adapt.

The director was Brian Gibson, who had moved across to drama from making scientific documentary films. In the summer of 1978, with Nat Crosby as cameraman, he shot the other outright masterpiece, *Blue Remembered Hills* (televised 1979), in which seven adult actors recreate the activities of seven seven- or eight-year-olds on a summer's day in the middle of the Second World War; and for the first time it is quite impossible to consider the author's contribution apart from the director's. There is a scene, for instance, in which the craven Willie, having been subdued in a fight by the bully Pete, is getting his own back by means of a resourcefully improvised scare-story on the dangers of eating dirty apples ('They drop them on Germany, the R.A.F. do, so the Germans will eat them and die . . .'). As Pete, who has been eating a dirty apple, begins to half-believe him and lose his top-dog assurance, Gibson has Willie idly scuffing along a fallen tree-trunk so as to put himself first on a level with the other boy, then above him. Or when the two girls in the gang are pushing their battered old pram through the grass and it gets stuck, Gibson lets them struggle with it instead of going to a retake, and instinctively the plain, devoted one does all the work while the pretty one looks on.

The convention of the play works perfectly to throw into sharp relief the differentness of childhood – the lightning shifts of mood and loyalty, the fantasies, the schemes, the cruelty, the remorse. Childhood innocence, Potter is saying, is really unspoiled original sin. It is also the only convention he uses here: none of the other devices from the armoury – no cross-cutting, no time-jumps, no flashbacks, no inner visions, no pop tunes (instead, a jaunty little march by Marc Wilkinson). The unities are observed. You are reminded of a painter who has discarded the stylistic tricks which brought him fame in favour of simplicity of line.

Perhaps the permanence of film makes a television dramatist aim a little more consciously for immortality. On celluloid his handiwork is more accessible, more easily consulted, more readily distributed, more of a property. It is going to be seen again and again in years to come. Certainly Potter has bemoaned the destruction of his lost plays, and it is not unreasonable to find in *Where Adam Stood* and *Blue Remembered Hills* signs of someone

7 Blue Remembered Hills by Dennis Potter, shown on BBC-1 as Play for Today on 30 January 1979, with Janine Duvitski (left) as Audrey and Helen Mirren as Angela – adults playing the part of children.

who, after years of revelling in the hit-and-miss, hurrying traffic of television, is now ready to leave a few monuments. But to infer too much would be to misunderstand what makes Dennis run. His impulse is not to store up, it is to splash out. All that output, all that journalism on top – he is the last of the big spenders. After the débâcle of *The Bonegrinder*, Potter devoted his column in the *Sun* to his compulsion to be a writer.[17] He knew he was destined either to be a laughable failure or a good writer – perhaps he dare not say 'a great writer'. He was interested in nothing between. All he knew was that he could only write by using himself, indeed using *up* himself. 'So when I die I want to be completely emptied and completely exhausted. Which means of course, that I am still rejoicing. Only a happy human being can write a sentence like that.'

Appendix

Television plays

24.2.65	*The Confidence Course*	BBC-1 *Wednesday Play*
13.10.65	*Alice*	BBC-1 *Wednesday Play*
–	*Cinderella*	–
8.12.65	*Stand Up, Nigel Barton*	BBC-1 *Wednesday Play*
15.12.65	*Vote, Vote, Vote for Nigel Barton*	BBC-1 *Wednesday Play*
11.4.66	*Emergency Ward 9*	BBC-2 *Thirty-Minute Theatre*
2.11.66	*Where the Buffalo Roam*	BBC-1 *Wednesday Play*
3.5.67	*Message for Posterity*	BBC-1 *Wednesday Play*
13.3.68	*The Bonegrinder*	Rediffusion
10.11.68	*Shaggy Dog*	LWT 'Company of Five'
20.11.68	*A Beast with Two Backs*	BBC-1 *Wednesday Play*
12.4.69	*Moonlight on the Highway*	LWT/Kestrel
16.4.69	*Son of Man*	BBC-1 *Wednesday Play*
23.5.70	*Lay Down Your Arms*	LWT/Kestrel
5.11.70	*Angels Are So Few*	BBC-1 *Play for Today*
13.6.71	*Paper Roses*	Granada
14.10.71	*Traitor*	BBC-1 *Play for Today*
23.11.71– 21.12.71	*Casanova* (6 parts)	BBC-2
4.7.72	*Follow the Yellow Brick Road*	BBC-2
12.2.73	*Only Make Believe*	BBC-1 *Play for Today*
21.11.73	*A Tragedy of Two Ambitions* (in series *Wessex Tales*)	BBC-2
14.2.74	*Joe's Ark*	BBC-1 *Play for Today*

20.6.74	*Schmoedipus*	BBC-1 *Play for Today*
1.3.75– 22.3.75	*Late Call* (4 parts)	BBC-2
6.4.76	*Double Dare*	BBC-1 *Play for Today*
–	*Brimstone and Treacle*	–
21.4.76	*Where Adam Stood*	BBC-2
22.1.78– 12.2.78	*The Mayor of Casterbridge* (4 parts)	BBC-2
7.3.78– 11.4.78	*Pennies from Heaven* (6 parts)	BBC-1
30.1.79	*Blue Remembered Hills*	BBC-1 *Play for Today*

Other television

3.6.60	*Between Two Rivers*	BBC	Documentary film
20.4.69	*'Son of Man' Reviewed*	BBC-1	Discussion programme with the author and a number of clerics, critics and laymen
14.10.71	*Late Night Line-Up*	BBC-2	Interview with Potter on *Traitor*, transmitted earlier same evening, but turning into an extemporised monologue
13.2.77	*Anno Domini*	BBC-1	Potter interviewed by Colin Morris on his religious beliefs
11.2.78	*South Bank Show: Man of Television*	LWT	Potter assessed and interviewed by Melvyn Bragg, with excerpts from his work

Publications

The Glittering Coffin, London: Gollancz, 1962
The Changing Forest, London: Secker & Warburg, 1962
Hide and Seek, London: André Deutsch/Quartet, 1976

Published texts

(For Potter's published TV plays, see Appendix 1.)
That Was the Week That Was, ed. D. Frost and N. Sherrin, London: W. H. Allen, 1963

Journalism

Too extensive to list, but for an encapsulation of Potter's attitude to television see his review (*The Times*, 15 March 1973) of Milton Shulman's

The Least Worst Television in the World, published by Barrie & Jenkins (London). For a representative piece of television criticism see his extended review of *Holocaust* in *The Sunday Times*, 10 September 1978. An extract may be more easily located in *Encounter* for December 1978, pp. 16–17.

Selected interviews with Potter, profiles, critical assessments

Philip Purser, *Daily Telegraph Magazine*, 2 April 1969

T. C. Worsley, *Television: The Ephemeral Art*, London: Alan Ross, 1970 (includes short review of *Stand Up, Nigel Barton* and extended criticism of *Message for Posterity*)

Paul Madden, interview in *Complete Programme Notes for a Season of British Television Drama 1959–1973, Held at the National Film Theatre, 11th–24th October 1976*, London: British Film Institute, 1976

Joan Bakewell, *The Sunday Times Magazine*, 14 November 1976

Jeremy Bugler, *The Listener*, 2 December 1976. (Potter's aims as a critic, together with those of a number of other practitioners)

Ray Connolly, *Evening Standard*, 21 March 1978

MARTIN BANHAM

JEREMY SANDFORD'S TWO broadcast plays for television, *Cathy Come Home*[1] (shown as a BBC-1 *Wednesday Play* on 16 November 1966 and subsequently) and *Edna the Inebriate Woman*[2] (BBC-1 *Play for Today*, 21 October 1971 and subsequently), are established as classics of television drama. *Cathy Come Home* is probably the best-known piece of contemporary TV drama, and its heroine's name has become a synonym for the homeless and underprivileged in British society. Although Sandford is widely known only for these two pieces, his work for television should be seen in the larger context of extensive writing for radio, newspapers, journals and the stage, and scripts (at the time of writing completed but not produced) for two further television or film pieces. These are *Smiling David*[3] (the story of David Oluwale, a vagrant who died in Leeds in 1969) and *Till the End of the Plums*.[4] Supporting and informing the two famous TV pieces and the other scripts are Sandford's documentary-style books including *Down and Out in Britain*,[5] *Cathy Come Home* (as a novel),[6] *Prostitutes*,[7] *Gypsies*,[8] *In Search of the Magic Mushroom*[9] and others. It is important to be aware of the range and concern of the total body of Sandford's writing in order to explain the apparent oddity of a writer whose work has attracted so much praise and attention being represented by only two televised plays in twelve years. It is also helpful to be aware of the considerable cross-fertilisation between the various forms of writing that Sandford has employed. Thus *Down and Out in Britain* is a parallel text to *Edna the Inebriate Woman*, containing specific descriptions and general or complementary material that informs one or the other piece. The novel of *Cathy Come Home*, with its appendixes, is a necessary companion to the play. But, despite an enviable reputation for innovative and important writing, the fact remains, as Sandford has himself written, that 'I have found it hard to persuade those who control the media to present my work.'[10] He instances the 'two and a half years of rejection' before *Cathy* was finally produced; and similar problems seem to have beset *Edna*, some of which are discussed from a producer's angle by Irene Shubik in her book *Play for Today*.[11] In the *Theatre Quarterly* article of 1973 quoted above Sandford is optimistic about *Smiling David* and *Till the End of the Plums* going into production 'this summer'. Neither of these important pieces has yet been produced on television. In this essay, in addition to discussing *Cathy* and *Edna*, brief reference will be made to the unproduced work, an assessment of which contributes to the general debate concerning the role of 'social epics' (Sandford's term) on television and the attitude of the broadcasting organisations and producing companies towards such work.

It is clear that Jeremy Sandford, as an individual, is deeply concerned about aspects of our society and anxious to urge us to action to deal with the plight of the unfortunate, the misunderstood, the ignored. It is outside our immediate scope to speculate on the cause for Sandford's overwhelming concern with the outcasts of society; it is sufficient to say that he is clearly a person of compassion and a writer who sees and seizes the opportunity of using his craft to urge the same compassion in others. In *Down and Out in Britain* he writes, 'our State is needlessly cruel'[12] and in the same book asserts, 'Certainly my play *Cathy* was about Britain's intolerable housing lists. But it was about other things too, more important things. It was about compassion and it was about that curious scheme of values which results in local authorities turning people out of "inadequate" accommodation which in other countries would have at any rate kept them together.'[13] Writers, Sandford offers, can have no higher ambition than to be Shelley's unacknowledged legislators of mankind, each doing 'what he is best at in trying to bring about the just society'.[14] Elsewhere Sandford has been happy to describe himself as a campaigning journalist, and it is evident that in the bulk of his work Sandford complements the writer's appeal to our senses with the legislator's eye for practical action. It is worth noting, though, that in an interview in late 1978 Sandford said, 'I am becoming more interested in spiritual enlightenment as opposed to social engineering as a solution to the problems of this world.'[15] It is not possible, of course, to anticipate in any detail the future direction of Sandford's work (though he has expressed the view that 'the position of the blacks in Britain should be brought into the forefront of public consciousness')[16] but as an important section of Sandford's completed work still remains to be given public viewing it is perhaps more immediately useful to concentrate our attention on encouraging the production of that before speculating on any future work.

With *Cathy Come Home* and *Edna the Inebriate Woman* Sandford powerfully exploited the form of drama/documentary. The sense of authenticity that is conveyed in both pieces by the reportage style of writing and by the deliberate application of filming techniques patterned on newsreel immediacy caused considerable controversy and unease when they were first televised. Sandford was accused of bias, of being unfair to or neglectful of the efforts of social workers and local authorities, or at the very least of what might be referred to as viewer disorientation. In a medium where news and documentary exist as 'objective' truth, should not drama be labelled clearly as 'fiction'? This may be to beg the question of what objectivity means in news and documentary programming, but it is the area where the debate has been most heated and where Sandford's approach, method and purpose have been most closely scrutinised. Irene Shubik refers to Sandford's 'impressionism', contrasting it, in one reference, with the 'meticulous approach and reasoned attitude' of Tony Parker's *Mrs Lawrence Will Look After It* (a play concerning a baby-minder) and later to Parker's 'painstaking research'.[17] But this is not to imply, as Shubik allows, that by contrast to Parker, Sandford indulged in a selective and distorting fiction in the preparation of *Cathy* and *Edna*; rather that he involved himself directly in the experience of his characters and wrote from that understanding. In this sense Sandford's research may reasonably be described as subjective, but this is in no way to devalue it – probably quite the opposite. It should also be pointed out that *Cathy* is clearly labelled 'a story by Jeremy Sandford' and *Edna* as 'a play' in the opening titles. But both use the techniques of factual and documentary reporting to present a personal view, the writer's, of the Cathys and the Ednas of our society. There is no doubt that Sandford's purpose was to influence public opinion – to urge action. It is involved writing, but it neither seeks nor needs to confuse the viewer in order to achieve its ends. Some reference to the critical response to this approach is relevant here. It ranged from outrage at what some saw as grotesque distortion of the way society treated its unfortunates to claims that the pieces were (because of the technical approach which might divert the eye and the mind by the very artistic skill that was being practised) too soft; from suggestions that the drama/documentary approach was misguided and misleading to wholesale endorsements of the initiative of the writer and the production team. Clive James, in *The Listener*, wrote of *Edna*,

What to do with *Edna the Inebriate Woman* is one of society's nagging problems. The quickest answer is to put her in a play. *Cathy Come Home* . . . proved that you can have the roof removed from over your head and still look like Carol White. *Edna* proved that you can hump your bluey all over the country, cop a bout of electro-convulsive therapy, be tossed out of the spike for wetting your bed, and still come up looking as chipper as Patricia Hayes. Mr Sandford descended in person into the bilges of existence to research the play – a brave venture which anyone but a churl would respect. But he couldn't get the intensity of his concern into the script, with the result that the actors and directors couldn't get it out again. The dialogue came jokey/pat: 'I like to sleep out' croaks Edna, dossing down: ' 'ats wo' keeps me in good 'ealth' (*Cough, cough, Fade*) . . . She looked like Princess Lee Radziwill beside some of the wrecks I've seen . . . Mr Sandford tries to rub our noses in the reality: but the truth is, the reality is worse.[18]

In *The Observer* Mary Holland wrote of *Edna* and *Cathy* (admitting that at that time she hadn't seen *Cathy Come Home*),

It will be said that it is not the function of television . . . to solve social ills, merely to draw attention to them. And perhaps 'Cathy' did make people pause; did make homelessness for a time a fashionable cause; did extract some money for charity. What it patently failed to do was to make any meaningful assault on the fundamental causes of the problem or to draw any conclusions. Nor does 'Edna'. It is significant that the most immediately visible results of the play are advertisements for charities that care. It makes people aware not of a situation which it is within their power to change . . . but of a social problem out there in the distance, arousing us perhaps to compassion, but not to action.[19]

A view more sympathetic to the effect of *Edna* is expressed by Edward Lucie-Smith in the *New Statesman*, though he has an interesting qualification concerning Sandford as a writer. 'Just as Orwell was no novelist, Sandford is no dramatist. As an observer, he remains unequalled.' The body of his comment on *Edna*, and marginally on *Cathy*, reads,

It is no small achievement to have written the one television programme which everybody remembers. If you want to defend the medium to its detractors, mention *Cathy Come Home*. Naturally, Jeremy Sandford's latest effort, *Edna the Inebriate Woman*, aroused one's expectations.

Expectations of what? Chiefly, I think, of a very generous and human compassion linked to detailed knowledge of the milieu which was to be depicted. By and large, we got what we expected.[20]

The comment concerning the detailed knowledge of the milieu is fundamental to any discussion of the impact and relevance of *Cathy* and *Edna*. Sandford's research methods involve considerable personal exploration of the plight of his characters and the conditions under which not only they operate, but also those in missions, social services, charities, police stations, courts and hospitals who have contact with them. In *Down and Out in Britain* Sandford describes this personal involvement with his subject's life. 'I descended into the bilges of society. Wearing boots that gaped at the seams and an ancient great-coat, I allowed my beard to grow and my hair to become matted with dirt. I wanted to meet and talk with down and outs, dossers, tramps, the inhabitants of kiphouses, derries, Spikes.'[21] Later he describes an old lady sitting beside him on a bench at Waterloo Station. She 'wore an ancient great-coat and a pork-pie hat, from beneath which she peered out with moist and luminous eyes'.[22] In the script for the play of *Edna* the character is described in exactly the same words ('peers out at the world through moist and luminous eyes . . . a pork-pie hat stuffed down over her head'). The gathering of real experiences in preparation for *Cathy* is also described in detail in the preface to the published play. 'I worked from a very large number of newspaper clippings that I had accumulated through the years, transcripts of tape recordings, actual tape recordings, notes of people I had met, and places I had been to . . .'[23] The specific quality that gives such impact to both characters as they are represented on television is that instead of the usual view that society has of its Cathys and Ednas, viewed from the outside, Sandford offers a view that is from the character's eye and has the character's assumptions. To them 'authority', in whatever shape or form it comes, looks harsh and uncaring: society looks uninterested and complacent. With *Cathy* Sandford has described his involvement (via the situation of the real-life Cathy who stimulated the story) as 'seeing the situation through her eyes and feeling it through her heart'.[24] This approach determines and shapes the visual composition of the TV play. Thus we are often offered the actual viewpoint of the character, and if there is a distortion in the image of the magistrate or the welfare officer or whoever is presented on the screen, it is not offered as an absolute comment but as the inevitable image of that person as seen by an individual who feels herself to be persecuted or ignored. Sandford does not neglect to offer positive proposals for avoiding this futile incompatibility of attitudes, even though his solutions may not be greatly attractive to all those concerned. 'I have always felt that a crash course for magistrates, judges, and other law-keepers and officials of one week as inmates of a Home for the Homeless and one week in prison before they assume office would be most valuable,' he says.[25]

The possible confusion on the part of the viewer between fact and fiction, reality and illusion, has dominated much of the critical controversy over *Cathy* and *Edna*. Matters of research and authenticity, or social significance, are inevitably subject to the scrutiny of integrity. A thoughtful and honest response to *Edna* which could in all respects be applied to the genre of 'fictional documentary' comes from the television playwright Paul Ableman.[26] Ableman voices the dilemma of many who, sensing the importance and essential worthiness of Sandford's plays, nevertheless question the legitimacy of the method. 'Is it fair to regard a play such as *Edna the Inebriate Woman* as being essentially a skilful forgery, a work which derives its credentials by counterfeiting "reality" which it does not actually possess? Or can we, in spite of the ambiguity implicit in its naturalistic treatment, credit it with true artistic qualities?' Ableman writes. And again, 'Such a play cannot show the actual truth about other people's lives. No matter how exhaustively researched, no matter how thickly-studded with phrase, gesture, costume, location, either exactly copied from, or actually employed in, the living world, the final creation must be synthetic . . . *Edna the Inebriate Woman* is neither a play nor a documentary but a huge commercial . . . *Edna* cannot provide a truly artistic experience.' Ableman (and I have slightly unfairly relocated the sequence of his comments) is clearly disturbed by the concept of artistic honesty, worried that the poetic, creative role of the artist is being degraded by easy access to the emotions and responses of an audience via brainwashing visual and literary tactics. His reference to *Edna* as a commercial implies a kind of single-minded promotional dishonesty that will extract and present only those facts that show the product in a specific light. Of the author and producers of *Edna* Ableman says, 'One may legitimately question . . . whether they considered the ethical implications of the form they used, with anything like the devotion they lavished upon achieving its remarkable verisimilitude.'[27] His solution is to suggest that such programmes should be clearly identified in advance in all promotional material and advertising as 'pure fiction'. Sandford's response[28] is perceptive and important. He announces himself 'delighted' by Ableman's description of *Edna* as 'a huge commercial . . . That's how she was meant to be.' He draws attention to the facts mentioned earlier that (*a*) both *Cathy* and *Edna* are labelled clearly as story and play and (*b*) that in the complementary material (*Down and Out in Britain*, the published *Edna* script with its introductory notes and essay, the novel of *Cathy*) and his own activities touring the country with the films of both plays, a considerable attempt has been made to identify the creative pieces as fiction but to relate them to the actuality upon which they are based. On the more substantial matter of the integrity of 'fictional documentary' Sandford explains his position thus:

What Ableman calls 'fictional documentary' I know as 'dramatized documentary'. I grew up with the radio and gained some of my knowledge of life when working for it both as writer and as interviewer and documentary maker. Dramatized documentary was a favourite form with them, so the furore about my translating some of its techniques to television came as a surprise to me . . . The arguments for and against 'Dramatized Documentary' go roughly like this:
Against dramatized documentary. It can be tedious and appalling, and has none of the unexpected which makes real things interesting.
It can be dangerous if it falls into the wrong hands.

Here he instances Nazi propaganda against the Jews and Orson Welles's radio play on an invasion from Mars which threw people into panic.

It can be dangerous if it produces a distorted picture of something. For example, a dramatized documentary series about the police which suggested that there were *no* corrupt coppers, that the police *never* planted or fixed evidence, could inspire a blind confidence in them which would be socially harmful. Equally harmful would be one which suggested that they are all bad.
In favour of dramatized documentary. Most people find it hard to be themselves in front of a tape-recorder or movie camera. And there are many places to which these cannot get without destroying the very thing they come to show. But the researcher–writer can get into most of these places or can talk to those who have been there, and can then script an objectively accurate re-creation of what really happens and what people are

really like when they are not posturing for the cameras. Also, the camera can only interview particular people about their particular view of some event. The dramatized documentary writer can quintessentialize the wider implications. Dramatized documentary can be a more powerful social medium than the play or the documentary . . . It's only when I've felt really strongly about something (usually some form of social injustice) that I've turned to dramatized documentary.[29]

Essentially Sandford is accepting the risks of a powerful weapon being allowed to get into the 'wrong hands', arguing that to allow that caution to restrict the use of the method would be to deny to the writer, especially in the modern conditions of radio and television, a perfectly legitimate vehicle for his statement. Why should the devil have all the good tunes?

The BBC, in facing the comments and criticisms from public and private quarters that greeted *Cathy*, offered a mild contribution:

obviously there are limits beyond which experimental techniques ought not to trespass. All the time the BBC is walking a tightrope, but even in its most experimental programmes it seeks to keep faith with the viewers. People like and have a right to know what it is they are looking at. In the history of protest about broadcasting, trouble has most frequently been caused when the audience got – not what it did not want – but what it did not expect.[30]

T. C. Worsley, the perceptive TV critic for *The Financial Times*, describes this statement as 'almost a parody of official timidity' and offers a simple response to *Cathy Come Home*. 'Its message was so startling that it half escaped notice that *Cathy* would have been altogether less effective if it hadn't been put across in an equally startling way. It was, in fact, the combination of the message with the particularly pungent technique adopted which combined to make the impact; and the producer and director, Tony Garnett and Kenneth Loach . . . have pioneered a form that is about as pure television as you can presently get.'[31] From all this we are left with the apparent fact that despite a label of play or story and despite methods borrowed from news reporting and documentary, 'dramatized documentary' is assumed by Sandford to be a form with its own integrity and identity – a specific response to the opportunity uniquely offered by the medium of television.

So what are the particular techniques to be noted in the creation of *Cathy* and *Edna*? First it is that they are almost entirely made in film. Roger Hudson has described the way in which it became apparent in the late 1960s and early 70s that technically (and from an economic point of view inasmuch as it related to crewing, studio time etc.) 16mm filming 'was quite adequate for TV transmission',[32] and in the same article in *Theatre Quarterly* Tony Garnett, the producer of *Cathy*, comments of the situation in the mid-sixties,

The whole logic of the scripts we were getting was forcing us to use film and to shoot outside the studios on location. We were interested in social forces and the fabric of people's lives and the kind of conflicts that go on particularly at places of work, where people spend quite a lot of their lives. It seemed to be driving us towards actually going out there ourselves. Because there's no argument for doing something at the Television Centre in a studio when you can actually do it where it would be taking place. So we started to push for more film. Also, in being as economical as possible, moving on to a fresh scene whenever the content dictated it, and not feeling we had to cross every 't' and dot every 'i' for the audience: this meant that you needed to cut, your cutting tempo was quicker – which threw the studios into a bit of turmoil, because at that time I think they only allowed us six VTR recording breaks in the hour. We used to act deaf and carry on shooting.

Film may also have been a better medium for Sandford's work from other points of view. Irene Shubik has suggested that Sandford is 'strong on dialogue and weak on structure',[33] and though this may be questioned (indeed, the whole comment seems to make assumptions about dramatic form that do not entirely coincide with Sandford's observations about the structure of dramatised documentary) it is apparent from Shubik's comments that Sandford's scripts logically offered themselves as film rather than as studio pieces. This appears to be despite Irene Shubik's wish, when she commissioned *Edna*, that it would be entirely designed as a studio piece, one part of a trilogy that was to include a work on Gypsies (now written as *Till the End of the Plums*), a play called *Arlene* (on unmarried mothers) and *The Lodging House*, which was the original title for *Edna*. The first two were seen as possible film pieces, but *The Lodging House* was destined for studio production. In the event only brief scenes in *Cathy* and *Edna* were studio-made, though Sandford has drawn attention to one of the possible disadvantages of film in the context of modern television when, in a letter to *The Observer* in response to Mary Holland's review quoted earlier, he refers to 'the absurd BBC rule that productions must be in colour, even when they are more suited to black and white'.[34] There is a strong case for arguing that *Edna* was made too attractive and glossy by being made in colour, and certainly the black-and-white-film prints of the play are in many respects visually more effective for the kind of squalid actuality that Sandford wished to show. But film does offer an authority and authenticity, particularly of location and background action, that the studio would have been unlikely to reproduce and gives a visual fluency that would certainly not have been achieved by any other medium. Apparently artless camerawork combines with a style of acting that avoids 'performance' to give a feeling almost of eavesdropping on reality. The care with which this casual image is created in both *Cathy* and *Edna* does not need to be emphasised. Editing, framing, lighting decisions, all contributed to the fine quality of the finished product. Fiske and Hartley have analysed in detail the construction of a sequence of five camera shots taken in one of the institutions in which Cathy and her children find themselves.[35] Their explanation points to the artistic skill and professional care that create the final image, offering simultaneously visual fact and metaphor.

Both *Cathy* and *Edna*, however, despite their documentary air, use deliberately contrived artistic effects to frame and punctuate the action. These alone may be seen as messages to the viewer concerning the nature of the work that they are seeing. In *Cathy Come Home*, for instance, an opening shot is a sentimental scene, with the young lovers, Cathy and Reg, kissing under the privacy of some trees, their faces and bodies decorated and dappled by the light of the sunshine through the leaves. It is a visual cliché of love's young dream. The only disturbing feature of the scene is that the stream by which they are walking is described as 'half stream, half sewer' with 'iceberg white mounds of detergent' floating on the top. In *Edna* various shots of Edna 'tramping' are quite beautiful to look at – the lonely figure walking quite jauntily down a country lane in summer, or traversing the brow of a downland hill with a sense of determination if not of destination. Even scenes around a fire of débris in a derelict building can momentarily be given the quality of a campfire idyll. (Do such moments soften the biting edge of the work?) Both pieces move rather jaggedly along, one scene complementing another, but presenting a selection of moments of action rather than a continuous narrative. This contributes to some extent to the criticism of *Cathy* that says that all the misfortunes she experienced couldn't realistically have happened to her in the time scale implied by the action. As for the possibility, it may be unlikely, though evidence from social workers certainly suggests that it isn't impossible. But of course the play is not necessarily concerned with that kind of absolute veracity, and arguments about the *probability* of such a rapid decline only divert attention away from the very real *possibility*. Here it is the artistic statement that is important and not the documentary.

The coherence given to the montage of scenes relies in both pieces on the personality of the central character, and if there is no evident *control* in the sequence of events that, in particular, afflict Edna, then that in itself is a deliberate statement. Control, planning, organisation, conformity, understanding of the wheels of society, the consequences of action, are exactly what Edna and Cathy (and Reg) lack. This is subtly reflected in the arrangement of the filmed action. Reg dreams of having an 'E'-type Jaguar without brakes on it, and this awful fantasy of inevitable destruction is an acute symbol. Reg sees the lack of concern about such things as insurance on the part of his employer as an advantage – giving him freedom from meaningless restrictions and petty bureaucracy. When the inevitable accident comes and his badly maintained lorry crashes and injures him, Reg protests to the Boss, but only half-heartedly pursues his vague claim for compensation. 'Don't worry! Live in the present, eh Cath?' is Reg's philosophy. It is of little consequence to moralise that Reg and Cathy shouldn't have taken a luxury flat that stretched their newly-married income, should have thought ahead to the financial implications of having children, should have exercised birth control so that they only had one child until they could afford two, should have taken any of the sensible and prudent precautions that society advocates. Feckless they may be, but in no sense are they wilful malingerers or milkers of the system or whatever emotive description may be coined to account for them. The innocence and the increasing hopelessness with which they slide into the downward spiral is emphasised by the production technique and specifically by the removal of an obvious thread of logical planned action in the visual presentation. An instance of this is the last effort of Cathy and Reg to find something for themselves – the move to a totally decrepit slum which is shown first in close-up as an apparently reasonable room, and then revealed in long shot as an appalling broken-down house in a wasteland. No plaster on the walls, no windows; Reg is putting 'bannisters and boards on the fire on which they're boiling water'. It is almost as if the first shot illustrates their dream of a home and the second the sordid reality. The visual comment is literally shocking.

With *Edna* a slightly different feeling emerges – one is not on a spiral but on a treadmill. Edna moves on compulsively. 'I am on the Tramp all night and I've kept on tramping after the day has broken. And I've kept on tramping.' There are other differences of style and emphasis between *Cathy* and *Edna*. *Cathy* was made with generally lesser-known actors, and this initially contributed to the documentary feeling in a manner that is not possible, nor presumably intended, in *Edna*, where Patricia Hayes (an actress well known for comedy roles) was cast in the name part. *Cathy* is a saddening and deeply moving experience, leaving the viewer with a feeling of despair, whilst *Edna*, because of her courageous spirit and the humour deliberately written into the play, often engages one's admiration for the independent character. There are moments of almost slapstick humour in *Edna*, as when she sets fire to her clothes trying to hide a cigarette behind her back, or in her ingenuous performance in front of the magistrate to whom she offers an inadequate fine in order to ensure a warm bed in prison (and the gleeful joy with which she jumps up and down on it). *Cathy* is unrelieved by such touches. *Cathy* too, as Jeremy Sandford has said, 'contained no solution, but when I came to write *Edna* I decided to embody in the play what seemed to me to be the solution. It is not a very original one; the Government report on the habitual drinker offender suggests that the small permissive hostel is the answer. The Criminal Justice Act and RAP [Radical Alternatives to Prison] are two other products of informed opinion which advocate this. What stands in the way is the hostility of the public to having such things in their streets and the shortage of funds. I wrote *Edna* to change this.'[36] Thus in *Edna* we get a strong advocacy of one solution, whilst in *Cathy* the immediate object was to raise the level of concern.

Cathy and *Edna*, however, share one feature that is interesting in the context of the relationship between the writer and the audience. This is the technique of what one might call the visual editorial. This is done in two ways. One is the use of voice-over comments or captions giving facts and statistics, and the other, and the most powerful, is by direct statements to camera that uncompromisingly address the viewer. These instances are used sparingly but deliberately, and I think one can identify one major instance in each play. In *Cathy* it occurs when Cathy appears before the members of the Board of Administration of Cumbermere Lodge, the temporary accommodation in which she and the children (but not Reg) are living. The growing desperation of her position and the break-up of the family have been emphasised in the previous scenes, and at this point Cathy, apparently humble and hopeless – a petitioner standing before people who seem to be able to command and manipulate her life – suddenly loses control and attacks. The scene is quoted in full, as the context is important.

BENSON. Now, Catherine Ward, you've been here three months, as you know this is the maximum period that we allow homeless families to remain in our temporary accommodation. Now, the first thing I think we'd all like to know is, have you found a place of your own yet?

CATHY. Well . . . I have been trying.

BENSON. How?

CATHY. Me and Reg've been looking on the notice boards. And we went to the agents. But we don't never seem to have no luck. We wouldn't be here if there was a chance.

BENSON. You see, we've been housing you without statutory obligation and without legal responsibility to do so. The idea was to give you a breathing space in which to make your own arrangements. As a result of people like you we are severely restricted in the number of beds we are able to offer to the elderly and the insane.

CATHY. I understand all that.

WARDEN. This is only temporary accommodation, you see, we do in fact have the power to evict you. We could very easily say, Well that's enough of that, so much for her. As they still do in many towns in Britain. We could turn you out and take your children into care just like that.

CATHY. Please don't.

WARDEN. But we're not going to. Instead, we're going to give you one more chance. But I must emphasise to you that this is your last chance. You must make your own arrangements. We've made arrangements for you to go to what we call Part III Accommodation. This, like the place here, is one of our accommodations where the husband is not admitted. You're not going to like it there – the amenities aren't anything like as good as in this place, but, it's the best we can do.

CATHY. But don't you think, the thing is sir, couldn't you find somewhere, some sort of place where I could get my husband back with me?

8 **Cathy Come Home** *by Jeremy Sandford. When shown on BBC-1 as* The Wednesday Play *on 16 November 1966, this drama documentary caused a great stir. Ray Brooks as Reg and Carol White as Cathy.*

WARDEN. Some families here have really been trying to get back on their feet.

CATHY. Who d'you mean? And how? I've not met any. It's not possible, not from this place. They can smell that you're from this place. They can smell it a mile off.

A CLERK. Now, don't be saucy young lady.

CATHY. I'm sorry. Something's happening like – I don't exactly know how to put it in words, this, it's having a bad influence on my family life. I did hear say that you had some places they call 'Halfway House' where the husband can be there too. And if I got to Halfway, I might be able to persuade Reg to come back, cos I feel well, it's not for me so much – I feel he's drifting away and the kids need him. I wish you could put us in Halfway House. The other thing is it would only be for a month. Because after that we got a place.

BENSON. You've got a place in one month's time?

CATHY. If it's finished. Yeah. We're going to the Smithson Estate. They're giving us a flat there.

BENSON. We've checked on your claim. We are told that you lost your place on the list long ago, owing to moving. Five hundred families have already moved in.

CATHY. But we was meant to be one of them families.

[*The Clerk whispers a word in Benson's ear. Cathy shouts at them.*]

CATHY. Runts! I saw you laughing there. Wipe that smile off your face! Aint you got room in your houses? Aint you got one single room? Or aint you got offices, empty half the night I shouldn't wonder. Runts! You don't care really do you? You only pretend to care. Oh Gawd. I shouldn't have shouted at you. I didn't mean it. I'm sorry.[37]

The confusion in Cathy's mind, the bewilderment that is her reaction to the way in which she is constantly being outmanoeuvred by circumstances, is pointed by various comments in this scene, particularly the poignant 'But we was meant to be one of them families' and the irony of 'it's having a bad influence on my family life'. But the explosion in the scene occurs with 'Runts!' The camera view of Cathy through much of this scene has been from around and behind the interviewers, but at this point Cathy is brought into full-face close up and her cry fills the screen. She is talking here straight at the viewer, and has intruded her despair and desperate articulacy directly into the room in which the viewer is comfortably sitting. It is a direct challenge and a most powerful and disturbing moment.

In *Edna* the editorial statement is handled by another character, Josie (played by Barbara Jefford) who runs a hostel called Jesus Saves in which Edna has found shelter. In this incident we also find something of the difference of approach between the two

plays that Sandford has indicated, for this editorial straightforwardly proposes a specific solution. The setting of the scene is a
public enquiry into the desirability of allowing the hostel to
operate, against the hostility of other local residents.

COUNSEL *for Jesus Saves*. Unless hostels are found for them, you say that
many in fact end up in the gutter?

JOSIE. Were it not for this hostel, they would be going to court very
frequently at a very great cost to the taxpayer, and going on to prison
or psychiatric hospitals at a cost to the taxpayer of many pounds per
week.

COUNSEL *for Jesus Saves*. If there is no hostel provided for these people
. . .

JOSIE. They have nowhere to go, poor dears, except to the mental
hospital or the streets. Or to prison.

NEIGHBOUR. Prison!

JOSIE. Going there, not because they are really criminals or mad but
because there's nowhere more suitable for them. These people are
referred to in official reports as inebriates, alcoholics, schizophrenics,
drug addicts, the disabled, layabouts, failures. These words are alibis
to help us to ignore why they're really like they are. Stack the cards
against us, these people are the same as us – you and me in a mess.
The answer, so I believe most sincerely, is in the sort of hostel that we
have set up. Let us help them. They can exist and be happy in a hostel
like ours. They *can* live fulfilled lives. There should be hostels like this
everywhere. One every four or five streets.
The places where they're put at present are no answer. The huge
institution, so vast, so impersonal. What they need is a small place, a
place to be a typical home, the home that most of them never had.
They escape the help that is their right because they can't dress up
their needs in the correct form. And so they get knocked from pillar to
post. And there are thousands of them. I reckon something like one
hundred thousand of people littering lunatic asylums, prisons, common lodging houses, spikes, sleeping out in the open, mostly men,
but a few thousand women.
And the need is desperate. Every day I have to turn women and girls,
even men, families away from my door. I don't want to have to turn
these away as well. By looking only at their symptoms, society has
made an alibi for throwing them away.[38]

As with the scene from *Cathy*, Josie faces the camera squarely
through the body of this speech, making it clear both from the
aspect and the delivery of the piece that her remarks are ad-
dressed beyond the confines of the fictional tribunal and out to
the viewer. This effective and important device is worth our
attention, as it relates very pertinently to Sandford's sense of his

function as a writer, described earlier. These are the moments when the medium of television is exploited in a deliberate way to allow a confrontation between action and audience – to invade and intrude into the privacy of the viewer's home. Whether this is ethical is, of course, at the heart of the debate between the creators of drama/documentary and their critics, but artistically it is certainly effective. Accepting this we have to return to the two major questions that need to be asked not only of this technique but of the whole nature of dramatised documentary. In the context of the means it employs and the style it creates, specifically as evidenced by *Cathy* and *Edna*, is it fair, and is it more than merely artistically effective?

Inevitably, as I have suggested earlier, the answer to the question 'Is it fair?' depends greatly upon the point of view that you are taking. There are no absolute heroes or total villains to be found in this sad conflict between elements of our society. There is no doubt that the reaction of housing authorities and social workers to the image of them offered in *Cathy* and *Edna* was sometimes hurt and angry. There are many instances in both plays where the face of public authority is physically unattractive, the manner heartless and callous. But the experiences of the recipients of society's charity are not always attractive or happy ones. So an inmate of Cumbermere Lodge in *Cathy Come Home* talks of the Welfare man who kept them waiting while he had his dinner, said come back at two-thirty, kept them waiting until three and then 'had the cheek to ask if the babies had been born out of wedlock'. Here we have the melodramatic picture of the self-satisfied heartless and insensitive bureaucrat, complete with long lunch breaks conjuring up images of steak and wines and cigars. Such an image would clearly astonish the average welfare worker whose dedication and life-style are in direct contrast to this instance. The neighbours who conspire to close down Jesus Saves in *Edna the Inebriate Woman* tend to be middle-class caricatures, fur-coated and behatted like a Tory ladies garden party, intolerant and only wishing that the nasty thing in their street would go away. Perhaps it is possible to have more sympathy with the protests of those in areas of social work who feel that a gross distortion of their role is portrayed by drama/documentaries of this kind than it is with society as a whole, which leaves its dirty work to them. If ten people sit in a room viewing *Cathy*, and one is a social worker, at the end of the play nine of them are

likely to turn accusingly on that individual. Presumably this is
not the intention of the writer or producers of the piece. The
blame belongs to all ten, and perhaps only one of them fully
understands or confronts the dimension of the problem. Fair-
ness, therefore, becomes an irrelevance, and the motive of Sandford in creating work of this nature may best be seen as seeking to
move society to self-appraisal by offering the outcasts' view of *us*
to redress in some way the constant propaganda travelling in the
other direction which forms the public attitudes and responses
that themselves contribute to the creation and tolerance of mis-
ery. But we can only argue for this acceptance of an element of
deliberate unfairness or selectivity if we see that the greater good
is served by the effectiveness of the work. How effective were
Cathy and *Edna*?

Cathy Come Home is acknowledged by Des Wilson, founder of
the charity Shelter, as having 'created a public uproar',[39] and it
certainly contributed to the foundation of Shelter itself and to
official action in the housing field. Husbands, for instance, were
allowed to stay with their wives and families where before they
had been separated. But Wilson also points out that between 1966
when *Cathy* was first screened and 1969, the problem of housing
and homelessness in Britain grew worse. Cathy may have been
reunited with her husband and children in due course of time,
but if so they probably now 'struggle to survive as a family in an
overcrowded and squalid slum. Homeless by any civilised
definition.'[40] If, therefore, one were to measure the effectiveness
of the play by a decline in the statistics on homelessness the
results would be very discouraging. Equally it would be naive to
assume that with one flash of the magic box a fundamental social
problem can be transformed into a success story. What *is* clear is
that public awareness of the problems of the homeless is greater
than it was before *Cathy*. Nowadays that is mainly through the
activities of bodies such as Shelter, but they had their initial
impetus from a play's deliberate exploitation of the possibilities
of a mass-media exposure of a social evil. What an aware public
chooses to do with its knowledge is another matter. Does it treat
it, as Mary Holland suggested, as simply a 'fashionable cause'
with all that that implies in terms of a long-term commitment to
action? Or is a more humane climate of public opinion substantially created? One has to believe so, and perhaps to have any
greater expectation of the effectiveness of the play is to be un-

realistic. It is possible that this reaction is implicit in the style of the piece itself and that Sandford's firmer proposals for action in *Edna* are an acknowledgement of this. Sandford has claimed specific success for the explicit advocacy in *Edna* of the creation of small permissive hostels. In a further letter to *The Observer* in response to Mary Holland's query in her review of a repeat performance of *Edna*, he writes,

The opening of small permissive hostels has accelerated since *Edna* was first shown and so has the planning of them. The Cyrenians alone now have over 25 in operation and 12 new ones planned. Many copies . . . of *Edna* have been on tour through Britain for information and fund-raising purposes, and above all for the important task of recruiting volunteers to run the hostels. I think it would be fair to say that there have been breakthroughs on all these fronts.

One example of the many new breakthroughs is an unprecedented local authority–charity relationship: this has resulted in no less than six new hostels being given to the Cyrenians and the St Mungo Community by Hammersmith Borough Council.

The Government, too, seems to be awakening from that lethargy which allowed 250 'spikes' to be closed by local authorities. A new circular is expected to remind local authorities of their duties under the National Assistance Act and the Mental Health Act . . .[41]

Inevitably, as a decade or more has passed since *Cathy* was first televised, and almost that for *Edna*, their impact is lessening, and the response to them – now that they are dignified as TV classics – has altered. In some details the facts and attitudes represented in the plays may no longer be accurate or precise. Legislation has been altered; conditions for the homeless and for 'vagrants' have altered. Television viewers, too, have altered perceptions; they are growing more used to the presence of drama/documentary and perhaps as a consequence are more difficult to shock and move. Dennis Potter suggests that the people who watch television drama 'regard it simply as a television programme, like the rest. It is a series of pictures on the screen and nobody is very much bothered about artificial boundaries between one segment of viewing and another.'[42] Sandford's comment quoted earlier about now being more concerned with spiritual enlightenment may reflect some feeling on his part as a writer that the tools of drama/documentary as used in *Cathy* and *Edna* no longer carry the power they once did and that new forms and new stimuli must be brought to bear on the minds and hearts of audiences and readers.

At the beginning of this chapter reference was made to the two
major pieces that Sandford has had completed for several years
but which have not yet been produced – *Smiling David* and *Till the
End of the Plums*. The first of these plays was commissioned by
BBC Radio Brighton and broadcast in May 1972. It was then
known as *Oluwale*, being the name of the Leeds dosser who came
originally from Nigeria and who died in the River Aire in Leeds in
April 1969. Subsequently two members of the Leeds police force
were accused of assault on Oluwale. But Sandford's concern is
with the way in which Oluwale was able to go to his death despite
the fact that for many years the social services and the 'entire
Panoply of the Welfare State' knew of him and his problem.
Reasonable people taking reasonable action within the options
open to them were unable to prevent the fall of this sad man – 'the
harassing of the unwanted'. Again the play is meticulously researched, using for instance only the words that people can
actually remember Oluwale having spoken in composing his
part, and applying once more the technique of gathering material
that has been described with *Cathy*. The method of presentation
is the familiar one of fictionalised fact, with small self-contained
images structured together. The opening sequences are set in
Lagos, where David Oluwale is shown venturing confidently
abroad to England to make his fortune – again, as with *Cathy*, a
hopeful and almost romantic opening. The remainder of the play
carefully chronicles his downfall and its implication not only for
Oluwale but for society. Sandford writes *Smiling David* in a form
that looks and sounds a little like verse, the effect of which is
to elevate the action into some sense of the dream world that
Oluwale floated through – seen and unseen, recognised and
ignored. The following scene may illustrate this:

Prison Reception Area
[*David stands, handing in his clothes.*]
BLACK. October 1967.
[*We hear the voices of the*]
CLERK. Wandering abroad.
MAGISTRATE. 56 days.
BLACK. Date of discharge: 1st December, '67.

Solicitor's Office

SOLICITOR. What is this crime of 'wandering abroad'?
It comes from the Vagrancy Act of 1824.
'An Act for the punishment of idle and disorderly

persons, and rogues and vagabonds . . .
be it . . . enacted that every person
wandering abroad and lodging in any barn or
outhouse,
or any deserted or unoccupied building,
or in the open air, or under a tent,
or in any cart or wagon,
not having any visible means of subsistence,
and not giving a good account of himself
or herself . . .
shall be deemed a rogue and vagabond . . .

> *Magistrates Court*

BLACK. A little later David was back again.
January, 1968.
CLERK. Wandering abroad. Indecent exposure.

> *Magistrates Court (later)*

MAGISTRATE. 56 days. 3 months consecutive.
BLACK. Effective duration 146 days.
Date of discharge: 29th March, '68.

> *Solicitor's Office*

SOLICITOR. Indecent exposure sounds bad until we
learn
that it can be used to describe those who
urinate
in public places, even though after dark.

> *Back Entrance of Magistrates Court*
> [*David enters court from police car.*]

BLACK. Two weeks after discharge
he was in court again,
for disorderly conduct.

> *In Magistrates Court*

MAGISTRATE. We're taking a lenient view.
I'm giving you a suspended sentence.[43]

The use of the black commentator underlines the point made in *Smiling David* about the factor of racial prejudice that may have contributed to the alleged persecution of Oluwale by the police, and the greater issue of the confidence of the black communities in the impartiality of the police. Sandford's interest, commented on earlier, in looking closely at the position of the black communities in Britain may have its roots in this perceptive and curiously neglected play. The play itself and the accompanying notes to the published text pose questions that are in some respects familiar from *Edna*, but *Smiling David*, with its constant reminder of the real man upon whom it is based, is a harsher work.

Till the End of the Plums is a play about Gypsies. Sandford's own sympathy for the situation of the Gypsies has been illustrated in his book, *Gypsies*, which, as *Down and Out in Britain* is to *Edna*, can be seen as a notebook for the play text (though the chronology is not important). Sandford's visual eye as a writer is very evident in *Gypsies*, where the information and anecdotes are set out in such a way that a shooting script could almost be made straight from it. Again the book and the play look at legislation governing the life of Gypsies in Britain and the reality of its application by local authorities. The crusading style of both pieces is familiar, as are the love and interest expressed in the subjects of the study. *Till the End of the Plums* has as its basis a simple narrative story concerning a family of Gypsies and may, in some respects, be regarded as a romantic vision, with the call of the roaming life seen to be irresistible. But it is also a realistic view of harassment and confrontation between the opposing life styles of the Gypsies and the 'Gorjio'. As in *Edna* and *Cathy* a strong editorial point is made, and we are once again challenged to face up to and analyse the prejudices that determine so much of our action as a society. The other side of the coin is offered to us for scrutiny, as in this scene between the young Gypsy Jim and the Gorjio wife, Maggie, that he has married:

JIM. . . . who makes more mess? The Gorjios with their roads and factory, pollution, houses – or the Gypsy with his old load of scrap?
MAGGIE. The other thing they say is that Gypsies are thieves. Are they?
JIM. Well, there's some thieves among the Gypsies, just as there are among the Gorjio folk. We got no more thieves than the Gorjios.
MAGGIE. Why do they say you all *are* then?
JIM. They can't stand us being different. Anyway, who's the thieves. We had this whole land once to roam through. We fought for this land in the war. Gypsies died for this land in the army. The Gorjios have stolen it all from us – everything. They say we're thieves because – they've stolen from us and they feel guilt.[44]

The neighbours who want to move on Jesus Saves, the police who cannot leave David Oluwale asleep in a shop doorway, the local authorities who move Gypsies on from a wasteground campsite, the housing authority that want Cathy out of their area of responsibility, all seem to share in common a wish to sweep under the carpet something that disturbs us or which we cannot understand. Sandford in his broadcast and published plays uses his art to educate. Television, which he has described as our national theatre, is a medium ideally suited to his campaigning and his compassion.

Appendix

Television plays transmitted

16.11.66	*Cathy Come Home*	BBC-1 *Wednesday Play*
21.10.71	*Edna the Inebriate Woman*	BBC-1 *Play for Today*
17.8.80	*Don't Let Them Kill Me on Wednesday* (in series *Lady Killers*)	Granada

Other play scripts

Intended for TV but produced on radio
Smiling David
Till the End of the Plums

For the stage
Dreaming Bandsmen
Prostitutes
Street Hustler (with Philippa Finnis)
The Fatted Calf

Other relevant work
Hotel de Luxe (TV documentary on the Savoy Hotel, London)
Radio documentaries for the BBC

Criticism by and about Jeremy Sandford

Paul Ableman, 'Edna and Sheila: Two Kinds of Truth', *Theatre Quarterly*, 2, 7 (July–September 1972), 45–8

Alan Rosenthal, *The New Documentary in Action: A Casebook in Film Making*, Berkeley and Los Angeles: University of California Press, 1971, pp. 166–75

Jeremy Sandford, 'Edna and Cathy: Just Huge Commercials', *Theatre Quarterly*, 3, 10 (April–June 1973), 79–85

T. C. Worsley, *Television: The Ephemeral Art*, London: Alan Ross, 1970 (references to *Cathy Come Home* on pp. 63–4, 156–7, 225–7, 230–1)

See also articles in *Plays and Players*, May 1972, p. 58 and, August 1972, p. 6

S. M. J. ARROWSMITH

PETER WATKINS MADE ONLY two films expressly for release through British television. His later work will be summarised towards the end of this essay, but it is not our primary concern here. The limitations of an aesthetic response to Watkins on such an incomplete basis should be underlined at once. Without proposing this as a totally accurate evaluative model, I would ask the impatient reader searching here for a conventional critical verdict on Watkins's merits and defects to consider the project of assessing Howard Hawks on the basis of *Scarface* and *The Crowd Roars*. A full and responsible evaluation of Watkins here presents similar problems, circumscribed as it must be by the dictates of a particular market – British television drama.

Watkins's contribution in this field, however, is undeniable. He discharged a crucial function in the historical development of TV drama in the mid-1960s. It is also clear that the social impact of *The War Game* and, to a lesser extent, *Culloden* was considerable and may continue to have repercussions, either directly or in the form of an apparently internally generated revision of the terms of reference of dramatic articulation in television. This impact may originally be said to have taken two directions; first towards an assault on conventional assumptions of how television was made, what it should and should not discuss, and how this discussion might be staged; secondly, towards an assault on conventional assumptions about the social function of television, and more particularly the mechanisms for self-regulation adopted by the institutions governing television. Hence the available areas for debate ranged from the merits of a particular text as social commentary to the nature and purpose of a notional or actual ruling class in British life.

Within certain circumscriptions, this debate or at least its origins can and should be traced by this essay. But circumstances preclude the use of Watkins as a trigger for a wholesale debate of the relative virtues and deficiencies of British broadcasting systems compared to other national models or indeed other articulative and industrial systems within Britain – for example, that of the British cinema. Suffice it to say that, even at the time, Watkins's contribution to the debate (which, by its very nature, may wax and wane but never disappears) was considerable in alerting a wide spectrum of English-speaking people to the self-regulatory mechanisms of British broadcasting and British society at large. Regardless of its other qualities, *The War Game* was a consciousness-raising device for people who never saw it at the time, as well as for those who did. Watkins's own fate as a practitioner of his chosen craft, however, is related to the most general of social and industrial practices which circumscribe political conduct far beyond the confines of British television drama. As a result, they may be sketched in the immediate context but will not receive detailed attention.

By the middle of the 1960s the BBC had begun to formulate a response to the industrial pressures exerted by the emergence of an independent network. The BBC's initial reflex to the stimulus of ITV appears to have been dismissive on a variety of levels, but the supercilious and defensive mentality which had been responsible for such short-term answers to ITV as the 'killing' of Grace Archer[1] on the opening night of the commercial channel had been largely replaced. It appears that fewer executives believed either that the correct competitive response to ITV lay within the limited province of radio or that time would tell and that the poverty of imagination associated with the commercial impulse would prevent ITV from competing for an educated audience. Part of this more sophisticated response was technologically derived: the BBC began to place a greater public importance on the launching of BBC-2 as a step towards transposition of services from 405 to 625 lines, for example. In the first instance, too, BBC-2's 'selling point' was that it would cater to educated/highbrow minority interests. While time and industrial logic were progressively to dissolve most possible intellectual distinctions between the two BBC channels, the original policy is interesting because, in its avowed grouping of programmes of limited appeal in one area, it led logically towards the more robust policy of direct competition for ratings which tended increasingly to characterise the BBC's attitude to its market after the 1960s.

More specifically, television drama began to undergo a revision in the light of industrial movement and also in response to other external pressures. Drama was just one of the areas – but perhaps the most notable – in which ITV had demonstrated, perhaps to the BBC's surprise, that it had the money to hire the talent to compete in the prestige areas of television hitherto monopolised by the BBC. Its primary function, of course, was to appeal to as many viewers as much of the time as possible, in order to increase its advertising revenue. But during the 1960s ITV began to come to terms with the fact that it, too, was circumscribed by British social attitudes and by the Reithian heritage of sturdy maintenance of the moral and educational function of broadcasting.

This circumscription is ratified in Britain by a system of institutional certification of the right of an 'independent' television company to transmit, and so it makes perfect sense for an independent station to look to its own franchise from time to time. Industrially, success will be judged by advertising revenue. Socially, estimated according to the criteria at play at the time of franchise hearings, ratings and income are largely irrelevant. The rise of 'prestige' productions in the general area of the arts, for example, seems an inevitable result. It is also worth noting that ITV, operating on one channel only, was encouraged by its own structure to integrate the 'serious' with the 'entertaining' (if I may use these rather strained categories in the interests of clarity), although as the years passed so commercial pressures came to impose a distinction between peak and other viewing hours, which programming policy tended at any given time to reinforce. But ITV in the 1960s would certainly make limited investments in drama as a form of social insurance, and talent was attracted for the simple reason that contributing to the formation of a tradition in a procedural vacuum is more clearly stimulating an opportunity than is the reform of a consolidated tradition within an existing institution, which may be more immediately sensitive to the notional 'dangers' of, for example, programme content.

Similarly, the BBC may have lost its impetus in the field of drama in the early 1960s because of the feeling of potential playwrights and producers that only technological development could effect change in production procedures and because of the assumptions about the value of drama and television as a whole which underlay them. At the same time, for as long as it took to circumscribe ITV drama with its own precedents, it might have been assumed that the commercial ethos would direct ITV drama departments towards ignoring traditional distinctions between 'culture' and 'mass entertainment', if for no other reason than because drama, too, would turn out to have a market value in terms of ratings – and the bigger, the better.

These circumstances combined with another impetus of the day, one which is traditionally signalled by the original production of *Look Back in Anger* in 1956. The influence of the Angry Young Men may have been registered in two ways by television drama during the 1960s. First, the assault on the tradition of the 'well-made play', however slowly digested by dramatists in practice, implies a structural overhaul of dramaturgical procedure which might be expected to produce its highest dividends in an area which would inevitably involve itself in any revision of dramatic structure and convention, by virtue of its new technological articulative determinants. Secondly, dramatists after *Look Back in Anger* were highly conscious of the need (as they saw it) to revise, at the level of plot content and characterisation, the social range of drama outwards across the social spectrum and downwards on the economic scale.

Television drama exists in close proximity, day by day, to news and current-affairs coverage. Such coverage embraces by definition a greater social range than any stage play, and proposes a greater immediacy (and thus disposability) of treatment and, hence, of product. Television drama was, again, uniquely placed to take advantage of this reformation. Indeed, the unprecedented hunger for manageable and transformable experience exhibited by television may have demanded in turn persistent initiatives in this dramatic field. For several years in the early 1960s, ABC's *Armchair Theatre* slot exploited this field and filled this vacuum with considerable success – in terms both of revision of aesthetic values and of the establishment of an unexpectedly large and consistent audience.

The BBC's response to all this was in part dictated by further technological development, in part by its own dramatic traditions. The first *Armchair Theatres* went out live, but film and videotape became increasingly available to drama producers and directors. They in turn gravitated logically towards production procedures and technological processes which would guarantee them a greater degree of 'quality control'. In relation to the possibility of institutional supervision by the BBC, a possibility always more strongly felt than regularly experienced, it may be that the use of film, in particular, became attractive, precisely because direct physical supervision of activity in a studio is far more feasible than is serious interference with the daily business of an expensive film unit shooting on location. Film footage achieves the status of a *fait accompli* to employers. Interference with a working crew still has such serious repercussions in the areas of finance and labour relations that it remains easier for the BBC, once script approval has been granted, to let a film be completed and then ban it than to scrap shooting as soon as any hostile executive is alerted to the existence of socially 'irresponsible' or otherwise contentious productions.

This was the dramatic context in which Watkins's career at the BBC began. The strong tradition of British documentary film also exerted an influence. As with dramatic convention, documentary was revising itself in response to identifiable technical and social pressures. Although aiming to root itself firmly in mundane experience, British documentary had never hesitated to adopt self-consciously artificial modes of discourse (e.g. *Night Mail*) – to make its own use, in fact, of dramatic technique. Naturally enough, it had not backed away from inserting itself into issue-related social debate (e.g. *Housing Problems*). In some of the work of the Free Cinema group, it had effected its own social response to the broadening of vision of fictional dramas. Most particularly, the documentary was coming under pressure formally to define itself as distinct from the increasing flood of actuality footage being broadcast nightly in news and current-affairs programmes. Logically enough, documentary adapted for a television age had recourse to those of its characteristics which reinforced such a distinction – most notably the notion of a highly designed organisation of a systematically isolated individual or event or subject; the careful design and planning of a film to distinguish it from the 'underdesigned' or superficially 'random' or opportunistic incidence of news footage; the systematic isolation of a nominated subject to distinguish its narrative qualities from the relatively undifferentiated practices of news-gathering.

TV news reached out further, faster and into more subject areas with the passage of time and technological development, which was always likely to be accelerated after the BBC had another news service with which to compete. At the same time, television drama had evolved the techniques for designing drama which was structurally more sophisticated than had been the case in the studio-bound and/or live broadcast-bound 1950s, as well as responding to external cultural pressures (e.g. from the stage) to expand its dramatic range into, for example, areas of social deprivation or concern which had traditionally been primarily the province of the documentary. It is scarcely surprising that documentary should adopt 'dramatic' modes of discourse with increasing frequency in its response to these twin pressures.

Another feature of the British documentary tradition is worth noting. Its founder, John Grierson, had developed a certain reputation as what was in effect a film theorist – although much of his writing is practical criticism shading into didacticism. There had never been any doubt in the minds of British documentarists, for this reason, about the issue of authorship. Authorial status could as well be attributed to a documentarist as to his counterpart in the fiction film – perhaps better. Even if his sole nominal function was that of director, the documentarist's discretionary powers would in practice almost invariably expand to include the close supervision of the script (which would sometimes be written solely as a commentary after shooting had taken place).

Under these circumstances, the documentarist in the 1960s would bring to his flirtation with traditionally dramatic techniques and/or subjects a strong sense of his own authorial status and responsibility, expecting to exert a degree of control over the finished product far closer to that of the writer than of the director of television drama. Peter Watkins in this sense has always drawn strongly from the documentary tradition, anticipating that he may initiate a project and will certainly prescribe its production at every stage. His function is therefore not precisely analagous to that of the television writer, but it is certainly comparable in terms of creative input and is sometimes superior in terms of quality control over the finished product.

Retrospectively, there seems little reason to doubt that documentaries which encroached on the traditional territories of drama, and vice versa, benefited in terms of the impact of product on consumer from the tension inherent in the still-emerging concord between the two disciplines. In his close supervision of casting and his exaggerated care for the gesticulative and intonative detail of performance, it appears certain that Watkins was acutely aware of the artificiality (on one level) of his work. On the other hand, he drew strongly on presumed response to actuality footage in news bulletins etc. and certainly took advantage of the growing technological and articulative sophistication of news-gathering and transmission. His key position within this area of public controversy between the actual and the fictional is illustrated by the fact that he never betrayed the bias towards conventional fiction exhibited even in the early work ('art' documentaries, for the most part) of his professional contemporaries (e.g. John Boorman and Ken Russell, each of whom served his apprenticeship during this period).

Culloden presents for its audience's consideration an account of the campaign of Bonnie Prince Charlie against the Hanoverian throne and establishment ('the '45'); its gradual loss of momentum in the face of poor military decisions and the overwhelming historical logic of Hanoverian supremacy; the battle of Culloden; and some of its consequences, tracing the fates of several major and some minor and representative historical figures through the opening of the Highland Clearances.

The mythological centre of these historical events is identified as the production of Georgian historians, intent upon chronicling a great military episode in the island story. The film proceeds to assail this myth on two levels: incidental and contextual. As an incident, it is suggested, the battle is frightening, confusing and/ or degrading for those involved. At the same time, an economic context is furnished for this episode, in which the relative status and condition of, for example, a Highland foot-soldier is juxtaposed with that of the Duke of Cumberland. The disastrous end to the campaign is circumscribed by an explanation of its economic inevitability, and the personal consequences of the Clearances are severely juxtaposed with a commentary on the brutal logic of the pursuit of the defeated Scots. It is suggested that the subsequent persecution of the Highland Scots and their culture was an ambiguous tribute based on the inability of English culture to assimilate this ethnic group.

As an historical analysis *Culloden* is, by contemporary standards, unexceptionable and probably unexceptional. Its social function as a document is rather more interesting, and this is something Watkins was quick to grasp. *Culloden* is itself arguably a function of a decade which saw the last acceleration into slump of the postwar economic boom and (catching up at last) the most public and radical articulation of the social movement generated by that boom. Such high-energy periods in Western life turn for fuel upon existing national histories and redefine the historical movement to sustain their own. An academic reorganisation of English history, however, has quite distinct effects in the classroom and on television, for it does nothing to redefine the function of the former and (in this context) everything to overhaul popular notions of the reading and function of the latter.

In revising the accounts of contemporary historians, Watkins effectively had recourse to the techniques of those twentieth-century historians, news cameramen. Handheld camerawork was to remain a standard weapon in his technical armoury. This might be said to make *Culloden* the most straightforward of historical revisions, merely acknowledging that the event will change because the technological determinants of its analysis have changed. In declining to display further analytical ambition, Watkins deliberately restricted his field of fire, so to speak. He assumed that there must remain in the articulation one fixed point. Conventional documentaries may stage a discussion of a particular event, but its historical status is likely to be neglected in favour of its characterisation as an incident contributing to an assumed historical continuum. In *Culloden*, as far as everyone except professional historians was concerned, the historical status of the event was being questioned; and, hence, the continuum of glorious British military history. It is to Watkins's credit that his chosen weapons were the handheld camerawork, 'impromptu' interview *in situ*, detached commentary and other modes of the contemporary documentary report. In themselves, however, these modes went unexamined. Subsequently, the more contentious Watkins's analysis became, the more likely his critics were to point out this one apparent area of acute *un*self-consciousness.

At the time, *Culloden* was greeted with some critical acclaim. It had genuinely extended the boundaries of the historical survey on television. Its partiality was invigorating to many viewers in the 1960s, whereas a later audience, circumscribed by the conservatism of response endemic to periods of economic recession and perhaps more cynical about a television service proposing to offer new perspectives, might have been more distrustful. But then Watkins would have (and indeed has) furnished later audiences with a more advanced range of perceptual determinants. It may well be characteristic of the form that television, placing as it does one programme in an extended image continuum, circumscribes the individual television programme and its analytical potential in a way that the cinema and the theatre do not. The individual drama or documentary may not be able to escape this circumscription to examine consistently its own manufacture, technology and place in the given continuum of broadcast articulations. But it may be noted that while Watkins is certainly a didactic film-maker/dramatist of human experience, didacticism is not necessarily incompatible with auto-criticism. *Culloden* appears highly successful within its own terms of reference, but the replacement of one tool for recording a historical verdict by another isolates the subject and renders any resultant historical reappraisal inevitably revisionist.

Watkins's camera describes arcs around groups of shivering Highlanders awaiting the battle, as the commentator informs us of the impoverished background and dubious prospects later in the day of these soldiers. It is precisely this imaginative extrapolation from news-gathering orthodoxies which captures the audience's attention; it appears to endow minor historical characters with (in this case) an almost literal three-dimensionality. While it undeniably dramatises their condition, this movement does so by refusing implicitly to comment on the arbitrary presence of the camera and the highly self-conscious nature of its deployment. The effect is oriented towards a legitimate pathos, but this in itself defines *Culloden* as an act of reform.

This, however, represents only one species of historical verdict. Innovation has its own historical value, and in a form as ephemeral as television it is dangerous to describe such values as superficial. Watkins revealed early on his capacity to enlist the sympathy of the audience, aware as he was that a scrupulously unemotional verbal description of the conditions of poverty in the eighteenth century would operate as an emotional stimulus to most television-watchers in the middle of the twentieth century. *Culloden* reveals also Watkins's appreciation of a persistent dramatic technique, creating an articulative space between the verbal and visual modes in order that the audience may integrate the two and thus commit itself to the narrative movement. Despite occasional linguistic and intonative ironies, the commentary in *Culloden* tends to stand off from the image stream, and the consistency of this technique indicates that Watkins is fully aware how far such a technique, carefully deployed, actually militates against audience detachment. Similarly, the image track tends to espouse a more or less rigorous conventional sequentiality, as the voice-over elaborates circumstantially behind and before the juxtaposed image. The resulting distance between discourses is conventionally ironic and pathetic (in the technical sense), and the instructional quality of all Watkins's voice-overs establishes that the audience is not being cheated – the status of the narrator is assumed. Watkins's adherence to this narrative technique is rigorous, and the concomitant dramatic effect considerable, but limited. In the same way that the narrative is secured internally by actual recorded accounts by the historical principals, recreated in interview form, so externally the function of the narrator is unchallenged. How far does an old story change if a new voice tells it, in a language comparable to the old?

The War Game proposes a politico-military chain reaction leading to a limited nuclear assault on the British Isles. It then proceeds to deal with the effects and consequences of the attack on an area in the county of Kent, where the film was shot with the cooperation of local dramatic societies etc. The action is interspersed with inserted quotations from nuclear texts, civil-defence manuals, leading public figures and scientific authorities, and so forth.

The film establishes beyond question Watkins's acute self-consciousness as a dramatist of human experience. As far as the specific articulation is concerned, 'Well, really getting down to basic roots, my sort of film is a gross cheat.'[2] Although that statement was made during an interview prior to the film's completion, and deliberately anticipated criticisms of the verisimilitude of the dramatic mode, it was not intended defensively. It simply indicates that Watkins was acutely aware of the notion of, for example, dramatic economy: 'This sort of film has to be incisive, has to make points and move ruthlessly.'[3] Similarly, there was no question of Watkins retreating behind a mask of documentary neutrality – he was already fully aware, if not of precise reactions, then certainly of the scope for contention he had created by treating thermonuclear warfare assertively as legitimate dramatic, even propagandistic, material: 'The problems will start when the hierarchy sees it . . . I can't "prepare" myself. It's just sort of . . . well, I *have* prepared myself, I've got all sorts of counter-arguments, and I think I'm going to get them in a very difficult position.'[4]

He was quite right. Leading BBC executives watched the film

and refused to transmit it. Themselves aware of the vulnerability of this position in a wider social context, the BBC decided to seek endorsement for its decision in a way that itself endorsed one of Watkins's basic political tenets: stratification of society at large by the Establishment into the haves and have-nots of that crucial index of political power – access to information. *'The War Game* is being shown next week at the National Film Theatre at two special morning showings to a selected audience drawn from amongst Members of Parliament, Peers from the House of Lords, members of the Home Office and Civil Defence, members of the Ministry of Defence and Armed Forces Personnel and members of the British Film Industry . . .' (Watkins in late January 1966).[5] The Corporation rejected Watkins's request for (*a*) admission of the general public to the showings and (*b*) the right to purchase copyright of the film from its owners, the BBC.

These showings, to which film critics were apparently admitted, took place in the first days of February 1966. The median of response was acutely summarised by the *Birmingham Evening Mail* on 8 February: 'Horrifying, but so would be a nuclear war'.[6] Two days previously, under the headline 'A Warning Masterpiece', Kenneth Tynan had led the liberal argument with the statement in his column in *The Observer*: 'It may be the most important film ever made.'[7] This view was widely shared. Elsewhere, in Parliament and the press, criticisms varied. As Watkins had predicted, the authenticity and legitimacy of his dramatic idiom and vision were attacked. Peter Bostock in the *Daily Sketch* summarised another response under the communicative headline 'Brilliant, But It Must Stay Banned': 'It excluded hope. In that I judge it to be irresponsible. It excluded any reasoned argument on why we must have The Bomb.'[8] One critic rechristened the film 'The C.N.D. [Campaign for Nuclear Disarmament] Game'.

In a crucial sense, these reactions are of marginal interest. Any response in this situation suited the BBC, although more especially those deriding Watkins's prejudice or irresponsibility. In a statement prior to the showings, Watkins had already penetrated the argument at a rather more important level: '[*The War Game*] was made . . . in an attempt to . . . break down the present trend of what amounts to "privileged information" in this particular subject. These two restricted showings . . . are using my film to help perpetuate this very situation.'[9] It was nevertheless a state of affairs which a number of those present were apparently conscious of and very much inclined to maintain: 'They [the BBC] should go on showing it to future audiences consisting of people occupying positions of influence in national or local policy or information' (*South Wales Argus*).[10] It is, by the way, a revealing instance of the political assimilation practised endlessly by British institutions that all these quotations and others, pro and con, are drawn from a thirty-page release of clippings issued by the BBC. The ban, of course, was maintained. The BBC, however, had discharged its social obligations by making a particular policy decision, reflecting faithfully all shades of political response, and then executing its original decision. In this sense, Watkins's strategic purpose in making the film may have gone down to inevitable defeat, but no single television programme has ever clarified the relationship of the BBC to the general public and existing political practice quite so extensively.

Liberal and Labour MPs urged the BBC to release the film for theatrical exhibition. Unsurprisingly, the Corporation offered a degree of cooperation with this proposal. A more damning indictment of the mounting irrelevance of the cinema as a social force in the television age can hardly be imagined. It also substantially reduced the possibility of the enterprising Mr Watkins gaining more publicity for the cause by remaking *The War Game* as a feature film amidst enduring and heated public debate. In fact, partial censorship and partial endorsement of this action probably suited the BBC better as an institution than total suppression and total acquiescence by the privileged first audiences could have done.

This is the enduring contribution of *The War Game* – its precipitation of debate about information-as-power, its hoarding and dissemination. Watkins was perhaps in a cleft stick: it takes a highly contentious treatment of a politically sensitive subject to launch such a debate, but the extreme nature of the effort involved may deflect the argument into localised discussion of the specific issue which has been dramatised. This in itself is of considerable value, but it has clear political limitations and establishes the debate as ephemeral because of its isolation at a phenomenological level. In this case the fiction, too, is quite shrewdly aimed at the issue of access to information. The horrors of nuclear devastation (and, in fact, a number of critics both pro and con pointed out that budgetary limitations had prevented the representation of anything which had not already taken place in the aftermath of conventional bombardments of Germany and Japan during the Second World War) served the purpose of arresting the attention of a British audience because British people were being devastated.

D. A. N. Jones indicated the technique operating when he observed in the *New Statesman*, 'What happens to them, singly, is no worse than what the Vietnamese are getting – and no-one complains when German pilots fry in "All Our Yesterdays".'[11] While not a particularly attractive argument to humanitarians, this observation establishes the force of the idiom. That a further dramatic purpose operates in the film is clear from the accelerating attack within the film on the public statements of a variety of socially, politically and even theologically engaged parties on the subject of nuclear war and disarmament. These are statements apparently originally designed to allay public misgivings on various practical and moral grounds, and tend to be juxtaposed with scenes depicting acute personal suffering or social and moral disintegration in the face of mounting panic by an ill-informed public.

This is Watkins's basic material for the fabrication of a history of the future. Such detachable statements, and an extrapolation from e.g. known civil-defence procedures into an actual nuclear assault, are organised dramatically to carry the same weight as the historical records and memoirs from which *Culloden* was constructed. This is what I mean by a history of the future – *The War Game* is thus not dramatically open to categorisation as some species of science fiction; although technically it is speculation, it is not idiomatically speculative. Each scene of possible/probable devastation or social disintegration is punctuated by facts, figures, accounts of existing contingency procedures, representations of responses made by contemporary public figures to contemporary public events and so on. Such devices are cumulative in effect, but they do not construct a coherent dramatic unity; they organise by punctuation.

In this respect the greatest possible disservice was done to *The War Game* by banning it from television and restricting its exhibition to the cinema. For it draws for its immediate impact on the conventions of e.g. TV actuality footage; further, its organisational logic is not derived from the 'seamless' fluency of orthodox cinematic narrative, but rather on the efficiency-as-punctuation of statements made now for immediate public dissemination and in response to the immediate stimulus of the passage of historical events. Hence *The War Game* is very much a television filmed drama, designed for impact now rather than hereafter, designed to compete under intense pressures for mass attention for a very limited period of time, and hence to precipitate debate rather than stage or maintain it. It is thus a weapon for social interaction and political conflict in a way that a great deal of politically contributory cinema is not. Its articulation is unilaterally assertive. This does not particularly suit the environments of voluntary engagement over a longer period of time (relative to television) by cinema audiences or the prolonged and detached survey of an academic audience long after the event.

Perhaps, then, *The War Game* does not stand up particularly well to the passage of time and transposition to the context of a classroom. It was not intended to do so. It is one of those texts which represent their own publication very self-consciously as political events, which is to say that the assault on specific ideological practices is paramount, and in such cases precise historical timing is everything. *The War Game* offered a specific and challenging response to a specific material pressure within a specific historical context. That is more directly the function of television than of theatrical or cinematic narrative. To embarrass the BBC was Watkins's service, because it exposed some of the Corporation's more dubious regulatory practices, an exercise which is educational in itself. But to secure a television audience for *The War Game* in the first months of 1966, which was beyond Watkins's contractual powers, would have constituted a legitimate and independent historical achievement.

The War Game controversy saw the end of Watkins's direct professional connection with British television, but a review of what followed reveals that his crusade against misinformation and official history continued unabated. *Privilege* represents his one flirtation with the British film industry; it is a low-budget independent colour production which traces the rise, redirection and further rise of a pop star in a quasi-authoritarian Britain of 'the near future'. Watkins's association with Johnny Speight[12] ensured that no opportunity would be lost to pursue social analogy. The star (played by Paul Jones) is treated as a product to be marketed in the interests of an economic, social and political Establishment. The analysis is unexceptionable but unsubtle. Watkins may have underestimated the extent to which colour film would reveal budgetary deficiencies in scenes of mass action, and there is a slightly hollow ring to (for example) the 'mass rally' at Wembley Stadium as a result.

On the other hand, one of the film's greatest strengths lies at its core in the utterly vacuous relationship between the romantic stars (Jones and Jean Shrimpton). Scripting and performance are both so shallow and so determined to decline any possible narrative movement that these passages achieve a remarkably effective revelation of a peculiarly British application of the inertia factor in the manufacture of glamour as a commodity; so effective, in fact, that later audiences have been almost completely alienated, deprived as they are of the prevailing context of fashionable values which 'explains' such glamorous appeals.[13] To establish this vacuum at the centre of the fiction's leading identification-figures offers a particularly incisive model for the political vacuum which allows itself to be filled by such manipulated and manipulative personalities. The casting of a real pop star and a real model as the lovers underlines Watkins's penchant for casting close to type from real life – exploiting again this area of tension between actuality and manifest patterns of dramatisation (e.g. allegory). Otherwise the implicit analysis is without obvious parallel in Watkins's other work.

The game of *The Peace Game* is played according to rules in a prescribed battle zone between national teams of soldiers. The controlled contests are internationally televised. In many ways this is Watkins at his least satisfactory. All possible narrative movement is entirely circumscribed by the game or response to it, but the rules are never adequately explained and movement depends on a convenient malfunction in the computer which screens and regulates the exercise. In the ensuing confusion, romance cuts across national boundaries as a couple try to break out of the game. An anti-game protester inadvertently sets the computer right while trying to sabotage it. Watkins represents a complete division between the manipulators and their victims, which may very well be a political fact; but, presented in such diagrammatic terms, this relationship lacks flexibility or any dramatic tension. The narrative is even more transparently programmed than the game. Watkins's usual fierce optimism in the face of bureaucratic misinformation seems to have crumbled into a kind of wan depressive romanticism. And the retreat into allegorical structures for aggression and conflict robs him of the capacity for thoroughgoing contextual analysis which did so much to hold the structure of, for example, *Culloden* together.

Punishment Park reverts to the war-games format. In America in 'the near future' a repressive government has clamped down on all forms of protest. Dissenters attend civic tribunals, which arraign them for abuse of the Constitution and sentence them to prison terms. Alternatively, they can try to avoid prison by evading National Guardsmen in a pursuit through one of a national network of punishment parks. Convicts invariably opt for the pursuit, trekking through desert terrain towards a point marked by the American flag; they are invariably caught by their pursuers, who break the rules of the game if necessary to forestall the prisoners' release.

Watkins covers one group during a hearing and another through the pursuit. The narrative is considerably stabilised by a fairly clear statement of the rules of the game, which assists its operation as a social analogue. No full break is made through the game-playing structure, and as a result Watkins can place it under highly productive stress. Working in America seems to have provided a salutory lesson in capitalising on rather than disguising a limited budget. The professional veneer of the production (reflecting the theoretical organisation of the game) is first resisted by the uncooperative demeanour of many of the actors towards the camera, and then subjected to outright assault when the narratorial voice begins to criticise and then rant hysterically against the conduct of the National Guard. This collapse of detachment is accomplished by the insertion of the complainant into the action, rendering the ethical dispute at the core of the film genuinely contentious because it achieves a provisional spatial articulation as the Guardsmen virtually assault the camera crew. Retrospectively, all images in the film revert to a problematic status (rather than one of unquestioned authorial detachment), and legitimate dramatic tensions are set in play.

Edvard Munch enjoys the benefits of historical enclosure, as well as enclosure in the realm of art and further enclosure as an everyday story of a socially restrictive aggregation of people, events and ideas. Watkins's regular techniques fragment against the hard concentration of this subject matter; that this is a conscious strategy may be deduced from the logical progression of the separate image streams employed towards final impact. His normal escalation of pitch or acceleration of pace is thwarted by the impossibility of defining a clear camera movement and/or detachable political argument when dealing with an artistic bio- graphy, a form even less flexible than an enclosed historical event. Watkins's task, after all, is to examine a single perspective rather than the contentious amalgam of many perspectives which only discernible ideological conflict can synthesise in the form of an accomplished historical fact.

Thwarted, this acceleration towards hysteria rebounds, frag- menting the narrative into obsessive repetition of emotive ima- gery and frustratingly incomplete movements through indi- vidual frames and on a distinct level, through the sustained fiction. Watkins discovers a way of collapsing the narrative according to an existing or constructed logic, in this case that of representation of a single artist and, by extension, the generic potential of a recognised discipline, the art film. Unusually sub- dued camerawork underlines this distancing from his material, characterised by some temporally relatively extended shots (by Watkins's former standards), relatively conventional set-ups, ex- aggerated use of the telephoto lens and a rationale for editing which might be described as cautious rather than simple. It is Watkins's most accomplished work.

Evening Land concerns the ramifications on a variety of political/ industrial levels of a growing protest against a proposal to in- volve Denmark in the trade in military equipment with a nuclear potential. Its strength is that it extrapolates on the basis of known and acknowledged industrial, political, military and journalistic practices. (*The War Game* is arguably less effective because of its sporadic tendency to revert from extension of established pro- cedures to ironic attacks on Establishment attitudes.)

Perhaps because of the unprecedented complexity of his sub- ject matter, perhaps because of his problematic status as a foreigner observing a series of interlocking internal disputes ab- out the ethical conduct of a nation not his own, Watkins is not particularly didactic or even aggressive in his treatment. He may have observed with some interest the rise of documentaries after the manner of Roger Graef and his *Decision* films. Watkins has sophisticated his exposition of the mechanics of decision-making and the exertion of pressure, and sensibly rejects the obvious possibility of organising narrative progression through a single investigative action. There is still no separate analytical articula- tive mode for the camera, but the relationship between unfiltered incident, television news and the editorial politics of print journalism, each credibly locked in on its own distinct level of bland distortion or furious incomprehension, is sensibly made available for examination and reconstruction by the audience.

Some of our legitimate interest in Watkins is certainly illuminated by his subsequent pursuit of themes and techniques identifiable in *Culloden* and *The War Game*. For the moment, however, our brief is limited, so at this point I think it would be useful to offer a provisional summary of Watkins's contribution to British television in particular.

Far from inventing his own dramatic terms of reference, Watkins adopted narrative techniques derived in the main from the documentary tradition, as it had been mutated through its own adaptation to the demands of televisual rather than cinematic communication. His deployment of these narrative resources was characterised by his awareness of how generalised actuality procedures might be made to serve specific dramatic ends; how, in fact, events which conventionally fell within the realm of actuality footage (history of the past or the future) might serve a particular didactic purpose by their single-minded dramatisation.

Clearly, technological and economic developments were gradually enforcing a revision of the traditional distinction between the social and dramatic functions of television (let us say, the different levels on which television might reasonably propose to inform and instruct). But it was left to Watkins to demonstrate with unprecedented vigour that, far from any divorcement of these functions being logical or even possible, they are in practice inextricably interconnected, and that only by insisting upon and pursuing this connection will television either extend its dramatic range or discharge any constructive (critical) social function at all. One may criticise Watkins's short-range vision, his affection for game-playing and other enclosed historical exercises, but his passion appeared at the time (and this may still be true) the most likely solvent to traditional categorisations. Watkins saw quite clearly that the maintenance of such artificial distinctions could only serve the prevailing ideology in its economic practices. His assault upon these was of sufficient force that within the space of two films he saw just such a model in operation, as the BBC decided which small groups of distinguished and responsible citizens should be allowed to watch *The War Game* at private views, in order to endorse the Corporation's decision, already taken, to ban its transmission on national television.

That the BBC should be embarrassed by *The War Game* need come as no surprise. Watkins had already showed (but in the relatively neutralised zone of a fictional reconstruction of past history) in *Culloden* that 'official' history can be assailed as a perceptual and hence a political system by the systematic application of its own technology. In practice, however, it is immaterial whether there was a failure on the part of BBC executives to decode *Culloden* accurately and thus grasp its political implications, for it remains axiomatic that the influence of the BBC on, for example, its Drama Department is obliquely exerted. Like many other national institutions, it proceeds by suggestion in preference to dictation. Censorship is a last resort, although one which retrospectively it appears was bound to be exercised towards Watkins, whose work denotes that suggestibility is not his most striking characteristic. It is interesting to note, however, that Corporation orthodoxies operated successfully on at least one level: Watkins wasn't dismissed; he resigned.

This does not compromise Watkins's achievement in exploiting to the full contemporary methods of news-gathering in their application to the news of the past and the future. Technological developments have been directed by news services towards the creation of an impression of greater verisimilitude to the quality of personally encountered experience (more intense 'actuality') and towards greater immediacy, both in the sense of ever decreasing time-lags between recording and transmission and in the qualitative effect of this acceleration of process on the viewer's response. We should accord Watkins a measure of respect for his pioneering work. The techniques of news-gathering for nightly broadcast, the production and consumption of actuality footage may subsequently have been used to serve a variety of dramatic purposes. But *Culloden* broke new ground in its time.

True, the ethical value-systems inherent in such techniques went largely unquestioned; the techniques themselves are exploited and not examined. But it is a signal event in the history of television when the technological coding systems of the twentieth century are first turned on the hitherto coded history of the eighteenth century. It requires a peculiar commitment, a single-minded vision of the function of the documentary drama, to achieve this transposition. It may be that this very sense of purpose excludes by definition the possibility that the audience will be encouraged to examine the coding systems of contemporary reportage for themselves. Watkins may have hoped that the very artificiality of the enterprise would precipitate an unprecedented re-examination of our response to actuality footage. This is speculation; it is a fact that, in closing in on his political/historical prey, Watkins allowed his audience little discretion, excluding rather than creating responsive and hence analytical options.

A final service of Watkins at this date was to test the tolerance of institutionalised broadcasting systems in this country, extending that political tolerance to its furthest limits. In view of the subsequent eclipse of his career in Britain, it might be argued that Watkins at the BBC worked towards the limits of his effective contract with British television, only to find himself working thereafter not towards the limits but in the margin. But the effect of *The War Game* in particular was to reveal to public scrutiny certain assumptions underlying the operation of the BBC. It doesn't matter whether the politics of confrontation was Watkins's conscious aim; everything about his choice of subjects, his perspective on them, and the techniques he employed to communicate this perspective reveals a man working to place existing articulative convention (and thus the convention of audience response, too) under acute stress. The extension of this debate into the public arena of the conduct of broadcasting systems as a whole was logical and inevitable.

Watkins's chosen methods played a crucial part in the evolution of public awareness of the BBC's code of dramatic conduct, for want of a better phrase. The BBC has always been fairly flexible in its attitude towards dramatic subjects, for example – and, phenomenologically speaking, even the idiom adopted in the treatment of the subject is rarely cause for concern. Each of these factors is more or less incidental to the mechanisms by which the Corporation organises its articulations. What bothers the BBC on a far more basic level is the assertive quality of the fiction – and hence its capacity to undermine prevailing attitudinal structures with damaging social implications. It is less concerned as an institution with the operation of any dramatic idiom, however radical, than with the way in which information is shown to be passed and the way in which power centres may be displayed colluding in the restriction of the passage of information (and thus in the maintenance of their own power).

The pattern seems to have survived with little mutation: in 1979 director Allen Clarke insisted that the finished television play *Scum* had been refused transmission by the BBC not for its violence but for its cumulative assertion that Borstal officers are corrupt in that they connive in the maintenance of the brutal and brutalising infrastructure of 'prison power' in these institutions. The controversy remains; no one ever did more to project it into the public arena than Pater Watkins.

Appendix

Films written and directed

1959   *Diary of an Unknown Soldier* (amateur film)

1960   *The Forgotten Faces* (amateur film about the Hungarian uprising of 1956)

1964   *Culloden* (dramatised TV documentary, made for and transmitted by the BBC)

1965   *The War Game* (dramatised TV documentary, made for but not transmitted by the BBC; subsequently distributed by the British Film Institute)

1967   *Privilege* (feature film made for Worldfilm Services/Memorial Enterprises; script by Norman Bogner, based on a story by Johnny Speight)

1969   *Gladiatorerna/The Peace Game* (feature film made in Sweden for Sandrews)

1971   *Punishment Park* (feature film made in the USA for Chartwell Films/Françoise Films)

1976   *Edvard Munch* (dramatised TV documentary made for Norsk Riks-kringkasting, Oslo, and Sveriges Radio, Stockholm; transmitted by the BBC)

1977   *Aftenlandet/Evening Land* (made in Denmark; co-scripted by Peter Watkins, Poul Martinsen and C. Clante)

Criticism

Milton Shulman, *The Ravenous Eye*, London: Coronet Books, 1975, pp. 256–9

Basil Wright, *The Long View*, London: Secker and Warburg, 1974, pp. 554–8

Reviews of *The War Game*

Film Comment, 3, 4 (Fall 1965), 4–14

Amateur Cine World, 9 December 1965, p. 819, and 24 February 1966, pp. 227, 257

Films and Filming, April 1966, p. 44 and, June 1966, p. 62

Jeune Cinéma, no. 17 (1966), 28–31

Sight and Sound, Spring 1966, p. 92

Variety, 7 September 1966

Positif, October 1966, pp. 115–19

Cinéma 67, no. 112, pp. 27–9

Chaplin 71, no. 3 (March 1967), 98–9

T. C. Worsley, *Television: The Ephemeral Art*, London: Alan Ross, 1970, pp. 214–17

Filmwoche, no. 15 (12 March 1971), 14

Image et Son, no. 259 (March 1972), 9–14

Jack Sheheen, 'The War Game Revisited', *Journal of Popular Film*, 1, 4 (Fall 1972), 299–308

Michael Tracey, 'A Nightmare Vision That Shook the BBC', *Guardian*, 1 September 1980, p. 12, followed by letters to *The Guardian*, 3 and 6 September 1980

Appendix 1

Plays published
Plays marked with an asterisk are available for viewing on film or videocassette at the National Film Archive, London (see Appendix 2).

Abbreviations

BSP *The Best Short Plays*, ed. Stanley Richards (series)
CG   *Conflicting Generations*, ed. Michael Marland, London: Longman 1968
ER   *Elizabeth R*, ed. J. C. Trewin, London: Elek, 1972
NGP *New Granada Plays*, London: Faber, 1961
PL   *The Pressures of Life*, ed. Michael Marland, London: Longman, 1977
SGP *Six Granada Plays*, London: Faber, 1960
SS   *Scene Scripts*, ed. Michael Marland, London: Longman, 1972
SWH *The Six Wives of Henry VIII*, ed. J. C. Trewin, London: Elek, 1972
TD   *The Television Dramatist*, ed. Robert Muller, London: Elek, 1973
TP   *The Television Playwright: Ten Plays for B.B.C. Television*, ed. Michael Barry, London: Michael Joseph, 1960
WT   *Writing for Television in the 70's*, ed. Malcolm Hulke, London: Black, rev. repr. 1976
ZC   *Z-Cars*, ed. Michael Marland, London: Longman, 1967

Adrian, Rhys, *The Protest*, in: *NGP*
Antrobus, John, *The Missing Links*, in: his *Why Bournemouth?*, London: Calder & Boyars, 1970
Arden, John, *Soldier, Soldier; Wet Fish*, in: his *Soldier, Soldier and Other Plays*, London: Methuen, 1967
Baron, Alexander, *A Bit of Happiness*, in: *SGP*
Barstow, Stan, *Joby: A Television Play Dramatised from His Own Novel*, Glasgow: Blackie, 1977
Bast, William, *The Myth Makers*, in: *SGP*
Beckett, Samuel, *. . . but the clouds . . .*; *Ghost Trio*, in: his *Ends and Odds*, London: Faber, 1977
Behan, Dominic, *The Patriot Game*, in: *Camera One*, ed. Ron Side and Ralph Greenfield, London: Holt-Blond, 1972
Bermange, Barry, *Invasion*, in: his *No Quarter and the Interview*, London: Methuen, 1970

239

Scenes from Family Life, in: *Collection: Literature for the Seventies*, ed. Gerald and Nancy S. Messner, Lexington, Mass.: D. C. Heath, 1972

Black, Campbell, *And They Used To Star in the Movies*, *Transatlantic Review*, 45 (Spring 1973)

Blair, Jon and Norman Fenton, *A Miserable and Lonely Death*: *A Reconstruction of the Inquest Into the Death of Steven Biko*, London: Thames TV, 1977

Bowen, John, *The Essay Prize, with A Holiday Abroad and The Candidate*, London: Faber, 1962
  Robin Redbreast, in: *TD*
  Hail Caesar: A Modern Version of 'Julius Caesar', London: BBC Publications, 1974

Brandel, Marc, *Five Men for Freedom*, in: *Camera Two*, ed. Ron Side and Ralph Greenfield, Toronto: Holt, Rinehart & Winston, 1972

Brenton, Howard, *The Saliva Milkshake*, London: TQ Publications, 1977

Bussell, Jan, *Sea Fever*, in: her *The Art of Television*, London: Faber, 1952

Cahill, Michael, *It's Me – Eileen*, in: *SS*

Callow, Philip, *The Honeymooners*, in: *NGP*

Campton, David, *Incident*, in: *Playmakers One*, Huddersfield: Schofield & Sims, 1976

Clarke, Roy, *The Last of the Summer Wine*, London: BBC Publications, 1976

Clarke, Tom, *Victims of Apartheid*: *Play for Today*, London: Eyre Methuen, 1978

Cleese, John and Connie Booth, *Fawlty Towers: Three Episodes*, n.p., Contact Publications, 1977

Coke, Peter, *In Confidence*, in: *Best One-Act Plays of 1963–64*, ed. Hugh Miller, London: Harrap, 1965

Cottrell, Richard, *Marking Time*, in: *NGP*

Cregan, David, *George Reborn*, in: his *The Land of Palms*, London: Eyre Methuen, 1973

Crisp, N. J., *The Expert: Death in the Rain*, in: *WT*

Cross, Beverley, *Catherine Howard*, in: *SWH*

Curteis, Ian, *The Gentle Invasion; Battle at Tematangi; The Last Enemy*, in: his *The Long Voyage Out of War*, London: Calder & Boyars, 1971

Daly, Wally K., *Butterflies Don't Count*: *Play for Today*, London: Eyre Methuen, 1978

Dewhurst, Keith, *Running Milligan*, in: *ZC*
  Last Bus, in: *SS*

Douglass, Stewart, *The Shadow of the Ruthless*, in: Howard Thomas (ed.), *The Armchair Theatre*, London: Weidenfeld & Nicolson, 1959

Duncan, Ronald, *The Rehearsal*, in: his *Collected Plays*, London: Hart-Davis, 1971

Dunn, Douglas, *Ploughman's Share*: *Play for Today*, London: Eyre Methuen, 1978

Duthie, James, *Donal and Sally*: *Play for Today*, London: Eyre Methuen, 1978

Edwards, Rex, *Hero in the Dust*, in: SS

Esmonde, John and Bob Lacey, *A Touch of the Tiny Hacketts: Play for Today*,
London: Eyre Methuen, 1978

Exton, Clive, **No Fixed Abode*, in: SGP

Eyre, Ronald, *Window Dressing*, in: ZC
The Victim, in: CG
Clean Sweep, in: SS

Flower, Pat, *The Tape Recorder*, in: BSP 1969, New York: Chilton, 1969

Fry, Christopher, *The Brontës of Haworth*, 2 vols., London: Davis-Poynter,
1975

Galton, Ray and Alan Simpson, *The Reunion, Impasse, and The Telephone
Call*, Leeds: E. J. Arnold, 1966
Steptoe and Son: Four Episodes, London: Longman, 1971
Hancock's Half Hour: Six Episodes, London: Woburn Press, 1974

Gear, Brian, *A Pretty Row of Pretty Ribbons*, in: BSP 1970, New York:
Chilton, 1970

Gray, Simon, *Sleeping Dog*, London: Faber, 1968
Spoiled, London: Eyre Methuen, 1971
Two Sundays; Plaintiffs and Defendants, in: his *Otherwise Engaged and
Other Plays*, London: Eyre Methuen, 1975

Griffiths, Leon, *Dinner at the Sporting Club: Play for Today*, London: Eyre
Methuen, 1978

Griffiths, Trevor, *All Good Men, and Absolute Beginners*, London: Faber,
1977
Through the Night, and Such Impossibilities, London: Faber, 1977

Hale, John, *The Lion's Cub*, in: ER

Hall, Willis, *Airmail from Cyprus*, in: TP
A Glimpse of the Sea; Last Day in Dreamland; Return to the Sea, in: his *A
Glimpse of the Sea*, London: Evans, 1960

Hampton, Christopher, *Able's Will*, London: Faber, 1979

Hare, David, **Licking Hitler*, London: Faber, 1978

Harris, Richard, *Reasonable Suspicion*, in: PL

Hines, Barry, *Billy's Last Stand*, in: BSP 1971, New York: Chilton, 1971
Speech Day, in: PL
The Price of Coal, London: Hutchinson, 1979

Holmes, Robert, *Doctor Who: Carnival of Monsters, Episode 1*, in: WT

Hopkins, John, *A Place of Safety*, in: ZC
*Talking to a Stranger, Harmondsworth: Penguin, 1967
A Game – Like – Only a Game, in: CG

Hughes, Ken, *Sammy*, in: TP

Hughes, Patrick, *A Place of My Own*, in: NGP

Jones, Elwyn, *Private Mischief; Power of the Press; In the Public Gaze; Priorities;
On the Third Day*, in: his *Softly, Softly*, London: Longman, 1976

Jones, Julia, *The Piano*, in: PL

Jupp, Kenneth, *The Photographer; The Explorer; The Tycoon*, in: his *A
Chelsea Trilogy*, London: Calder & Boyars, 1969

Kent, Graeme, *The Queen's Corporal*, in: *SGP*

Kneale, Nigel, **The Quatermass Experiment*, Harmondsworth: Penguin, 1959
  *Quatermass II, Harmondsworth: Penguin, 1960
  *Quatermass and the Pit, Harmondsworth: Penguin, 1960
  Mrs Wickens in the Fall, in: *TP*
  The Road; The Stone Tape; The Year of the Sex Olympics, in: his *The Year of the Sex Olympics*, London: Ferret Fantasy, 1976

Knowles, Leo, *The Last Victim*, in: *BSP 1974*, Radnor, Pa.: Chilton, 1974

Lehman, Leo, *Thirty Pieces of Silver*, in: *TP*
  End of Story, in: *TD*

Leonard, Hugh, *The Late Arrival of the Incoming Aircraft*, London: Evans, 1968

Livings, Henry, *There's No Room for You Here for a Start*, in: his *Kelly's Eye and Other Plays*, London: Methuen, 1964

Long, Peter et al., *Crossroads; Episode 1751*, in: *WT*

Lyons, Bill, *£60 Single, £100 Return*, in: *SS*

McCarty, Nick, *Anne Boleyn*, in: *SWH*

MacCormick, Iain, *The Small Victory*, in: *TP*

Mackie, Philip, *The Right Person*, London: Evans, 1956
  The Whole Truth, London: Evans, 1956
  Open House, London: Evans, 1958
  The Key of the Door, London: Evans, 1959

McSmith, Andy, *One Bummer News Day: Play for Today*, London: Eyre Methuen, 1978

Mann, Stanley, **Better Luck Next Time* (excerpt), *Contrast* 3, 3 (Spring, 1964)

Manvell, Roger, *The July Plot*, Glasgow: Blackie, 1966

Marcus, Frank, *The Window*, London: French, 1970
  Blank Pages, in: *BSP 1974*, Radnor, Pa.: Chilton, 1974

Markham, Jehane, *Nina: Play for Today*, London: Eyre Methuen, 1978

Mercer, David, **Where the Difference Begins; A Climate of Fear; The Birth of a Private Man*, in: his *The Generations*, London: Calder, 1964
  A Suitable Case for Treatment; For Tea on Sunday; *And Did Those Feet, in: his *Three Television Comedies*, London: Calder & Boyars, 1965
  Let's Murder Vivaldi; *In Two Minds; *The Parachute, in: his *The Parachute with Two More TV Plays*, London: Calder & Boyars, 1967
  On the Eve of Publication; The Cellar and the Almond Tree; Emma's Time, in: his *On the Eve of Publication and Other Plays*, London: Eyre Methuen, 1970
  The Bankrupt; You and Me and Him; An Afternoon at the Festival; Find Me, in: his *The Bankrupt and Other Plays*, London: Eyre Methuen, 1974
  Huggy Bear; The Arcata Promise; A Superstition, in: his *Huggy Bear and Other Plays*, London: Eyre Methuen, 1977
  Shooting the Chandelier, in: his *Cousin Vladimir and Shooting the Chandelier*, London: Eyre Methuen, 1978

Mitchell, Adrian, *Man Friday*, in: his *Man Friday and Mind Your Head*, London: Eyre Methuen, 1974

Mitchell, James, *Soldier in the Snow*, in: *NGP*

Mitchell, Julian, *Shadow in the Sun*, in: *ER*

Morgan, Elaine, *The Soldier and the Woman*, London: French, 1961

Morris, Colin, *The Unloved*, in: *TP*

Morris, Jean, *Anne of Cleves*, in: *SWH*

Mortimer, Elaine, *You're a Long Time Dead*, in: *TP*

Mortimer, John, *Call Me a Liar; David and Broccoli*, in: his *Lunch Hour and Other Plays*, London: Methuen, 1960

  A Choice of Kings, in: *Playbill 3*, ed. Alan Durband, London: Hutchinson, 1969

  Desmond, in: *BSP 1971*, New York: Chilton, 1971

Muller, Robert, *Afternoon of a Nymph*, in: *Anatomy of a Television Play*, ed. John Russell Taylor, London: Weidenfeld & Nicolson, 1962

Nichols, Peter, *Promenade*, in: *SGP*

  *Ben Spray, in: *NGP*

  *The Gorge, in: *TD*

O'Neill, Michael and Jeremy Seabrook, *A Right Dream of Delight*, in: *PL*

Orton, Joe, *The Good and Faithful Servant; The Erpingham Camp; Funeral Games*, in: his *Collected Plays*, London: Eyre Methuen, 1976

Osborne, John, **A Subject of Scandal and Concern*, London: Faber, 1961

  The Right Prospectus, London: Faber, 1970

  Very like a Whale, London: Faber, 1971

  The Gift of Friendship, London: Faber, 1972

  Jill and Jack, in: his *The End of Me Old Cigar*, London: Faber, 1975

  You're Not Watching Me, Mummy, and Try a Little Tenderness, London: Faber, 1978

O'Toole, Jon, *The Bush and the Tree*, in: *SGP*

Owen, Alun, *No Tram to Lime Street; After the Funeral; *Lena, Oh My Lena*, in: his *Three TV Plays*, London: Cape, 1961

  *The Rose Affair, in: *Anatomy of a Television Play*, ed. John Russell Taylor London: Weidenfeld & Nicolson, 1962

  Dare To Be a Daniel, in: *Eight Plays: Book 1*, ed. Malcolm Stuart Fellows, London: Cassell, 1965

  George's Room, London: French, 1968

  Shelter, London: French, 1968

  Doreen, in: *BSP 1971*, New York: Chilton, 1971

  The Wake, in: *Theatre Choice*, ed. Michael Marland, Glasgow: Blackie, 1972

  The Male of the Species, London: French, 1972; also in: *Camera Three*, ed. Ron Side and Ralph Greenfield, Toronto: Holt, Rinehart & Winston, 1972, and in: *Best Short Plays of the World Theatre 1968–1973*, New York: Crown, 1973

Palin, Michael and Terry Jones, *Ripping Yarns*, London: Eyre Methuen, 1978

Parker, Tony, *Mrs Lawrence Will Look After It; Chariot of Fire; When the Bough Breaks*, in: his *Three Television Plays*, London: Davis-Poynter, 1975

Perry, Jimmy and David Croft, *Dad's Army*, London: Elm Tree Books, 1975

Pinter, Harold, **A Night Out*, in: his *A Slight Ache and Other Plays*, London: Methuen, 1961
   The Collection and *The Lover, London: Methuen, 1963
   *Tea Party; The Basement; Night School, in: his *Tea Party and Other Plays*, London: Methuen, 1967

Plater, Alan, *A Quiet Night*, in: ZC
   See the Pretty Lights, in: *Theatre Choice*, ed. Michael Marland, Glasgow: Blackie, 1972
   Terry, in: *SS*
   On Christmas Day in the Morning; Seventeen Per Cent Said Push Off, in: his *You and Me*, ed. Alfred Bradley, London: Blackie, 1973
   Close the Coalhouse Door, London: Eyre Methuen, 1974
   Annie Kenney (abridged), in: *Act 3*, ed. David Self and Ray Speakman, London: Hutchinson, 1979

Potter, Dennis, **Stand Up, Nigel Barton; *Vote, Vote, Vote for Nigel Barton*, in: his *The Nigel Barton Plays*, Harmondsworth: Penguin, 1967
   *Son of Man, London: Deutsch, 1970
   *Follow the Yellow Brick Road, in: *TD*
   Strawberry Fields, London: Eyre Methuen, 1977
   *Brimstone and Treacle, London: Eyre Methuen, 1978

Powell, Vince and Frank Roscoe, *Here's Harry: Five Harry Worth Scripts*, Altrincham: John Sherratt, 1963

Prebble, John, *Catherine Parr*, in: *SWH*
   The Enterprise of England, in: *ER*

Raphael, Frederick, *An Early Life*, London: Faber, 1977

Raphael, Frederick and K. McLeish, *The Serpent Son: TV Adaptation of Aeschylus' 'Oresteia'*, Cambridge: University Press, 1979

Rattigan, Terence, *Heart to Heart*, in: his *Collected Plays*, vol. 3, London: Hamish Hamilton, 1964
   All on Her Own, in: *BSP 1970*, New York: Chilton, 1970
   High Summer, in: *BSP 1973*, New York: Chilton, 1973

Raven, Simon, *Royal Foundation; The Gaming Book; The Scapegoat; Sir Jocelyn, the Minister Would Like a Word*, in: his *The Royal Foundation and Other Plays*, London: Blond, 1966

Rodger, Ian, *Sweet England's Pride*, in: *ER*

Rosenthal, Jack, **Another Sunday and Sweet F.A.*, in: *TD*
   Bar Mitzvah Boy; *The Evacuees; *Spend, Spend, Spend, in: *Three Award-Winning Television Plays*, Harmondsworth: Penguin, 1978

Rudkin, David, *Penda's Fen*, London: Davis-Poynter, 1975

Sandford, Jeremy, **Cathy Come Home*, London: Boyars, 1976
   *Edna the Inebriate Woman, London: Boyars, 1976

Schuman, Howard, *Censored Scenes from King Kong*, Gambit 26 & 27 (Autumn 1975)

Shaughnessy, Alfred, *Holiday for Simon*, London: French, 1955

Shaw, Don, *Me Mackenna*, in: *Second Playbill Three*, ed. Alan Durband, London: Hutchinson, 1973

Sillitoe, Alan, *Pit Strike*, in: his *Three Plays*, London: W. H. Allen, 1978

Simpson, Alan and Ray Galton, *Hancock: Four Scripts for Television*, London: Deutsch, 1961

Simpson, Norman Frederick, *Some Tall Tinkles*, London: Faber, 1968

Sisson, Rosemary Anne, *Catherine of Aragon*, in: *SWH*
  The Marriage Game, in: *ER*
  Finders, Keepers (excerpt), in: *WT*

Speight, Johnny, *If There Weren't Any Blacks You'd Have To Invent Them*, London: Methuen, 1968
  Till Death Us Do Part, London: Woburn Press, 1973

Spooner, Dennis, *Jason King: An Author in Search of Two Characters*, in: *WT*

Spurling, John, *Death of Captain Doughty*, in: his *Shades of Heathcliff*, London: Boyars, 1975

Stevenson, John, *Nearest and Dearest: Getting To Know You*, in: *WT*

Stoppard, Tom, *A Separate Peace*, in: *Playbill 2*, ed. Alan Durband, London: Hutchinson, 1969
  Professional Foul, in: his *Every Good Boy Deserves Favour and Professional Foul*, London: Faber, 1978

Stott, Mike, *Soldiers Talking Cleanly: Play for Today*, London: Eyre Methuen, 1978

Taylor, Cecil P., *Charles and Cromwell*, in: his *Making a TV Play: A Complete Guide from Conception to BBC Production*, Newcastle upon Tyne: Oriel Press, 1970
  Words, in *Second Playbill 2*, ed. Alan Durband, London: Hutchinson, 1973

Terson, Peter, *The Ballad of Ben Bagot*, in *Prompt 2*, ed. Alan Durband, London: Hutchinson, 1976

Thorne, Ian, *Jane Seymour*, in: *SWH*

Trevor, William, *The Old Boys*, London: Davis-Poynter, 1971
  A Night with Mrs da Tanka, London: French, 1972
  The Grass Widows (excerpt), in: *WT*

Turner, David, *Way Off Beat*, in: *CG*

Voysey, Michael, *The Amorous Goldfish*, in: *TP*

Waddy, Laurence, *The Prodigal Son: A Musical*, London: French, 1963

Ward, Edmund, *The Challengers: Six Plays with Supporting Essays*, London: Elek, 1973

Ward, Philip, *Hawklaw; A Fence round the Property*, in: his *Television Plays*, Cambridge: Oleander, 1976

Watkins, Peter, *The War Game*, London: Deutsch, 1967

Weldon, Fay, *Time Hurries On*, in: *SS*

Welland, Colin, *A Roomful of Holes*, London: Davis-Poynter, 1971

Wesker, Arnold, *Menace*, in: his *Six Sundays in January*, London: Cape, 1971

   Love Letters on Blue Paper, London: TQ Publications, 1978

Whitemore, Hugh, *Horrible Conspiracies*, in: *ER*

Whiting, John, *A Walk in the Desert*, in: his *Collected Plays*, vol. 2, London: Heinemann, 1969

Williams, Raymond, *Public Inquiry*, Stand 9, 1 (1967)

   A Letter from the Country, Stand 12, 2 (Spring 1971)

Willis, Ted, *Woman in a Dressing Gown; Look in Any Window; The Young and the Guilty*, in: his *Woman in a Dressing Gown and Other Television Plays*, London: Barrie & Rockliff, 1959

Wilson, Donald, *Flight of the Dove*, in: *TP*

For an annotated bibliography of British television plays with brief plot synopses, see *Theatre Quarterly* 7, 27 (Autumn 1977) and 8, 30 (Summer 1978).

Appendix 2

The National Film Archive

The National Film Archive, which is part of the British Film Institute, has been collecting television programmes since the 1950s. It enjoys co-operation both from the BBC and the ITV companies (from the latter in the form of a grant to purchase selected ITV programmes). Numerous examples of television drama are preserved in the Archive's collection. Where viewing copies are available, these can be seen on film or videocassette on Archive premises. (They are not available for outside use, because of restrictions of copyright.)

Enquiries about the availability of specific titles should be made to the Viewings Supervisor, National Film Archive, 81 Dean Street, London W1V 6AA.

Notes

Chapter 1.   Introduction

1 Preface to Howard Thomas (ed.), *The Armchair Theatre*, p. 7.
2 Tony Garnett in *Journal of the Society of Film and Television Arts*, 23 (Spring 1966), 9.
3 See B. P. Emmett, 'The Television and Radio Audience in Britain', in: *Sociology of Mass Communications*, ed. Denis McQuail, p. 212.
4 *Hazell: The Making of a TV Series*, p. 1.
5 Raymond Williams, *Drama in a Dramatised Society*, p. 5.
6 *Daily Telegraph*, 30 May 1960.
7 *The Observer*, 30 July 1978.
8 'Writing for the Dreamer's Dustbin', in: Thomas (ed.), *Armchair Theatre*, pp. 50–1.
9 *Discrimination and Popular Culture*, ed. Denys Thompson (Harmondsworth: Penguin, 1964), p. 67. The revised edition (London: Heinemann, 1973) changes some details in Abrams's argument but not its substance.
10 *Discrimination and Popular Culture*, p. 52.
11 *Selected Masques*, ed. Stephen Orgel (New Haven and London: Yale University Press, 1970), p. 48.
12 *Discrimination and Popular Culture*, p. 70.
13 Vol. 3, no. 4 (Summer 1964), 211–14.
14 See also Clive James, *Visions Before Midnight*, and T. C. Worsley, *Television: The Ephemeral Art*.
15 John Drakakis, introduction to *British Radio Drama* (Cambridge: University Press, 1981), pp. 20–1.
16 John Swift, *Adventure in Vision*, pp. 46–7.
17 In: Joan Bakewell and Nicholas Garnham, *The New Priesthood*, p. 9.
18 Swift, *Adventure in Vision*, pp. 154–5; original italics.
19 *Ibid.* p. 153.
20 Jan Bussell, *The Art of Television*, p. 103.
21 *Ibid.* p. 105.
22 *Ibid.* pp. 103–4.
23 *Ibid.* p. 104.
24 *Ibid.* p. 43.
25 Arthur Swinson, 'Writing for Television', in: Paul Rotha (ed.), *Television in the Making*, p. 39.

26 Bussell, *Art of Television*, pp. 106–7.

27 Irene Shubik, *Play for Today*, p. 34.

28 Ted Willis, 'The Writer and Television', in: *Woman in a Dressing Gown*, p. 9.

29 Thomas (ed.), *Armchair Theatre*, p. 16.

30 *Ibid*. p. 18.

31 Philip Purser, 'Head of Drama', *Contrast*, 2, 1 (Autumn 1962), 35.

32 See the lists of *Armchair Theatre* productions in: Thomas (ed.), *Armchair Theatre*, pp. 102–15, and in: John Russell Taylor, *Anatomy of a Television Play*, pp. 212–23.

33 In: Michael Barry (ed.), *The Television Playwright: Ten Plays for B.B.C. Television*, p. 14; original italics.

34 See Shubik, *Play for Today*, for a first-hand account of the genesis and development of this play spot, and note the list of productions from 28 October 1964 to 11 December 1973 on pp. 60–74.

35 'Is the Script Editor Really Necessary?', *Theatre Quarterly*, 5, 18 (June–August 1975), 55.

36 Caryl Doncaster, 'The Story Documentary', in: Rotha (ed.), *Television in the Making*, p. 47.

37 See pp. 194–211.

38 See *Television and Radio 1979* (London: Independent Broadcasting Authority, 1978), p. 94.

39 *Ibid*. p. 93.

40 For the production history of *Upstairs Downstairs*, see *Theatre Quarterly*, 2, 6 (April–June 1972), 26–38, and 2, 8 (October–December 1972), 82, and Alfred Shaughnessy, *Both Ends of the Candle*.

41 *The Observer*, 30 December 1979.

42 In: Bakewell and Garnham, *New Priesthood*, pp. 103–4.

43 In: *ibid*. p. 47.

44 'Synthetic Gossip', *Contrast*, 3, 4 (Summer 1964), 230.

45 For Speight's views on TV scriptwriting, see Henry Mara, 'Conversation with a Script Writer', *Contrast*, 2, 1 (Autumn 1962), 50–6.

46 Stuart Hood, *A Survey of Television*, p. 153.

47 See pp. 185–8.

48 *Television and Radio 1979*, pp. 93–4.

49 *Ibid*. p. 89.

50 Thomas (ed.), *Armchair Theatre*, p. 15.

51 J. R. Taylor, *Anatomy of a Television Play*, p. 11.

52 Vol. 11, no. 2 (March–April 1964), 21–33.

53 See *Screen*, issues of Winter 1975–6, Spring 1976 and Spring 1977.

54 *Television as a Medium and Its Relation to Culture*, p. 97; original italics.

55 Stuart Hall and Paddy Whannell, *The Popular Arts*, p. 264.

56 See pp. 48–52.

57 Colin MacCabe, '*Days of Hope* – A Response to Colin McArthur', quoted in: Colin McArthur, *Television and History*, p. 51.

58 'Realism and Non-Naturalism', in: *Official Programme of the Edinburgh International Television Festival 1977*, p. 37.

59 'Edna and Sheila: Two Kinds of Truth', *Theatre Quarterly*, 2, 7 (July–September 1972), 47.

60 'Drama-Documentary 2', in: *Official Programme of the Edinburgh International Television Festival 1977*, p. 22.

61 29 September 1975.

62 'The Politics of Television', in: *Sociology of Mass Communications*, ed. McQuail, p. 421.

63 *What Price Annan!* (Ardleigh, Colchester: National Viewers' and Listeners' Association, 8 May 1978), pp. 6–19.

64 Paul Tayler, *The Guardian*, 29 August 1978.

65 *Television Violence and the Adolescent Boy*, p. 520; original italics.

66 *Sex, Violence and the Media*, p. 274.

67 *Ibid.* p. 269; original italics.

68 *Radio Times*, 28 October–3 November 1978, p. 25.

69 See Appendixes 1 and 2.

Chapter 2.   Jim Allen

1 Unpublished interview with Jim Allen by Paul Madden, 1979.

2 Roger Hudson, 'Television in Britain: Description and Dissent', *Theatre Quarterly*, 2, 6 (April–June 1972), 23–4.

3 John McGrath, 'The Case Against Naturalism', *Sight and Sound*, 46, 2 (1977), 100–5.

4 Jim Allen, 'The Way Back from the Legend', in: *Journey to a Legend and Back: The British Realistic Film*, ed. Eva Orbanz (Berlin: Volker Spiess, 1977), pp. 151–9.

5 Paul Madden, 'Interview with Jim Allen', in: *Complete Programme Notes for a Season of British Television Drama 1959–1973, Held at the National Film Theatre, 11th–24th October 1976*, ed. Madden (London: British Film Institute, 1976).

6 Unpublished interview by Paul Madden.

7 *Ibid.*

8 *Ibid.*

9 'The Way Back from the Legend'.

10 Hudson, 'Television in Britain', p. 20.

11 Paul Madden and David Wilson, 'Getting In Close: An Interview with Jack Gold', *Sight and Sound*, 43, 3 (1974), 134–7.

12 'A Lecture on Realism', *Screen*, 18, 1 (1977), 61–74.

13 Unpublished interview by Paul Madden.

14 *Ibid.*

15 'Interview with Jim Allen'.

16 'Years of Promise', *Radio Times*, 6–12 September 1975.

17 'Interview with Jim Allen'.

18 London: New Park, 1967.

19 'The Way Back from the Legend'.

20 'The Case Against Naturalism'.
21 Paul Madden, review of *The Spongers*, *Sight and Sound*, 47, 2 (1978), 126–7.
22 *Ibid.*
23 *Ibid.*
24 Unpublished interview by Paul Madden.

Chapter 3. Trevor Griffiths

1 Trevor Griffiths, *Through the Night, and Such Impossibilities* (London, 1977), Preface, p. 11.
2 *Ibid.* pp. 7–8.
3 Plus a stage version of *All Good Men*, first presented at the Young Vic, 13 May 1975.
4 For synopses and production details of all plays written by Griffiths up to and including *Bill Brand*, see Malcolm Hay, 'Theatre Checklist No. 9: Trevor Griffiths', *Theatrefacts*, 3 (1976), no. 1 – TF9, pp. 2–8.
5 Interview on 8 May 1979 (hereafter cited as 'Interview'). This interview also furnished much of the factual information contained in this chapter. I should like to record my gratitude to Trevor Griffiths for his patience and openness.
6 In addition, a version of *The Cherry Orchard* by Griffiths was staged at the Nottingham Playhouse in March 1977, directed by Richard Eyre.
7 *Through the Night*, p. 12.
8 *Ibid.* p. 127 (quotation from Tom Mann).
9 *All Good Men, and Absolute Beginners* (London, 1977), pp. 9–17.
10 Interview.
11 'Prickly Pair', *New Statesman*, 8 February 1974, p. 198.
12 Interview.
13 'TV Selections', (unsigned), *Time Out*, 19 April 1974.
14 Interview.
15 *Ibid.*
16 *All Good Men*, p. 87.
17 In fact, there was an actual agent called Kabakchev, who attended the 1921 Livorno conference of the Italian Socialist Party (PSI).
18 Interview.
19 *All Good Men*, p. 69.
20 *Ibid.* p. 110.
21 The published version is somewhere between the two.
22 'Transforming the Husk of Capitalism', *Theatre Quarterly*, 6, 22 (Summer 1976), 39.
23 *Through the Night*, p. 37. 'Stourton' becomes 'Staunton' in the published text.
24 *Ibid.* p. 43. Note that where here and elsewhere there are slight divergences from the published text, they are the result of my quoting from the text as transmitted.
25 *Through the Night*, Scene 36.

26 'The People Speak', *The Sunday Times*, 7 December 1975, p. 39.
27 *Through the Night*, p. 63.
28 For medical corroboration of Griffiths' contention, see Maureen Reynolds, 'No News Is Bad News: Patients' Views About Communication in Hospital', *British Medical Journal*, 24 June 1978, pp. 1673–6.
29 *Through the Night*, p. 64.
30 Interview.
31 *Through the Night*, author's preface, pp. 11–12. The correspondence on mastectomy was in fact conducted in the *Sunday Mirror*, not in *The People* as stated in this preface.
32 Quoted by Griffiths in his author's preface to the play.
33 *Through the Night*, p. 26.
34 Nigel Thomas, 'Trevor and Bill – On Putting Politics Before News at Ten', *The Leveller*, November 1976, p. 12.
35 The directors were Roland Joffe, Michael Lindsay-Hogg and Stuart Burge, who also produced the series.
36 'Haggard Odysseus', *The Listener*, 22 July 1976, p. 85.
37 *The Leveller*, p. 12.
38 All quotations are taken from the videotapes of the series made available by Thames Television.
39 Episode 6, which covered the prime minister's resignation, was shot well before Harold Wilson's resignation on 16 March 1976.
40 'Bill Brand and I', *New Statesman*, 30 July 1976, p. 140.
41 See Joe Ashton, 'Brand Images', *Guardian*, 3 August 1976; 'Good Television – But How Many MPs Are Bill Brands?', *The Economist*, 14 August 1976, p. 26; Audrey Williamson, 'Bill Brand – Monosyllabic Melodrama', *The Tribune*, 30 July 1976.
42 *The Leveller*, p. 12.
43 Expressed henceforth as '5.3'.
44 Jonathan Croall, 'From Home to House', *The Times Educational Supplement*, 25 June 1976, p. 19.
45 Georg Lukács, *The Meaning of Contemporary Realism* (London, 1963), pp. 93–4. Quoted from the introduction to David Craig (ed.), *Marxists on Literature – An Anthology* (London, 1975), which contains a discussion of the meaning of socialist realism.

Chapter 4. David Mercer

1 *Where the Difference Begins*, in: David Mercer, *The Generations* (London: Calder, 1964).
2 'The Birth of a Playwriting Man', *Theatre Quarterly*, 3, 9 (January–March 1973), 47.
3 *Death in the Family* was the title of the original draft of the play. See *The Generations*, appendix by Don Taylor, p. 244.
4 *The Generations*, p. 14.
5 *Ibid*. p. 15.

6 Ralph Stephenson and J. R. Debrix, *The Cinema as Art* (Harmondsworth: Penguin, 1965), p. 70.

7 *The Generations*, p. 16.

8 *Ibid.* p. 17.

9 *Ibid.* p. 18.

10 *The Observer*, 31 May 1964, p. 28.

11 *The Generations*, pp. 23–4.

12 *Ibid.* p. 56.

13 *Ibid.*

14 *Ibid.* p. 29.

15 *Ibid.* p. 20.

16 *Ibid.* p. 24.

17 When asked by *Theatre Quarterly* whether this was his idea or the director's, he answered, 'I can't remember now how much of what I might have written in by way of directions was literally followed up by the actual shooting and editing, but I think a fair amount of it was written in and intended' ('Birth of a Playwriting Man', p. 49).

18 *Ibid.* p. 43.

19 *The Generations*, p. 80.

20 'Notes on Broadcasting', *The Times*, 30 December 1961, p. 5.

21 *The Generations*, p. 53.

22 Peter Noble (ed.), *British Film and TV Year Book 1974–5* (published by Cinema TV Today), p. 244, under entry for Ken Loach, who directed the film *Family Life* (1971).

23 'Mercer and the Slag Heap', *Radio Times*, 23 November 1972, p. 11.

24 'Birth of a Playwriting Man', p. 48.

25 *The Generations*, p. 85.

26 *Ibid.* pp. 104–5.

27 *Ibid.* p. 105.

28 *Ibid.* p. 117.

29 *Ibid.* p. 118.

30 *Ibid.* p. 121.

31 *Ibid.* p. 153.

32 *Ibid.* p. 152.

33 *Ibid.*

34 *Ibid.* p. 153.

35 Andrew Sarris (ed.), *Hollywood Voices: Interviews with Film Directors* (London: Secker & Warburg, 1971), p. 100. John Huston, interviewed by Gideon Bachmann, discusses his scriptwriting technique.

36 *Ibid.* p. 114.

37 *The Generations*, p. 161

38 *Ibid.*p. 29.

39 *Ibid.*p. 80.

40 *Ibid.* p. 41.

41 *Ibid.* p. 125.

42 *Ibid.* p. 137.

43 *Ibid.* p. 174.
44 *Ibid.* p. 227.
45 *Ibid.* p. 156.
46 *Ibid.* p. 232.
47 *Ibid.*
48 *A Suitable Case for Treatment*, in: David Mercer, *Three Television Comedies* (London: Calder & Boyars, 1965), p. 18.
49 'British writers always tend to do first, and to theorize, if at all, afterwards' (John Russell Taylor, *The Rise and Fall of the Well-Made Play* (London: Methuen, 1967), p. 11).
50 *In Two Minds*, in: David Mercer, *The Parachute with Two More TV Plays* (London: Calder & Boyars, 1967), pp. 63–4.
51 *Ibid.* p. 58.
52 *Ibid.* p. 60
53 *Ibid.* p. 47.
54 *Ibid.* p. 68.
55 *Ibid.* pp. 59–60.
56 *Ibid.* p. 52.
57 *Ibid.* p. 53.
58 'Birth of a Playwriting Man', p. 48.
59 Dennis Potter, 'Sting in the Brain', *New Statesman*, 10 March 1967, p. 339.
60 'Birth of a Playwriting Man', p. 49.
61 *Sanity, Madness and the Family*, vol. 1, *Families of Schizophrenics* (London: Tavistock Publications, 1965), p. viii.
62 *Ibid.* p. 64.
63 *In Two Minds*, p. 65.
64 *Ibid.* p. 62.
65 *Ibid.* p. 91.
66 *Ibid.* p. 84.
67 *Ibid.* p. 85.
68 *Families of Schizophrenics*, p. 142.
69 *Ibid.* p. 184.
70 *In Two Minds*, p. 57.
71 *Ibid.* p. 55.
72 *Ibid.* pp. 55–6.
73 *Families of Schizophrenics*, p. 184.
74 *In Two Minds*, pp. 49–50.
75 *Ibid.* p. 52.
76 *Families of Schizophrenics*, p. 154.
77 *In Two Minds*, p. 60.
78 *Ibid.* p. 61.
79 *Ibid.* p. 92.
80 *The Politics of Experience and the Bird of Paradise* (Harmondsworth: Penguin, 1970), p. 81.
81 *Ibid.* p. 100.

82 *In Two Minds*, p. 90
83 *The Listener*, 9 March 1967, p. 335.
84 Letter to *The Times*, 8 March 1967.

Chapter 5. Peter Nichols

1 *Promenade*, in: *Six Granada Plays* (London: Faber, 1960), p. 49.
2 *Ibid*. p. 56.
3 *Ibid*.
4 *Ben Spray*, in: *New Granada Plays* (London: Faber, 1961), p. 190.
5 *Ibid*. p. 207.
6 *The Big Boys* (MS), p. 24.
7 *Ibid*. pp. 35–6.
8 *The Heart of the Country* (ATV camera script), p. 73.
9 *The Reception* (Granada TV camera script), pp. 3–4.
10 *Ibid*. p. 11.
11 *When the Wind Blows* (ATV camera script), pp. 3–4.
12 *Ibid*. p. 10.
13 *The Gorge*, in: *The Television Dramatist*, ed. Robert Muller (London: Elek, 1973), pp. 79–80.
14 *Ibid*. p. 85.
15 *Daddy Kiss It Better*, (Yorkshire TV camera script), p. 1.
16 *Ibid*. p. 3.
17 *Ibid*. p. 5.
18 *Ibid*. pp. 18–19B.
19 *Ibid*. p. 21.
20 *Hearts and Flowers* (BBC TV camera script), p. 2.
21 *Ibid*. pp. 45–6.
22 *Ibid*. p. 37.

Chapter 6. Alan Plater

1 Interview with Alan Plater, January 1979.
2 *Ibid*.
3 *Ibid*.
4 *Ibid*.
5 From *Jarrow Festival Brochure 1970*, quoted in: Alan Plater, 'Twenty-Five Years Hard', *Theatre Quarterly*, 7, 25 (Spring 1977), 39.
6 'Twenty-Five Years Hard', p. 38.
7 *Ibid*.
8 *Ibid*. p. 39.
9 *Ibid*.
10 *Ibid*.
11 *Ibid*. p. 41.
12 Interview with Alan Plater.
13 'Twenty-Five Years Hard', p. 34.
14 'Drama and the Dialectics of Violence', *Theatre Quarterly*, 2, 5 (January–March 1972), 14.

15 'Twenty-Five Years Hard', p. 41.
16 Interview with Alan Plater.
17 *Ibid.*
18 *Ibid.*
19 *Ibid.*
20 *Ibid.*
21 *Ibid.*
22 *Ibid.*
23 *Ibid.*
24 *Ibid.*
25 'Twenty-Five Years Hard', p. 41.
26 Interview with Alan Plater.
27 *Ibid.*
28 'Twenty-Five Years Hard', p. 44.
29 *Ibid.*
30 *Ibid.* p. 45.

Chapter 7.   Dennis Potter

1 The brainchild of a young scriptwriter from South Africa, Tessa Diamond, who sold the idea to Lew (later Lord) Grade of ATV. When the fashion changed to one-hour drama series in the early sixties, the weekly *Call Oxbridge 2000*, retaining the same location and some of the same regular characters, replaced the twice-weekly dispensation for a while. Later, a new one-hour format, *General Hospital*, replaced *Ward 10* altogether and, surviving until early in 1979, maintained a tradition of hospital drama from ATV that lasted almost without interruption for twenty-one years.

2 The adaptations for the stage include *Nigel Barton, Son of Man* and *Brimstone and Treacle*. Exceptions to the generalisation about screen plays would certainly include his own *Pennies from Heaven* for MGM.

3 *Daily Telegraph Magazine*, no. 234 (2 April 1969).

4 A true innovator. His broadcasting career began in radio in Manchester, where he was one of the first producers to experiment with the newfangled, relatively portable tape-recorder and certainly the first to take it out into the streets and pubs and revivalist chapels of the North to interview his subjects rather than bring them into the studio to cut twelve-inch discs, as was then the prescribed BBC method. When he crossed into television, the tape-recorder remained his first tool. Long before any cameras turned up he would be talking to the people who were going to be seen in the film, recording their meditations on every subject which might conceivably relate to his theme. Fragments of these thoughts would eventually find their way on the the sound track as an often ironic counterpoint to what the screen was showing. Mitchell called the technique 'Think-tape', and though it is now part of the basic vocabulary of film and television, it was at the time quite revolutionary. It would be naive to look for some magic

transference of genius from Denis Mitchell to Dennis Potter in the course of a few months' work together, but perhaps not too fanciful to wonder if Potter didn't pick up from his early mentor a knack of using voices and, in particular, music against the obvious mood of a scene.

5 4 June 1960.
6 *That Was the Week That Was*, ed. David Frost and Ned Sherrin (London: W. H. Allen, 1963). 'Mother's Day' is on p. 91.
7 Until its suspension on 30 November 1978, when with a characteristic splutter of indignation Potter conveyed his resignation to the Editor in the text of his last column.
8 'Tinkering with a fairy story', Potter said in my *Telegraph* profile, 'is worse blasphemy to them than tinkering with the Bible.'
9 *The Nigel Barton Plays*, (Harmondsworth: Penguin, 1967), p. 75.
10 London: Hutchinson, 1961. The anthology was edited by Brian Inglis.
11 *Sunday Telegraph*, 17 October 1971.
12 *The Television Dramatist*, ed. and with an introduction by Robert Muller (London: Elek, 1973), p. 324.
13 In the published text (*New Review*, no. 26 (May 1976), 41) the specification is merely 'The toenails are very long. Curling and claw-like.'
14 In a letter from Milne to Potter quoted in the *New Statesman*, 23 April 1976.
15 With Ray Connolly, *Evening Standard*, 21 March 1978.
16 In the Paul Madden National Film Theatre interview.
17 20 May 1968.

Chapter 8.   Jeremy Sandford

1 Published in London, 1976 (screenplay).
2 Published in London, 1976 (screenplay).
3 Published in London, 1974.
4 Unpublished MS.
5 Published in London, 1971; see also rev. edn. (London, 1972).
6 Published in London, 1967 (novel and special report).
7 Published in London, 1975 (rev. edn., 1977).
8 Published in London, 1973 (rev. edn., 1975).
9 Published in London, 1972.
10 'Edna and Cathy: Just Huge Commercials', *Theatre Quarterly*, 3, 10 (1973), 79–85.
11 London, 1975.
12 Rev. edn, p. 161.
13 *Ibid.* p. 105.
14 *Ibid.* p. 149.
15 Interview with Martin Banham, December 1978.
16 *Ibid.*
17 *Play for Today*, pp. 99, 126.

18 28 October 1971.
19 24 October 1971.
20 28 October 1971.
21 Rev. edn, p. 9.
22 *Ibid*. p. 13.
23 Pp. 11–12.
24 Alan Rosenthal, *The New Documentary in Action: A Casebook in Film Making* (Berkeley and Los Angeles, 1971), p. 169.
25 *Down and Out in Britain*, rev. edn, p. 153.
26 'Edna and Sheila: Two Kinds of Truth', *Theatre Quarterly*, 2, 7 (1972), 45–8.
27 *Ibid*.
28 'Edna and Cathy'.
29 *Ibid*.
30 'Keeping Faith with the Viewer', *Talking Points* (BBC Publication, London, January 1969), pp. 14–17.
31 *Television: The Ephemeral Art* (London, 1970), p. 63.
32 'Television in Britain: Description and Dissent', *Theatre Quarterly*, 2, 6 (1972), 18–25.
33 *Play for Today*, p. 106.
34 31 October 1971.
35 John Fiske and John Hartley, *Reading Television* (London, 1978), pp. 55–8.
36 Letter to *The Observer*, 31 October 1971.
37 *Cathy Come Home*, pp. 119–21.
38 *Edna the Inebriate Woman*, pp. 99–100.
39 *I Know It Was the Place's Fault* (London, 1970), prologue.
40 *Ibid*. p. 11.
41 12 March 1972.
42 'Cue Telecine – Put on the Kettle', in: Paul Barker (ed.), *Arts in Society* (London, 1977), pp. 193–7.
43 *Smiling David*, pp. 64–5.
44 Unpublished MS, p. 54.

Chapter 9.   Peter Watkins

1 A central character in the longest-running soap opera in British radio history. Her 'death' was a gambit calculated to steal the thunder of ITV's opening night.
2 Interview, *Film Comment*, 3, 4 (Fall 1965), 15.
3 *Ibid*. p. 17.
4 *Ibid*. p. 14.
5 *Ibid*. p. 4.
6 *Ibid*. p. 5.
7 *Ibid*. p. 4.
8 *Ibid*. p. 5.
9 *Ibid*. p. 6.

10 *Ibid*. p. 10.
11 *Ibid*.
12 A writer, primarily of television comedy, whose work has always been characterised by a high level of explicit political comment. His best-known work was the BBC series *Till Death Us Do Part*.
13 During the mid-sixties, Paul Jones was lead vocalist for Manfred Mann, a leading English rock band. Jean Shrimpton, epitome of the 'swinging sixties' in the fashion magazine, was for several years perhaps the most famous cover girl in the world.

Select bibliography

Books

Abrams, Philip, 'Radio and Television', in: *Discrimination and Popular Culture*, ed. Denys Thompson, Harmondsworth: Penguin, 1964; 2nd rev. edn, London: Heinemann, 1973

Annan Committee, *Report of the Committee on the Future of Broadcasting*, London: H.M.S.O., 1977, esp. ch. 21, 'The Arts in Broadcasting'

Alvarado, Manuel and Edward Buscombe, *Hazell: The Making of a TV Series*, London: British Film Institute in association with Latimer, 1978

Arnheim, Rudolf, 'A Forecast of Television' (1935), in: his *Film as Art*, London: Faber, 1958

Bakewell, Joan and Nicholas Garnham, *The New Priesthood*, London: Allen Lane, Penguin Press, 1970

Bartlett, Sir Basil, *Writing for Television*, London: Allen & Unwin, 1955

Belson, William A., *Television Violence and the Adolescent Boy*, Farnborough: Saxon House, 1978

Bennett, Rodney, *The Writer's Approach to the TV/Film Script*, London: Harrap, 1976

Black, Peter, 'The Base of the Pyramid', in: Thomas (ed.), *Armchair Theatre*
The Biggest Aspidistra in the World, London: BBC, 1972

Brandenburger, Barbara, *Working in Television*, London: Bodley Head, 1965

Brandt, George W., 'Radio, Film and Television', in: *Drama and Theatre: An Outline for the Student*, ed. John Russell Brown, London: Routledge & Kegan Paul, 1971

Briggs, Asa, *The History of Broadcasting in the United Kingdom*, vol. IV: *Sound and Vision*, Oxford: University Press, 1979

British Broadcasting Corporation, *Writing for the BBC: A Guide to Writers on Possible Markets for Their Work*, 4th edn, London: BBC, 1974

Brown, Roger L., 'Television and the Arts', in: *The Effects of Television*, ed. James Halloran, London: Panther Books, 1970

Bussell, Jan, *The Art of Television*, London: Faber, 1952

Campbell, Patrick, *You Want To Write for Television: An Informal Handbook for the Use of Writers, Would-be Writers and Writers' Agents*, London: Associated Rediffusion, 1959

Davis, Anthony, *Television: The First Forty Years*, London: Independent Television Publications, 1976

Davis, Desmond, *The Grammar of Television Production*, 3rd edn, rev. John Elliot, London: Barrie & Rockliff, 1974

Dicks, Terrance and Malcolm Hulke, *The Making of Doctor Who*, London: Target Books, 1976

Dunbar, Janet, *Script-Writing for Television*, London: Museum Press, 1965

Eigner, Edwin, 'British Television Drama and Society in the 1970s', in: *Themes in Drama 1: Drama and Society*, ed. James Redmond, Cambridge: University Press, 1979

Elliot, John, *Mogul: The Making of a Myth*, London: Barrie & Jenkins, 1970 (creation of series *The Troubleshooters*)

Elliot, Philip, 'Media Organisations and Occupations: An Overview', in: *Mass Communication and Society*, ed. James Curran, Michael Gurevitch and Janet Woollacott, London: Edward Arnold in association with The Open University Press, 1977

Ellis, Robin, *Making Poldark*, St Teath, Bodmin: Bossiney Books, 1978

Emmett, B. P., 'The Television and Radio Audience in Britain', in: *Sociology of Mass Communications*, ed. Denis McQuail, Harmondsworth: Penguin, 1972

Emmett, B. P. et al., *Violence on Television: Programme Content and Viewer Perception*, London: BBC, 1972

Esslin, Martin, *Brief Chronicles*, London: Temple Smith, 1970, esp. 'Contemporary English Drama and the Mass Media', pp. 272–84
'Radio and Television Drama in Britain', in: *The Reader's Encyclopedia of World Drama*, ed. John Gassner and Edmond Quinn, London: Methuen, 1970

Eysenck, H. J. and D. K. B. Nias, *Sex, Violence and the Media*, London: Temple Smith, 1978

Fiske, John and John Hartley, *Reading Television*, London: Methuen, 1978

Gielgud, Val, *Years in a Mirror*, London: Bodley Head, 1965, ch. on television drama, pp. 124–35

Glucksmann, André, *Violence on the Screen*, trans. Susan Bennett, London: British Film Institute Education Department, 1971

Goodland, J. S. R., *A Sociology of Popular Drama*, London: Heinemann, 1971

Graham, Burton, *Television: A Do You Remember Book*, London: Marshall Cavendish, 1974

Granada TV Network, *The First 75: A Cross Index of Granada TV Play Productions*, 1960

Green, F., *The Third Floor Front: A View of Broadcasting in the Sixties*, London: Bodley Head, 1969

Hall, Stuart, *Television as a Medium and Its Relation to Culture*, Media Series SP no. 34, Centre for Contemporary Cultural Studies, University of Birmingham, 1975

Hall, Stuart and Paddy Whannell, *The Popular Arts*, London: Hutchinson Educational, 1964

Halliwell, Leslie, *Halliwell's Teleguide*, London: Granada, 1979

Halloran, James, 'The Social Effects of Television', in: *The Effects of Television*, ed. James Halloran, London: Panther Books, 1970
  'The Production of Television Drama', in: *Entertainment Television*, ed. Heinz-Dietrich Fischer, New York: Hastings House, 1978

Hancock, Alan, *The Small Screen*, London: Heinemann Educational, 1965, ch. on *Z-Cars*, pp. 24–41

Hayman, Ronald, *Playback 2*, London: Davis-Poynter, 1973, interviews with Peter Nichols and David Mercer
  British Theatre since 1955: A Reassessment, Oxford: University Press, 1979

Heath, R. B., *Radio and Television*, London: Hamish Hamilton, 1969

Himmelweit, T. et al., *Television and the Child: An Empirical Study of the Effect of Television on the Young*, Oxford: University Press, 1958

Hood, Stuart, *A Survey of Television*, London: Heinemann, 1967

Hopkins, John, interview in: Bakewell and Garnham, *The New Priesthood*, pp. 80–2
  Interview with Giles Gordon, in: McCrindle (ed.), *Behind the Scenes*, pp. 31–43

Horton, Derek, *Television's Story and Challenge*, London: Harrap, 1951

Howitt, Dennis and Guy Cumberbatch, *Mass Media Violence and Society*, London: Elek Science, 1975

Hulke, Malcolm, *Writing for Television in the 70's*, rev. repr., London: Adam & Charles Black, 1976

Independent Television Authority, *Violence in Television Programmes: The ITV Code*, London: ITV, 1971

James, Clive, *Visions Before Midnight: Television Criticism from the Observer 1972–76*, London: Jonathan Cape, 1977

Kerensky, Oleg, *The New British Drama: Fourteen Playwrights since Osborne and Pinter*, London: Hamish Hamilton, 1977, chs. on Peter Nichols and Trevor Griffiths

Klotz, Günter, *Alternativen im britischen Drama der Gegenwart*, Berlin: Akademie-Verlag, 1978

McArthur, Colin, *Television and History*, Television Monograph 8, London: British Film Institute, 1978

McCrindle, Joseph (ed.), *Behind the Scenes: Theatre and Film Interviews from the Transatlantic Review*, London: Pitman, 1971, interviews with Christopher Hampton, John Hopkins, David Mercer, Joe Orton, Tom Stoppard and others

McLuhan, Marshall, *Understanding Media: The Extensions of Man*, London: Routledge & Kegan Paul, 1964

McQuail, Denis, 'The Audience for Television Plays', in: *Media Sociology: A Reader*, ed. Jeremy Tunstall, London: Constable, 1970
  'The Influence and Effects of Mass Media', in: *Mass Communication and*

Society, ed. James Curran, Michael Gurevitch and Janet Woollacott, London: Edward Arnold in association with The Open University Press, 1977

McQuail, Denis, Jay G. Blumler, and J. R. Brown, 'The Television Audience: A Revised Perspective', in: *Sociology of Mass Communications*, ed. Denis McQuail, Harmondsworth: Penguin, 1972

Madden, Paul, *Complete Programme Notes for a Season of British Television Drama 1959–1973, Held at the National Film Theatre, 11th–24th October 1976*, London: British Film Institute, 1976

Manvell, Roger and Albert William Bluem, *The Progress of Television: An Anglo-American Survey*, London: Focal Press, 1967

Mercer, David, interview in: Bakewell and Garnham, *The New Priesthood*, pp. 84–6

Interview with Giles Gordon, in: McCrindle (ed.), *Behind the Scenes*, pp. 88–98

Millerson, Gerald, *The Technique of Television Production*, 9th edn, London: Focal Press, 1973

Miyajima, Sumiko, 'La télévision dramatique au Royaume-Uni', in: *Théâtre et télévision*, ed. Gilles Marsolais, Paris: Unesco, 1973

Murdock, Graham, 'Fabricating Fictions: Approaches to the Study of Television Drama Production', in: *Organisation and Structure of Fiction Production in Television*, vol. I, Turin: Edizioni Radiotelevisione Italiana, 1977

Mustafa, Khalid El Mubarak, 'The Television Play as Art', unpublished Ph.D. dissertation, University of Bristol, 1974

Nathan, D., *The Laughtermakers*, London: Peter Owen, 1971

National Viewers' and Listeners' Association, *What Price Annan!*, Ardleigh, Colchester, 1978

Law – and Disorder, Ardleigh, Colchester, 1979

Newman, Sydney, 'The Producer', in: Thomas (ed.), *Armchair Theatre*

Nordenstreng, Kaarle and Tapio Varis, 'International Flow of TV Programmes', in: *Television: Ideology and Exchange*, ed. John Caughie, Television Monograph 9, London: British Film Institute, 1978

Pilkington Committee, *Report of the Committee on Broadcasting*, London: H.M.S.O., 1962

Potter, Dennis, interview in: Bakewell and Garnham, *The New Priesthood*, pp. 82–4

Purser, Philip, 'What Comes After Realism?', in: Thomas (ed.), *Armchair Theatre*

'Television Writers', in: Vinson, *Contemporary Dramatists*, 2nd edn

Richardson, Maurice, 'Planting the Iceberg', in: Thomas (ed.), *Armchair Theatre*

Rosenthal, Alan, *The New Documentary in Action: A Casebook in Film Making*, Berkeley and Los Angeles: University of California Press, 1971, interviews with Jeremy Sandford and Peter Watkins

Rotha, Paul (ed.), *Television in the Making*, London: Focal Press, 1956

Salem, Daniel, *La révolution théâtrale actuelle en Angleterre*, Paris: Denoël, 1969

Sandford, Jeremy, interview on *Cathy Come Home*, in: Rosenthal, *The New Documentary in Action*

Shaughnessy, Alfred, *Both Ends of the Candle*, London: Peter Owen, 1978, for background on *Upstairs Downstairs*

Shubik, Irene, *Play for Today: The Evolution of Television Drama*, London: Davis-Poynter, 1975

Shulman, Milton, *The Ravenous Eye*, rev. edn, London: Coronet, 1975, on the influence of TV

Spraos, John, *The Decline of the Cinema: An Economist's Report*, London: Allen & Unwin, 1962

Styan, John Louis, 'Television Drama', in: *Contemporary Theatre*, Stratford-upon-Avon Studies 4, ed. John Russell Brown and Bernard Harris, London: Edward Arnold, 1962

Sutton, Shaun, *The Theatre in the Living Room: BBC Lunch-Time Lectures*, 8th ser., 1, London: BBC, 1969

Swift, John, *Adventure in Vision: The First Twenty-Five Years of Television*, London: John Lehmann, 1950

Swinson, Arthur, *Writing for Television*, London: Black, 1955
Writing for Television Today, London: Black 1963

Taylor, Cecil P., *Making a TV Play: A Complete Guide from Conception to BBC Production*, Newcastle upon Tyne: Oriel Press, 1970

Taylor, Don, 'David Mercer and Television Drama', appendix to David Mercer, *The Generations*, London: Calder, 1964

Taylor, John Russell, *Anatomy of a Television Play: An Inquiry Into the Production of Two ABC Armchair Theatre Plays*, London: Weidenfeld & Nicolson, 1962
Anger and After: A Guide to the New British Drama, London: Methuen, 1962; rev. edn, 1969
The Second Wave: British Drama for the Seventies, London: Methuen, 1971, bibliography of Peter Nichols, David Mercer and Alan Plater

Thomas, Howard, *The Truth About Television*, London: Weidenfeld & Nicolson, 1962
With an Independent Air: Encounters During a Lifetime of Broadcasting, London: Weidenfeld & Nicolson, 1977

Thomas, Howard (ed.), *The Armchair Theatre*, London: Weidenfeld & Nicolson, 1959

Vinson, James, *Contemporary Dramatists*, 2nd edn, London: St James Press, 1977

Watkins, Peter, interview on *The War Game*, in: Rosenthal, *The New Documentary in Action*

Whitehouse, Mary, *Cleaning Up TV: From Protest to Participation*, London: Blandford Press, 1967

Wickham, Glynne (ed.), *The Relation Between Universities and Films, Radio and Television*, London: Butterworth, 1956

Wiggin, Maurice, 'Writing for the Dreamer's Dustbin', in: Thomas (ed.), *Armchair Theatre*

Williams, Raymond, *Television: Technology and Cultural Form*, London: Fontana, 1974

   Drama in a Dramatised Society: An Inaugural Lecture, Cambridge: University Press, 1975

Willis, Ted, 'The Writer and Television', in: his *Woman in a Dressing Gown and Other Television Plays*, London: Barrie & Rockliff, 1959

   'The Playwright' in: Thomas (ed.), *Armchair Theatre*

Worsley, T. C., *Television: The Ephemeral Art*, London: Alan Ross, 1970

Worth, Katherine J., *Revolutions in Modern English Drama*, London: Bell & Sons, 1972

Wyndham-Goldie, Grace, 'Television', in: *Cassell's Encyclopedia of World Literature*, vol. 1, London: Cassell, 1973

Articles

Abbreviations

JSFTA	*Journal of the Society of Film and Television Arts*
OP/EITF	*Official Programme of the Edinburgh International Television Festival*
TQ	*Theatre Quarterly*
St	*The Stage and Television Today*

Ableman, Paul, 'Edna and Sheila: Two Kinds of Truth', *TQ* 2, 7 (July–September 1972)

Aicken, Frederick, 'Writing with Pictures', *Contrast* 1, 4 (Summer 1962)

   'Whatever Happened to TV Drama?', *Screen Education* 24 (May–June 1964)

Allen, Douglas and Michael Voysey, 'Classic Serials', *JSFTA* 20 (Summer 1965)

Allen, Rod, 'International Co-Production: Cash for the Concept', *OP/EITF 1978*

Arden, John, 'Writers and Television 2: The Writer's View', *Contrast* 2, 2 (Winter 1962)

Atkins, Ian, 'Videotape and the Television Producer', *JSFTA* 1 (Winter 1959–60)

Aylestone, Lord, 'Television Drama and Public Taste', *ITA Note* 22 (May 1971)

Barlas, Chris, 'An Interview with Mike Leigh' and 'An Interview with Christopher Morahan', *Gambit* 7, 26 & 27 (1975)

Barr, Charles, 'Criticism and TV Drama', *OP/EITF 1977*

Barry, Michael, 'Problems of a Television Producer', *BBC Quarterly* 3, 3 (Autumn 1951)

   'TV Writing Today', *The Writer* (May 1953)

Barstow, Stan, 'The Writer in the Regions', *JSFTA* 9 (Autumn 1962)

Bazalgette, Cary, 'Reagan and Carter, Kojak and Crocker, Batman and Robin?', *Screen Education* 20 (Autumn 1976)

Black, Peter, 'The Television Playwright', *The Author* 70, 4 (Summer 1960)
    'Can One Person Criticise the Full Range of Television?', *JSFTA* 2, 7 (1973)

Bowen, John, 'The Worm in the Bud', *Contrast* 1, 2 (Winter 1961)

Brandt, George W., 'The Domestic Playwright: Some Thoughts About Television Drama', *Review of English Literature* 3, 4 (October 1962)

Bryce, John, 'Violence on TV', *JSFTA* 16 (Summer 1964)

Buckler, Robert, 'Is the Script Editor Really Necessary?', *TQ* 5, 18 (June–August 1975)

Campbell, Patrick, 'The Quiet Revolution in BBC Drama', *St*, 10 February 1972
    'Getting the Best from the Drama Writers', *St*, 1 February 1973

Caughie, John, 'The Television Festival (Edinburgh 1977)', *Screen* 18, 4 (Winter 1977–8)

Clarke, Cecil, 'Edward the Seventh', *Independent Broadcasting* 5 (August 1975)

Cooper, Giles, 'Adapting Classic Novels', *JSFTA* 20 (Summer 1965)

Cox, Constance, 'Dickens and Television', *JSFTA* 20 (Summer 1965)

Cox, Michael, 'Coronation Street and Its Audience', *JSFTA* 31 (Spring 1968)

Day-Lewis, Sean, 'The Specialisation Issue and Other Problems for the Critic', *JSFTA* 2, 7 (1973)

Dennington, John and John Tulloch, 'Cops, Consensus and Ideology', *Screen Education* 20 (Autumn 1976) (study of *The Sweeney*)

Dewhurst, Keith, 'Driving Force', *Radio Times*, 24–30 June 1978 (the story of *Z-Cars*)

Drummond, Phillip, 'Structural and Narrative Constraints and Strategies in *The Sweeney*', *Screen Education* 20 (Autumn 1976)

Dyer, Richard, Terry Lovell and Jean McCrindle, 'Soap Opera and Women', *OP/EITF 1977*

Eaton, Mick, 'Television Situation Comedy', *Screen* 19, 4 (Winter 1978–9)

Elliot, Michael, 'Television Drama: The Medium and the Predicament', *Encore* 4, 4 (March–April 1958)

Esslin, Martin, 'The Global Village and the Mass Mind', *TQ* (April–June 1972)

Fox, Avril, 'The Danger Is Real', *JSFTA* 25 (Autumn 1966) (censorship)

Furnival, Robert, 'The Wall of Glass: Some Notes on the Writer in Television', *Encore* 5, 4 (November–December 1958)

Garnett, Tony et al., 'Film Versus Tape in Television Drama', *JSFTA* 23 (Spring 1966)

Garnett, Tony, John Gould and Roger Hudson, 'Television in Britain: Description and Dissent', *TQ* 2, 6 (April–June 1972)

Giddings, Robert, 'Superproduct', *New Society*, 13 July 1978 (ATV's six-part *Will Shakespeare*)

Gielgud, Val, 'Drama in Television and Sound', *BBC Quarterly* 5, 4 (Winter 1950–1)

Gilbert, Stephen W., In and Out of the Box', *Plays and Players* (March 1975)

Goodwin, Clive, 'Censorship and Drama', *OP/EITF 1977*

Gray, S., 'Confessions of a Television Playwright', *Times Literary Supplement*, 19 September 1968, pp. 1042–3

Greatorex, Wilfred, 'Power Games', *JSFTA* 25 (Autumn 1966) (censorship in ITV)

Guthrie, Tyrone, 'Theatre Versus Television', *Plays and Players* (May 1966)

Hall, Stuart, 'Television and Culture', *Sight and Sound* 45, 4 (Autumn 1976)

Hawkesworth, John, 'The Special Connection: Writer/Director', *JSFTA* 2, 8 (1973)

Hawkins, Jim, 'A Foot in the Door', *Gambit* 7, 26 & 27 (1975)

Henriques, Robert, 'Writing for Television: A Novelist's Problem', *BBC Quarterly* 7, 2 (Summer 1952)

Hill, Derek, 'Which Way for Hancock?', *Contrast* 1, 2 (Winter 1961)
  'Writers and Television 1: Intellectual Attitudes', *Contrast* 2, 2 (Winter 1962)

Hoare, Ken, 'Situations Vacant', *Contrast* 1, 1 (Autumn 1961)

Hobson, Harold, 'What We Want in Television Plays', *BBC Quarterly* 5, 2 (Summer 1950)

Holt, Hazel, 'In Flight from Today: A Look at Period Drama', *St*, 23 October 1975
  'The BBC – A Prime Offender in the Area of Half-Truth', *St*, 27 April 1978 (polemic on documentary drama)

Hopkins, John, 'The Television Documentary Play', *Plays and Players*, July 1971

Hurd, Geoff, '*The Sweeney* – Contradiction and Coherence', *Screen Education* 20 (Autumn 1976)

Independent Television Authority, 'Violence on Television: Control of the Portrayal of Violence in the Programmes of Independent Television', *ITA Note* 20 (1970)

Itzin, Catherine, '*Upstairs Downstairs:* London Weekend Drama Series (A Production Casebook)', *TQ* 2, 6 (April–June 1972)

Kelsey, Gerald, 'The Inequality of Rewards: The Writer and Self-Protection', *JSFTA* 2, 8 (1973)

Kennedy Martin, Troy, 'nats go home: First Statement of a New Drama for Television', *Encore* 11, 2 (March–April 1964)
  'Up the Junction and After', *Contrast* 4, 5–6 (Winter 1965–Spring 1966)
  'From *War Game* to *Law and Order*', *Vision* 4, 1 (April 1979)

Kershaw, John, 'Synthetic Gossip', *Contrast* 3, 4 (Summer 1964) (TV serials, including *Coronation Street*)

Kuehl, Jerry, 'Drama Documentary', *OP/EITF 1977*
'The Motives for Making Drama Documentaries', *Vision* 3, 1 (April 1978)

Langley, Noel, 'The Nature of the Television Play', *BBC Quarterly* 8, 3 (Autumn 1953)

Lewis, Peter, 'Z-Cars', *Contrast* 1, 4 (Summer 1962)

Lovell, Alan, 'Television Playwright – David Mercer', *Contrast* 2, 4 (Summer 1963)

McGivern, Cecil, 'Television Needs Writers', *The Author* (Winter 1950)

McGrath, John, 'TV Drama: The Case Against Naturalism', *Sight and Sound* 46, 2 (Spring 1977)

Mackie, Philip, 'Self-Censorship', *JSFTA* 25 (Autumn 1966)
'The Writer: Servant or Master?', *JSFTA* 2, 8 (1973)

Madden, Paul, 'What Is Being Kept for Posterity', *St*, 5 January 1978 (the TV collection at the National Film Archive)

Madden, Paul and David Wilson, 'The Communal Touch: The Television Plays of Colin Welland', *Sight and Sound* 44, 2 (Spring 1975)

Maddison, John, 'What is a Television Film?', *Contrast* 3, 1 (Autumn 1963)

Manvell, Roger, 'Drama on Television', *BBC Quarterly* 7, 1 (Spring 1952)
'The Achievements of Television Drama in Britain', *JSFTA* 13 (Autumn 1963)
'"Realising" the Classics', *JSFTA* 20 (Summer 1965)
'Why Television Criticism Differs from Other Forms of Criticism', *JSFTA* 2, 7 (1973)

Mara, Henry, 'Conversation with a Script Writer', *Contrast* 2, 1 (Autumn 1962) (study of Johnny Speight)

Markstein, George, 'Censorship', *JSFTA* 2, 8 (1973)
'The Novel – A Bright Hope in a Bleak Outlook', *St*, 7 March 1974 (the 'TV novel')

Marshall, Norman, 'Television: Ally or Enemy?', *Drama* 48 (Spring 1958)

Mercer, David, 'Playwright's Postscripts', *Contrast* 3, 3 (Spring 1964)

Mercer, David, Lewis Greifer and Arthur Swinson, 'What Television Has Meant in the Development of Drama in Britain', *JSFTA* 13 (Autumn 1963)

Mercer, David and Roger Manvell, 'The Meaning of Censorship: A Discussion', *JSFTA* 25 (Autumn 1966)

Mitchell, Julian, 'Writing for Television', *Observer Magazine*, 7 October 1973

Muller, Robert, 'How the Author Would Have Done It Himself', *St*, 7 November 1974 (TV adaptations)

Murdock, Graham, 'Understanding Television Drama Production', *Screen Education* 26 (Spring 1978)

Murphy, Stephen, 'Censorship', *Independent Broadcasting* 11 (April 1977)

Newman, Sydney, 'Drama', *JSFTA* 15 (Spring 1964)

Page, Malcolm, 'Published British Television Plays: An Annotated Bibliography', *TQ* 7, 27 (Autumn 1977)

'Published British Television Plays: A Supplementary Bibliography', *TQ* 8, 30 (Summer 1978)

Paterson, Richard, '*The Sweeney*: A Euston Films Project', *Screen Education* 20 (Autumn 1976)

Plater, Alan, 'The Playwright and his People', *TQ* 1, 2 (April–June 1971)

'Twenty-Five Years Hard: A Playwright's Personal Retrospective', *TQ* 7, 25 (Spring 1977)

Plater, Alan, et al., 'Boxing the Arch: A Discussion About Television and the Theatre', *Gambit* 7, 26 & 27 (1975)

'New Gothics, Realists and Phantasists', *Gambit* 8, 29 (1976)

Potter, Dennis, 'Realism and Non-Naturalism', *OP/EITF 1977*

Pringle, Ashley, 'A Methodology for Television Analysis with Reference to the Drama Series', *Screen* 13, 2 (Summer 1972)

Prior, Allan, 'The Relationship of Art and Money in Writing Television Drama', *JSFTA* 13 (Autumn 1963)

'The Role of the Television Dramatist: His Achievements and Prospects in British Television', *TQ* 1, 1 (January–March 1971)

'What Is the Condition of the Single Play?', *St*, 16 December 1971

Prior, Allan and John Hopkins, 'The *Z-Cars* Team', *The Screenwriter* 12 (Spring 1963)

Purser, Philip, 'Landscape of TV Drama', *Contrast* 1, 1 (Autumn 1961)

'One Cheer for Fantasy', *Contrast* 1, 2 (Winter 1961) (Alun Owen's *The Rose Affair*)

'Head of Drama', *Contrast* 2, 1 (Autumn 1962) (the work of Sydney Newman)

Richler, Mordecai, 'Making Out in the Television Drama Game', *Twentieth Century*, March 1959

Richman, Stella, 'The Subject', *JSFTA* 31 (Spring 1968) (setting up a TV series)

Robinson, David, 'The Critical Problem', *Contrast* 3, 4 (Summer 1964)

'The Comedian's Labourer', *Contrast* 4, 1 (Winter 1964–5)

Saville, Philip, 'Writers and Television 3: Director and Writer', *Contrast* 2, 2 (Winter 1962)

Scott, Peter Graham, 'Producing a Television Series', *JSFTA* 31 (Spring 1968)

Sendall, Bernard, 'Portrayal of Violence on Television', *Independent Broadcasting* 3 (February 1975)

Seton, Marie, 'Television Drama', *Theatre Arts Monthly* 22, 12 (December 1938)

Shaw, Roy, 'The Freedom of Television', *JSFTA* 25 (Autumn 1966) (censorship problems)

Shivas, Mark, '*The Glittering Prizes*', *Sight and Sound* 45, 1 (Winter 1975–6) (the making of the serial)

Silverstone, Roger, 'An Approach to the Structural Analysis of the Television Message', *Screen* 17, 2 (Summer 1976)

Smith, Anthony, 'Censorship and Drama', *OP/EITF 1977*

Stonier, G. W., 'The Intimate Screen', *Sight and Sound* 27, 6 (Autumn 1958)

Sutton, Shaun, 'Television Drama and the Censor', *JSFTA* 43–4 (Spring–Summer 1971)

'BBC Drama Head Hits Back', *TQ* 2, 7 (July–September 1972), 96–7

Swallow, Norman, 'Television: The Integrity of Fact and Fiction', *Sight and Sound* 45, 3 (Summer 1976)

Taylor, Don, 'The Gorboduc Stage', *Contrast* 3, 3 (Spring 1964) (a writer's policy)

'An Essay of Television Drama: A Dialogue', *Contrast* 4, 3 (Summer 1965)

'When Directors and Writers Lost Their Freedom', *St*, 10 March 1977 (organisational change and creativity)

Taylor, John Russell, 'Drama '66', *Contrast* 4, 5–6 (Winter 1965–Spring 1966)

'An Alun Owen Festival', *Plays and Players* (August 1968)

'British Dramatists: The New Arrivals', *Plays and Players* (January 1971) (notes on John Hopkins, Alan Plater and Cecil P. Taylor)

Taylor, Ken, 'Sex and Violence on TV' *JSFTA* 16 (Summer 1964)

Tilsley, Vincent, 'Style in Drama: The Role of the Script Editor', *Contrast* 3, 4 (Summer 1964)

'The Doomsday Planners', *Contrast* 4, 1 (Winter 1964–5) (TV drama policy)

Tynan, Kenneth, 'Television and the Stage', *Drama* 26 (Autumn 1952)

Walters, Margaret and Sue Woodford, 'Race', *OP/EITF 1978* (minorities in British TV drama)

Ward, Bill, 'Videotape: A Summing Up', *JSFTA* 1 (Winter 1959–60)

Weatherby, W. J., 'What the Public Wants?', *Contrast* 1, 2 (Winter 1961)

'Granada's Camino Real', *Contrast* 1, 4 (Summer 1962) (a study of *Coronation Street*)

Whitehead, E. A., 'Writing for Television', *Movie* 25 (Winter 1977–8)

Whitehouse, Mary, 'Responsibility in Television Drama', *JSFTA* 25 (Autumn 1966)

Whitemore, Hugh, 'Learning the Lingo', *Contrast* 3, 3 (Spring 1964) (the nature of TV drama)

Williams, Raymond, 'A Lecture on Realism', *Screen* 18, 1 (Spring 1977)

'Realism and Non-Naturalism, *OP/EITF 1977*

Willis, Ted, 'Look Back in Wonder', *Encore* 13 (March 1958)

'A Writer and His Critics', *Contrast* 3, 2 (Winter 1963)

'TV and the Dramatist', *Plays and Players* (June 1965)

Wilson, Donald, 'The Background', *JSFTA* 31 (Spring 1968) (early series and serials)

'Series and Serials', *St*, 13 June 1968

'The Television Saga', *EBU Review* (September 1971) (blockbuster serials)

Wilson, Snoo, 'The Means of Production', *Gambit* 7, 26 & 27 (1975)

Wood, Duncan, 'The Situation Comedy Situation', *Independent Broadcasting* 8 (June 1976)

Index